The Abandoned Generation

Other Books of Interest from St. Augustine's Press

Dave Sterrett, *Aborting Aristotle: Examining Fatal Fallacies in the Abortion Debate*

Joseph Bottum, *The Decline of the Novel*

James V. Schall, *On the Principles of Taxing Beer: And Other Brief Philosophical Essays*

Rémi Brague, *The Anchors in the Heavens*

Christopher Kaczor, *The Gospel of Happiness: How Secular Psychology Points to the Wisdom of Christian Practice*

Marvin R. O'Connell, *Telling Stories that Matter: Memoirs and Essays*

Josef Pieper, *Traditional Truth, Poetry, Sacrament: For My Mother, on her 70th Birthday*

Peter Kreeft, *Summa Philosophica*

Leon J. Podles, *Losing the Good Portion: Why Men are Alienated from Christianity*

Gerard V. Bradley, *Unquiet Americans: U. S. Catholics and America's Common Good*

David Lowenthal, *Slave State: Rereading Orwell's 1984*

Charles E. Rice, *Right or Wrong?*

Charles E. Rice, *The Winning Side: Why the Culture of Death Is Dying*

Charles E. Rice, *What Happened to Notre Dame?*

George J. Marlin, *Mario Cuomo: The Myth and the Man*

Gene Fendt, *Camus' Plague: Myth for Our World*

Nathan Lefler, *Tale of a Criminal Mind Gone Good*

Nalin Ranasinghe, *The Confessions of Odysseus*

Will Morrisey, *Herman Melville's Ship of State*

Roger Scruton, *The Meaning of Conservatism: Revised 3rd Edition*

Stanley Rosen, *The Language of Love: An Interpretation of Plato's Phaedrus*

Winston Churchill, *The River War*

The Abandoned Generation

GABRIEL KUBY

TRANSLATED BY JAMES PATRICK KIRCHNER

ST. AUGUSTINE'S PRESS
South Bend, Indiana

Manufactured in the United States of America.

1 2 3 4 5 6 27 26 25 24 23 22

Library of Congress Control Number: 2022930357

Paperback ISBN: 978-1-58731-004-1
Ebook ISBN: 978-1-58731-005-8

First published in German 2020
Fe-medienverlags GmbH
88353 Kisslegg
ISBN 978-3-86357-276-1

∞ The paper used in this publication meets the minimum requirements of the American National Standard for Information Sciences – Permanence of Paper for Printed Materials, ANSI Z39.48-1984.

St. Augustine's Press
www.staugustine.net

To the laughter of children

Contents

Afflicted in body and soul

Chronically physically sick

26% of all children and teens have a potentially chronic somatic illness. Most frequent among children are neurodermatitis (8%) and asthma (7%). Every fourth child is chronically ill physically and every tenth child has a chronic mental illness.

DAK Kinder- und Jugendreport 2018[1]

Mental disturbances

At 26%, mental and behavioral disturbances are among the four most common pathologies among children and teens.

DAK Kinder- und Jugendreport 2018[2]

20% of children and teens are mentally vulnerable

For a good fifth of children and teens 3 to 17, there is a risk of psychological abnormalities, and boys are affected significantly more often than girls. Most common are anxiety disorders, followed by aggressive dissocial disorders, depression, and ADHD.

Federal Centre for Health Education, Kindergesundheit-info[3]

New morbidity

A new morbidity can be seen from acute to chronic diseases, from physical to mental disorders in emotional and mental development of social behavior, and motor and cognitive development.

J. Leidel, Entwicklungsstörungen bei Kindern und Jugendlichen, Prevention conference of the German Medical Association[4]

Speech disorders in 42% of 5-year-old boys

In 2017, speech and language disorders were diagnosed in 16% of all boys and girls aged 0 to 17 years. Developmental disorders occur most often at the age of 5, in boys 42% and in girls 30%.

DAK Gesundheitsreport 2019[5]

27% increase in developmental disorders in 5- to 7-year-olds
The number of developmental disorders diagnosed in children 5- to 7-year-olds has increased 27% in the past seven years, from 28% in 2008 to 35% in 2018. More than 82% of the diagnosed developmental disorders involve speech and language. Disorders of motor development are firmly in second place, with 22%.
Heilmittelbericht des Wissenschaftlichen Instituts der AOK[6]

28% of children and teens in therapy in the Rheinland-Pfalz region
28% of children and teens in Rheinland-Pfalz were treated for mental illnesses and disorders in 2018. That was 12% more than in 2009. Most of the diagnoses made in 2018 were problems with speech and language development (almost 22%), followed by hyperkinetic disorders like ADHD (12%).
Health minister Sabine Bätzing-Lichtenthäler in November 2019[7]

28% of boys and girls in Berlin have a mental illness
In Berlin, 30% of the boys and 26% of the girls suffer mental illness. In 2016, in 9% of children a potentially chronic mental illness was diagnosed (school anxiety 44%, ADHD 41% — boys almost three times as much as girls — and depression 13% — girls almost twice as much as boys).
DAK Gesundheitsreport 2019, Berlin

Lack of sleep and media consumption
Young people in all types of schools now suffer from a pronounced lack of sleep. There is a chain of effects: a lot of screen time leads to lack of sleep, high stress, lack of exercise, physical symptoms such as headaches and back pain, along with ADHD.
Präventionsradar, Schuljahr 17/18, DAK-Gesundheit[8]

Lack of exercise
Only 35% of children get enough exercise — 40% of boys and 31% of girls.
Präventionsradar, Schuljahr 17/18, DAK-Gesundheit

Stress
40% of schoolchildren indicate that they very often experience stress. At 48%, girls rated higher than boys at 33%, caused mainly by school. Stress

causes high blood pressure, increased irritability, disturbed sleep, headaches and backaches. 50% report fatigue and exhaustion every week or more often. Girls are more affected than boys.
Präventionsradar, Schuljahr 17/18, DAK-Gesundheit

Poverty
A fifth of children and teens under 18 live below the poverty line in homes that earn less than 60% of the average income.
Andreas Storm, Beiträge zur Gesundheitsökonomie, DAK Kinder- und Jugendreport 2018[9]

Poor education and stress from illness
Children from socially disadvantaged families are far more likely to show physical, mental, cognitive, linguistic and motor development issues than children from more well-to-do families. They are less likely to be breastfed, more likely to smoke, spend more time in front of screens, spend less time at sports, eat less healthily, have more cavities, more allergies, often more obesity, spend more time in the hospital and need more medications. Pediatricians speak of an "unholy alliance between poor education and stress from illness."
DAK Kinder- und Jugendreport 2018

Sick parents — sick children
In 2017, 37% of all children insured by the German Employee Health Insurance Fund had a parent who underwent medical treatment for psychological problems. The risk of childhood mental illness is up to 80% higher if one parent is mentally ill.
DAK Kinder- und Jugendreport 2019

Dear readers,

This book speaks of the plight of the young generation. It aims to turn the hearts of fathers and mothers back toward their sons and daughters, so that they will turn their hearts back to their parents. A veil has been placed over our consciousness and hides the plight from us. No one wants this distress. Everyone wants a better world. When we give children what they need, the world will be better. This is why we have to draw away the veil.

Under the veil, we will find ourselves. It can be painful to discover that, as fathers and mothers, we have contributed to our children's distress. Is there a father or mother who does not realize this at some point? There are no perfect parents and no perfect families, but there are people who want to grow. This is the only prerequisite for benefiting from this book.

I'm not looking down from a high horse. I am a child of divorce and am divorced myself. That is well within statistical probability. The youngest of my three children was 11 at the time I became a single mother. Not until I had turned to God right after the separation did my eyes gradually open to what marriage and family are all about, how great the promise of happiness is and what it demands.

Since then, 25 years have gone by. The stumbling blocks that a broken family throws on the path of life turned into challenges along a mountain path; through twists and turns, it led to a broad landscape that fills my heart with gratitude. Understanding, forgiveness and love have all grown. I have since become a grandmother and am enraptured by the way new life begins. We must protect it to make the world a better place!

Gabriele Kuby, Easter 2020

Introduction
The child — our future

> Children play a redeemer role in the family. They represent the victory of love over the insatiable ego. They symbolize the defeat of selfishness and the triumph of giving love.
> *Fulton Sheen*

How delighted we are when we see a mother duck leading her ducklings; a cat gently licking her kittens; a polar bear cup cuddling in its mother's paws; when a father penguin spends weeks rocking the egg under his flat feet and warms it under his plumage while the mother fetches food. The strong care for the weak. This is how life begins anew again and again — and we humans are touched by it.

We're also touched when a baby smiles at us. Just a few weeks after birth, without thought or judgment, the baby bestows us with a pure look of complete, loving acceptance. Heaven opens up to us. But do we feel the same enchantment from animals' care for their young as we do from a nursing mother? Does she not make great sacrifices from conception to birth? From birth to weaning and continuously throughout life? She gives her body — her physical substance — so could she not give her heart? But something strange is going on: People are not moved, do not respect a mother who cares for the weak and thus passes on life.

What is wrong? Aren't we in the West proud of our "humanity"? We don't sacrifice virgins to appease the gods, like the Aztecs did. We don't murder newborns if there are too many of them or they are defective, like the Romans did. In the affluent Western countries, we don't force children into labor, like those whose cheap products we buy, and we don't force them to be soldiers in a war. But do children really have it made in our culture?

No. They don't fare so well. A quarter to a third of children and youth in Germany are sick in body and soul — so sick that they need treatment by doctors and therapists. Behind the numbers hides sorrow, great existential suffering of children and youth with negative consequences to their personal life and to the future of all society. The figures also conceal the sorrow of parents whose children do not thrive, who give them no joy, who are sick, aggressive or depressive and soon slip from their embrace. Children whose psyches are ruptured have more trouble in school, are more likely to drop out, have little or no educational achievement, have poor opportunities for training and jobs, and are at greater risk of addiction and imprisonment.[10] Families have always had their hardships, but before the late 1960s a "happy childhood," a "carefree childhood," nestled in a family of father, mother, and siblings, an extended family, a natural environment safe for children, was still the norm that people strove for. Today, destruction of the family is encouraged as the back way to socialism: equality of the lowest common denominator of a collectivized people ruled over by the political classes.

The major studies documenting the mass suffering of the young generation link it to low socio-economic and educational status, but the deeper causes are not examined. Family disintegration never surfaces as a reason, and the word *divorce* never comes up. Medication and therapy are supposed to take care of it. In the best of cases, they can provide relief, but they cannot stop the further slide into a society that largely consists of ill individuals.

Refusing to accept so much suffering has nothing at all to do with nostalgia, but with the will to life and with hope for a return to a livable future.

Life is set up such that people in the earliest and latest periods of life depend on help, and that people in the middle of life have the strength to aid the young and the old. Life is a burden no matter which way we look at it. A humane society takes on this burden: The strong care for the weak, and the young for the old. When parents take good care of their children, the chances are better that the children will take good care of them when they're old. An inhumane society wants to throw off the burden and ends up on a collision course with life itself.

The word "humane" evokes the idea that it is characteristic of people to be good, but here the language is mistaken. It doesn't describe the reality, but just the potential — the human ideal: Father penguins go weeks without food and barely move, so that the chick can grow inside the fragile shell on his feet and hatch at the right time to become a penguin itself, and take its turn in the outermost row to protect the whole herd from the howling north wind.[11] He doesn't decide to do that. His instinct drives him to selflessness. People have to choose good. It doesn't come easy — it's an uphill battle. But we typically prefer to slide downhill, especially today. The path uphill brings life, joy, and a future. The path downhill brings sadness, depression, fear, hopelessness, and death. There is suffering on both paths — uphill and downhill. Uphill, hope is the companion. Downhill it's misery.

How can we become as humane as a penguin?

In our society, children are largely depicted as a burden. And bearing and raising children is, in fact, no child's play. It is the serious business of life. Great joy and great sacrifice come in a two-pack. During mass prosperity, a whole generation was sold a lie — that fun is the meaning of life, and that this fun comes with no sacrifice or suffering. From one moment to the next, parenting collapses this lie. There in your hands is a tiny bundle of humanity, completely helpless, fully dependent on love and care.

It can suckle and scream and grasp a finger, but not much else. Forget sleeping through the night. The whole day is devoted only to the baby. Up to the time of birth, the mother was an autonomous person, her wishes were the compass of her life. Now, all of a sudden, it is an infant's cry. Her ego has been pushed off the throne without warning — suddenly it should, it *must* serve instead of rule. And the astonishing thing: The mother *wants* to do it.

Oxytocin, the "happiness hormone," is secreted. It's also called the "bonding hormone." It is secreted during sexual union, during birth, and during nursing. A mother who not long ago got her self-esteem from her attractiveness and professional recognition looks at this newborn with deep emotion and wonder. Her face takes on the radiance of tender love. She loses herself upon looking at the child that she has borne. It has gone from a mystery in her body to a visible wonder in her arms. Life will never be the same. Her care for the child will never end. The journey of life now has new coordinates: Child — Mother — Father. Nature and oxytocin have administered the initial dose of love. Asserting this love in all coming phases of life requires continuous inner growth, constant new types of sacrifices, always letting go in new, more profound ways to give the child the appropriate level of freedom, without which love cannot thrive.

Life unfolds from the inside outward, all by itself. A few days after birth, the child looks into the mother's eyes. There is a self, endowed with a soul. How incomprehensibly precious this small person is. Who is this child? What will become of him? What are his gifts, his traits, his mission? With each new expression of life, the parents grope for signs that might reveal this mystery. No one teaches the baby to lift his head, to turn over, to take interest in a mobile, to sit up, to crawl, to exert himself to exhaustion, to climb the stairs, and to dare his first step. Is there anything more delightful than the smile of an infant, anything more contagious than a child's laughter? And there is celebration all round when Aiden learns something new. Photos and videos are sent, and grandparents, aunts, uncles, and friends are riveted when Isabella enthusiastically stomps in a puddle. Is there anything more beautiful than a joyful child running into your arms, giving off peals of laughter over things we grownups don't even notice; putting full trust in Dad when he throws him into the air, nestling into Grandma's arms all ears when she tells a story?

A mother needs a lot of staying power to feed, change diapers, protect, and speak to a child 24 hours a day, without receiving a single word in response. She always has her antennas aimed at the child and develops a sixth sense for the child's needs. A complete change in rhythm is required of the mother, from the frenzied pace of the digital world, the reward system of professional work, and the enjoyments of childlessness to a constant, patient presence. Between the joy of each new step the child takes, there are long dry spells, sleeplessness, and hours alone with the child when the father leaves the home and comes back tired in the evening.

Fathers have become more tender with their small children, get up at night, feed them, change their diapers, and rock them until they go back to sleep. Fathers who take a few months off from work to care for their babies experience what the mother does, and soon develop their own bond with the child.

Yes, it is stressful to smooth a child's path through life, always to look after the child and not after yourself, sometimes without being able to comfort, but just to wait out illnesses. But the payoff is huge, infinitely greater than the effort: A new child has come into the world. The parents can be renewed through the child's unconditional love. They are now inextricably connected to life itself. And there's no turning back. The child draws its parents along into the future.

Before long, maybe others will attend to the child in the crib, the child will go to kindergarten, to school, reach for the smartphone and seek a place among children of the same age. More and more, parents lose their power to shape the child's world. Fortunate are the parents and children if, in the first three years, a secure, indestructible bond to the mother and father has been formed that gives the child the inner certainty: I am wanted. I am loved. I am secure. The world is good. I can trust.

So much for the course of life for father, mother, and child. But what goes on today? Let's look at what we do to children. Children are our future. Let's look at what we do to our future.

It's painful to see reality as it is. We are all part of this reality and contribute to its creation. But pain can yield a decision to put the child at the center, to serve the weak, the child. This means sacrifice — sacrifices that bring blessings.

In a society that places adults' needs in the center, children don't have it so well.

- Children are prevented.
- Children are killed before birth if they are unwanted.
- Children are produced in a laboratory if they are wanted.
- Children are deceived about their lineage.
- Children are frozen as embryos and consumed for research.
- Children are carried in a rented womb.
- Children are bought and raised by same-sex couples.
- Children are placed in the hands of strangers from infancy.
- Children are sexualized as early as kindergarten.
- Children are made confused about their sexual identity.
- Children are sexually indoctrinated in primary school.
- Children are encouraged to "change" their gender.
- Children are exposed to smartphones.
- Children are exposed to pornography.
- Masses of children are sexually abused.
- Children are orphaned by divorce.
- Children must grow up in shattered families.

- Children become sad.
- Children become sick.
- Children are doped with Ritalin.
- Children are robbed of their childhood.

Children are our future. Children are human. Children have dignity — right from the beginning.

Let's give childhood back to the children, and the future back to everyone.

1.
I want to live — and you should live

From the moment of its fertilization every human egg cell is a human embryo.
European Court of Human Rights, 2011

Life — what a mystery! Life is within us. It rises from a seed, grows up, and eventually dies — relentlessly. No human being has ever succeeded in creating life — Adam and Eve have not eaten from the tree of life. But life has incessantly brought fruit, ever since it has existed. One is nourished from the fruit of others. The fruit conceals the seed that falls to the ground, dies and brings forth new fruit.

The seeds have a building plan inside them. The great oak is already programmed within the acorn. It is meant to become an enormous tree, and it can if it plants its roots in good soil, sun and rain come down upon it, and nothing happens to the seedling while it is still tender and defenseless. Any plan for life requires the right conditions to unfold. For people, this is a web of destiny and happenstance, imprinting and free will, freedom and providence.

Archaic religions worship fertility goddesses and celebrate fertility cults, because it is the woman who gives birth to new life. The Israelites made no distinction between the fruit of the body, the fruit of livestock, and the fruit of the field: "Blessed shall be the fruit of your body, and the fruit of your ground, and the fruit of your beasts, the increase of your cattle, and the young of your flock" (Deuteronomy 28:4). For them, fertility is a sign of the grace of God — infertility of the body, the land, the livestock, on the other hand, is a curse from God by which he punishes people who have broken from his commandments and broken the covenant.

For the ancients, it was clear that God himself opens and closes the womb. Jacob loved Rachel and served her father Laban for seven years to earn her as his wife, but her older sister Leah was placed in the bed on the wedding night. God had sympathy for the unloved sister Leah and "he opened her womb; but Rachel was barren" (Genesis 29:31). When Rachel complained to Jacob and demanded, "Give me children, or I shall die!" Jacob berated her: "Am I in the place of God, who has withheld from you the fruit of the womb?" (Genesis 30:2) Later God remembered the infertile Rachel, "opened her womb" and took away her reproach (Genesis 30:22–23). She gives birth to Joseph and finally to Benjamin.

These are people whom the Bible brings forth from the shadows of time so vividly that we recognize them as our brothers and sisters — so vividly that Thomas Mann could write a 1,000-page novel about *Joseph and his Brothers*. They knew and believed:

> Children are a gift from the Lord, the fruit of the womb is his blessing. (Psalm 127:3)

That was then. We're now light years from there. We've torn the roots out of nature, of which we are a part, and upset the order of creation. And no one can deny that there really is an order. Science discovers its laws and delves deeper and deeper into the mystery of the origin of life. Pope Benedict XVI writes:

> Man becomes a product, and this fundamentally alters man's relationship to himself. He is no longer a gift of nature or of the Creator God: he is his own product. Man has climbed down into the wellsprings of power, to the source of his very existence.[12]

That there is a creator who has equipped the seeds with their building plans is something we don't want to know. We would rather believe that the unfathomable intelligence that we discover in everything is a product of coincidence, that order has arisen out of senseless chaos through a continuous, autonomous higher development, a balance of billions of organisms and highly complex systems in which life pulsates.

As with every other higher being, people come in two sexes, man and woman, and procreate through their biological union. The man's member enters the woman's vagina, releases a stream of 40 million to 400 million sperm cells with genetic information, from which the woman's egg generally accepts *just one* and merges into itself. The woman's egg cells are numbered. Her body does not constantly produce new ones, as with the man's sperm. They age and die out. In the instant the egg and the sperm cell merge, a new person is created, and the entire genetic program is set in motion. From that point on, the human being, just like every animal and plant, needs nothing more than good growth conditions to develop continuously first in its mother's womb and then as a separate living being.

It is disputed whether the zygote, the very first merging of the egg and sperm cell, is already a person who has the right to life. Anyone who wants to use this embryo for research purposes or commercial interests argues in this way: Not until the embryo has adhered to the uterine wall — after nidation — can one really talk about a human being, or not until 12 weeks, or maybe only if it is self-aware or healthy?

On October 18, 2011, in the case of Brüstle versus Greenpeace e.V., the European Court of Human Rights reached a clear decision:

> Every human egg cell, from the time it is inseminated, is a human embryo.

It therefore has the right to state protection of its life.

The act of procreation gives pleasure to both animals and humans. Man and woman are attracted to each other with a power that can overcome will and reason to form a biological union. But there is a big difference between animals and people: In animals, this irresistible urge arises only during the annual cycle for reproduction. In people, sexual attraction is independent of an instinctual imperative to procreate. This creates freedom for soaring love, the bliss of lust, the heartbreaking dramas between love and lust, and the abyss of perversion.

Of course, we women can fly planes, run countries and companies, become engineers or mathematicians, win at karate or stand our ground as soldiers. All through time, women have taken over men's tasks when there was a shortage of men to do them, such as when millions of men went off to war and perhaps never came back. But strangely, the vast majority of women resist state attempts at reeducation and choose professions that have to do with people, with teaching and helping, with language and communication. There is an attempt to talk women out of the idea that they're different and convince them that they're actually better men. Men should make room in leadership positions — by quota, if necessary. Everybody knows that the body, spirit, and mind of men and women are fundamentally different and wonderfully complement one another. Nobody can change the fact that men's and women's bodies fit together like a lock and key, and that human beings come about through the unification of the woman's egg cell and the man's semen — whether in a night of love, or a rape, or a Petri dish. The man's seed must unify with a woman's egg to bring forth a new, genetically unique human being. Today men and women are considered interchangeable, even more now that gender is claimed to be an individual choice. We see images of women with rifle at the ready and men with a beard and pregnant belly. Have we really gained any freedom? Is the future rosier for man, woman, and child?

The woman's cycle

For the greater part of his life, a man is capable of procreating, while a woman can do so only a few days of the month and only for a lesser portion of her life. Her supply of viable eggs is limited. Something extraordinary, something that's hers alone, happens in her body — from puberty to menopause, which is really not a pause, but the end of her ability to bear life.

Every four weeks or so, blood comes out the woman's vagina. It can be associated with pain and mood swings. After a couple of days, the bleeding stops again. This repeats for about 30 years of a woman's life, about 450 to 500 times, starting in puberty. All women of this earth are subject to this cyclical event. Many cultures and religions consider the woman "unclean" during this time and subject her to specific rituals. People were always aware that the cycle had something to do with fertility, because the woman's fertility goes away when the blood does. But discovery of the complex hormonal system of a woman's fertility cycle didn't come until the 20th century and only gradually seeped into the general consciousness.

"Women bear children," a medical education website says. "This statement sounds simplistic and superfluous. However, it is fundamental to everything that happens in a woman's body in its monthly rhythm. The purpose of the periodic change is always to create optimal conditions for a possible pregnancy."[13]

Let's look more closely at this wonder of self-regulation. It is a finely tuned interplay of hormone glands in the brain, monthly maturation of a viable egg in the woman's ovary, and the uterus, which every four weeks prepares to accept a fertilized egg, so that for nine months a viable child can grow in it. If the egg does not get fertilized, the uterus's mucous membrane is rejected and excreted, which shows up as menstruation.

The brain is the control center of the woman's fertility. The operations manager for the whole event is the hypothalamus, a specific area of the mid-brain. In the first phase of the cycle, beginning on the first day of bleeding, the hormone gonadotropin (GnRH) is secreted, which triggers the fertility cycle. It causes the pituitary gland to produce the follicle-stimulating hormone (FSH), which is released into the blood. This does what its name says: It initiates follicle maturation in the ovary and increases production of the sex hormone estrogen. The follicle is the vesicle in which the egg cell and hormone glands are located.

Estrogen prepares the woman's organs for fertilization. The mucus in the neck of the uterus liquefies and draws long threads for transporting and nourishing the sperm. The neck of the cervix softens, the sex organs are better supplied with blood, and the mammary tissue can swell and become sensitive.

Several follicles from the ovary's limited reserve start to grow, but only one follicle — the strongest and best — wins the race. It grows up to 25 mm and produces progesterone, which gives the signal for the follicle to burst. The egg springs out of the follicle, or more precisely, it flushes out of the fluid in the follicle and lands in the fimbriated end of the fallopian tube, and ovulation has occurred. The other follicles die out. The egg begins the four- to five-day journey through the fallopian tube into the uterus. It is ready for fertilization only during the first 10 to 12 hours.

The estrogen produced in the follicle during its maturation gives the uterine lining the signal for new growth. New blood vessels sprout, and the mucous membrane becomes thicker and softer.

With ovulation, the second phase of the cycle starts. Plan A is pregnancy: The egg cell is fertilized and nests into the uterus. Plan B: Fertilization does not take place, all hormonal pregnancy stimulators are retracted, the receptive mucous membrane in the uterus is shed (menstruation), the cervix is closed with tough cervical mucus, and the cycle begins again — and again and again for 30 years until the egg cells become old and are used up. At age 35, fertility already starts to decline.

Or Plan A comes into effect: A single sperm out of 40 million to 400 million makes it into the fallopian tube and is taken in by the egg cell. Egg and sperm merge and create a zygote, which contains all hereditary information. A new human being comes into existence.

The fertilized egg is transported by the cilia of the fallopian tube in three to four days into the uterus and needs another two to three days to embed.

In the meantime, the corpus luteum is formed in the follicle cavity, which then produces plenty of progesterone. This converts the uterine lining. Nutrients are stored that can nourish the embryo for several weeks until the placenta has fully developed. As soon as the embryo has nested, the uterus produces the pregnancy hormone HCG, which can be found in the blood just two days after nidation. It skyrockets and is what causes many pregnant women to have morning sickness. Progesterone reliably prevents another ovulation. It raises the waking temperature, thickens the cervical mucus, and the cervix becomes hard.

The control and interaction of the hormones, their rise and retreat, the exact timing, the reciprocal, finely tuned resonance, work like a chamber orchestra playing an extremely intricate composition. The rise and fall, swell and retreat, crescendo and decrescendo follow the impulse of a mysterious conductor. Sometimes the violin comes to the fore, sometimes the cello, and at other times the flute. They all play the song of life.

How can humanity — no, not humanity, but ideological trend setters — fall for the idea that motherhood is merely incidental for women, something that someone could just as well forget about and sacrifice on the altar of career and sexual freedom?

To be fertile, to be receptive to a man's seed, to give life, to nurture and care for life, is the woman's deepest identity. It makes her courageous as a lioness while being tender and compassionate, deeply satisfied and happy, if she has a man who protectively embraces mother and child, allows himself to be seized by the miracle of life, and is ready to grow into the responsibility of fatherhood — and to stay with his wife and children for a lifetime.

For nine months, all matter from which the child is formed is matter from the woman's body. It may be no accident that the words *mother* (Latin *mater*) and *matter* are so similar. Even after birth, in nursing her child, she gives it everything it needs to grow. This child, formed from her own substance, evokes in her a love that astounds and brings the deepest joy — so small, so fragile, so helpless, so fully dependent on her. With every fiber of her being, she wants her child to live. Is there anything that belongs to her more than this child, "my child"? It only takes a couple of weeks for the baby to start smiling, when his eyes notice his mother's face. His smile is like a window to heaven — no animal smiles, and no robot will ever truly be able to smile.

None of this is romantic pie in the sky. No, it's the plan of creation that brings forth life and happiness.

If mothers are honored, then so are their children. But such a claim evokes only mockery and ridicule among childless feminists who fight for the right to abortion. Sixty-seven percent of female journalists in Germany have no children.[14] No wonder they toot the feminist horn. They have never been challenged by children to overcome their self-centeredness. That's not learned in the whirlwind of editorial offices, but in the honing process of marriage and responsibility for children. The other person comes first — husband or wife or the crying baby. That might mean getting up five times a night. The child must not be let down in the absolute trust he or she places in the mother, because someday this child must also be capable of seeing to the wellbeing of others.

Everyone has a mother — hopefully just one. All in all, if we like living, we have to be thankful to our mother, no matter how far she may fall short. But people let their state of mind be determined by the shortcomings and not from the much greater gift of life. That is the psychological fashion of our time. It has descended over the whole society like a cloud of smog. Mothers aren't worth anything. If women want recognition, they should work, and preferably be childless. If they nonetheless have a child or two, then they must be raised by strangers right from birth.

The average life expectancy of women in Western Europe is 84 years. If we assume that menstruation first occurs at 13 and lasts 30 years, then there remain another 40 years or so when the woman can no longer get pregnant. At 40, she is full of vitality, and her beauty has gained in maturity and femininity. If she had her children shortly after her education was finished, they are already more or less independent by that time. As a mother, she has learned an incredible number of things: To overcome her natural youthful selfishness. She has served her husband, children, the whole family, and has become willing to sacrifice. Now she can use these capabilities for even greater goals.

People seldom dare to utter the words "serve" and "sacrifice." Women are supposed to hold society's power positions. They have been oppressed by the patriarchy for too long. Finally, *finally*, we have overcome that, right?

But don't people — both men and women — need to *serve* the general welfare? That is only possible when the ego is restrained. Aren't there enough power-, sex-, and money-obsessed people in leadership positions?

Women who have chosen to live their identity as mothers seldom reach the highest leadership positions — and maybe that's not what they find most important. For them, it's more important to do meaningful work, to make life better and more beautiful — in her own family and beyond. Is that a loss to society? Does society not need women who use their strength and power as givers of life, who nurture and support, encourage and guide toward the good? More than men, women see the big picture. It's not as important to them to get from A to B as fast as possible, while overtaking others. They perceive everything that goes on between A and B. They are specialists in "inclusion." The woman has authority, because she sacrifices for the good of all.

Because a woman is essentially receptive, she has a greater openness to the spiritual dimension of existence. To bring this dimension to her husband, she needs to give up the struggle for power. A man listens to his wife only if she respects him. Women who are willing to do this stand a greater chance for a good marriage, for having healthy children who can cope, and for a happy, lively family.

Even women who have no children, for whatever reason, can have women's feminine, maternal, life-giving qualities. Women who do that receive the honorary title of "mother." One of the most famous examples is Mother Teresa of Calcutta. What is decisive is that the woman uses her life force to serve life. The world hungers for selfless love. When this hunger is sated, it makes two people happy: the giver and the receiver.

2.

Barren by choice: Sex yes, baby no

> *I will bereave them of children, I will destroy my people, since they return not from their ways.*
> Jeremiah (15:7), 600 v. Christus

We live in a time when individual freedom has become the highest virtue. We want to lord over life and death and consider this absolutely indispensable for our freedom. It's *I* who decides if and when I have a child — and when not. My rights and needs come first. There's no higher being than I. An ape is my ancestor, Nirvana my goal, and my will is my heavenly kingdom.

At one time, it was different. At the forefront was the wellbeing of the community we knew we belonged to — the family, the town, the nation. Their good was to be served. And there were times when all of a person's life was over-arched by belief in God, whose will people wished to discern.

Today, the individual's power trip is enabled and encouraged by the tremendous development of technology. It seems anything is possible — everything is subject to the power of the human will.

So, should we women still allow ourselves to be governed by our fertility cycle? Thank God, that's all over! Should women be at the mercy of men's sexual desires and the risk of pregnancy? No! No! No! The woman herself decides if she'll be fertile or not.

Not many decades ago, there would have been dramatic consequences for both the woman and child if she got pregnant out of wedlock. Banishment from the family, stigmatization of the illegitimate child. Mary, the mother of Jesus, might have been stoned if Joseph had not accepted the child and his mother. In Muslim societies, there is a threat of blood revenge. Today about 40 percent of children are born out of wedlock. In Western societies, no one points and whispers anymore at an unmarried woman with an illegitimate child. Now she's just a "single mother." Instead of marrying the father, she may marry the state. About a fifth of all mothers raise their children alone.

The woman fears getting pregnant when she doesn't want to — she may be filled with angst after a night of sex until the pregnancy test results come. A carefree romp in the sack should not have lifelong consequences.

For men, unintentional creation of a child is more of a peccadillo. He can get away with it, but the woman can't. For the woman, letting passions carry her away can alter her destiny. It can mean creation of a child that grows for nine months in her body, labor pains during delivery, and caring for the child, who will never again leave her spiritual orbit. The man just pays child support.

We think we now have a handle on that through contraception. "I" decide over lust, love, and life.

People's idea of contraception includes a notion of protection. An accident can be prevented, because someone was on guard. "May God protect us," was once a common expression that has now fallen out of fashion in the wasteland of disbelief. If we use contraception during the physical union of man and woman, we guard ourselves from the misfortune of a child. If despite all contraceptive measures a child is conceived, people now call it an "accident."

The woman

I want sex.
I do not want commitment.
I do not want a child.
I do not want to be a mother.
I don't want you as the father.

The man

I want sex.
I do not want commitment.
I do not want a child.
I do not want to be a father.
I don't want you as the mother.

Contraception, the most normal thing in the world. Collecting the semen in a rubber sack, blocking access to the cervix with a rubber diaphragm coated with spermicide, inserting a spiral into the uterus to prevent the fertilized egg from nestling into the receptive uterus, or swallowing a pill every day promises freedom from all cares. But are we really capable and authorized to systematically sever the sex act from its purpose — the creation of human life?

The question hidden behind it all is this: How do we understand the world we live in? Does the living world that surrounds us have meaning, or are we thrown into a universe of objects that we can exploit and manipulate as we please?

Aristotle said that every object has a *telos*, an internally hidden meaning and plan for development. Man himself has an internal *telos*, and to follow it makes his existence successful. Philosopher Robert Spaemann speaks of a type-specific way in which each living being is "after something." It is part of that being's very existence.[15] If we respect that existence and its inner destiny, what ought to be will be, and that becomes the norm. This means: It is good for us when we seek our *telos*, and it is bad for us when we use our freedom to arbitrarily satisfy our own interests, desires, and passions.

Do we believe, with Aristotle, that the cosmos, nature, the body, have an internal meaning, an objective with an inner drive to be fulfilled?

What does this mean for sexuality? What is its *telos*, its inner meaning, its objective? Any child knows half the answer: Creation of new life. This can apply to animals, whose sexual activity is governed by instinct and is limited to specific times during the year. Meanwhile, humans are the only creatures with a free will. Humans have a thinking mind that is aware of itself, that can decide whether to do something or not. They have an internal mechanism for distinguishing good and evil, which is called the conscience. They have dignity, because according to Judeo-Christian tradition they are formed in the image of God. They have souls that survive death, as all religions teach, and they have a heart that can love.

Because a person cannot separate mind from body without robbing himself of integrity and dignity, sexuality has a second basic meaning for him: a union of love. Only this allows him not to use another person as an object to satisfy his lust. No person wants to be an object. People want to be recognized and respected in both the body and in the soul, which expresses itself through the body.

Let's take a closer look at whether the contraceptive industry's most frequently used products — condoms and the pill — keep their promises.

Condoms

Condoms are the most frequently used form of contraception. As children are now taught from a young age, condoms protect from pregnancy, AIDS, and other sexually transmitted diseases, and they guarantee "safe sex," or at least "safer sex." Where reality does not confirm this, it is supposedly because not enough condoms have been distributed among the people. Even before puberty, children in mixed classes learn how to pull condoms over plastic penises. They are to learn that sex is okay anytime, from childhood on. Everything bad is prevented if they just have this rubber sheath at hand.

But that's a lie.[16] Condoms are not a sure thing: They rip, they slip off, they may leak, and they may pull hairs, creating perfect tiny wounds for diseases to enter. If a hundred couples use condoms absolutely reliably for a year, two couples will conceive a child. With "typical use," 18 couples conceive. What then?

Condoms also don't reliably guard against AIDS and other sexually transmitted diseases. It's a game of Russian roulette. For every 16 uses, one condom fails. Would we use parachutes if every 16th one didn't open?

If condoms were as secure as the worldwide propaganda tells people, the explosive spread of venereal diseases would not be possible. That includes syphilis (now more common than HIV[17] among men in Europe who have sex with men), gonorrhea (risk: infertility), human papilloma virus (risk: genital warts, uterine cancer, male infertility[18]), and chlamydia, the most common sexually transmitted disease (risk: ectopic pregnancy, female infertility[19]).[20]

Women can become pregnant only a few days a month. But women and men can catch venereal diseases through any kind of sexual behavior — vaginal, anal, and oral — and thereby risk cancer, infertility, and death. Dr. Helen Singer, founder of the Human Sexuality Program at Cornell University, therefore says: "Trusting condoms is flirting with death."[21]

How do condoms affect the intimacy of man and woman? How would it feel to be petted by a hand that is wearing a rubber glove? Men who make love feel the rubber sheath as a barrier to union, because they want to become "one flesh" and can't. This brings up the question: How do condoms contribute to our era's divorce culture?

The pill

We want to be healthy, live to an old age, and reach death in the best health we can. Clean air, healthy food, wellness and fitness offerings are everywhere we look. Smoking, one of the surest paths to cancer, has been banned in most public places by law and through years of campaigning by governments. But strangely enough, healthy habits and government's concern for public health — especially for the young — go right out the window when it comes to sex. Why do women willingly poison their bodies with a daily chemical cocktail that interferes with their body's deepest control system?

According to a survey by Germany's Federal Center for Health Education, one out of two women between 18 and 49 are on the pill in that country. Young girls have no trouble getting a pill prescription, without their parents' knowledge, the first time they visit the gynecologist. Many young women take the pill when they aren't even in a sexual relationship yet, because it improves their complexion, enlarges their breasts, and adds sheen to their hair. The pill is attractively packaged, with little flowers and hearts, as if it were a cosmetic product.

We normally take pills to restore disrupted functions in the body and to activate life processes. The pill does the opposite: It prevents life and can even extinguish life.

What liberation when a tiny pill, swallowed daily, frees one from the responsibility of being a woman! I decide for my body, not my body for me, and not the man for me, and not the family for me, and definitely not the kid. What an irresistible temptation!

Legalization of contraception and abortion, to gain control over women's fertility, were the life's mission of American Margaret Sanger (1879–1966). Her driving motive was to prevent the underclass — especially blacks — from reproducing, because their birth rate was higher than that of the white upper class.[22] This is called eugenics, the idea of taking biological measures to "improve" the human race. In 1921, she founded the

American Birth Control League, which in 1942 was renamed the *International Planned Parenthood Federation* (IPPF).

Today, Sanger would be shunned and legally penalized for her racism. But her methods and disrespect for human dignity were adopted by the IPPF, a worldwide organization that tries to decrease the world population by aborting millions of unborn children.

Scientific progress played right into Margaret Sanger's hands. Gregory Pincus and Carl Djerassi had discovered how a woman's pregnancy cycle can be suspended by introducing artificial hormones. The hormones trick the body into thinking it has become pregnant and thereby prevent ovulation. Hooray! Women were no longer slaves to their biological cycle! It was tremendous progress, but away from the very complex, natural operation of the female fertility cycle. The price of this progress came to light only later, and women had to pay with their physical and mental health.

The pill was tested by the Searle Pharmaceutical Corporation on unsuspecting women in Puerto Rico and Haiti. Someone in the United States seemed to think there were too many of them, and no one there would protect them from the pharmaceutical industry's experimentation anyway.

In 1960, the first product, "Enovid," came on the US market, and in 1961 it arrived in West Germany as "Anvolar." The pill was introduced as a treatment for menstrual cramps, with contraception listed as a "side effect" on the package insert. The German magazine *Stern* trumpeted the market rollout as a "historic day" — which it really was. It started the industrialized countries' decline into the demographic winter. Within ten years, it became a clear baby-bust caused by the pill.

Soon millions of women were swallowing pills every day, which doctors willingly prescribed. The women were willing to choke off, trick, and disable their most innate attribute — the ability to bring forth life — having been enticed by the promise of sex with no fear of pregnancy.

Then the women's bodies and souls got stuck with the bill. The pill has severe side effects. There is barely any serious illness whose probability is not exacerbated by taking the pill: breast cancer, cervical cancer, liver damage, thrombosis, stroke, heart attack, severe migraines, high blood pressure, thyroid problems, glaucoma, weakened immune system, reduced fertility, shrinking of the ovaries by up to 50%, and miscarriages.[23]

The risks increase the earlier the pill is taken and the longer it continues. They massively increase when other risk factors are present, such as smoking or sexually transmitted diseases.

The greatest threat for women is breast cancer. Statistically, every eighth woman in Germany comes down with breast cancer. Previously, three-quarters of them died, but now — thank God — a bit fewer than half of them do. Who doesn't know of tragic cases of women taken from their families by breast cancer? Studies show that taking the pill increases the risk of breast cancer.[24]

To reduce the risks, the pharmaceutical industry developed the three-phase "mini-pill." "Great!" women thought, "Fewer hormones!" But most of them didn't know this: The pill with the lowest dose may allow ovulation and then fertilization. A human being is conceived and is then prevented from implanting in the uterus. The fertilized egg does not survive the journey through the fallopian tube or is rejected by the uterus. With the mini-pill, therefore, conception can take place, but implantation is prevented, which is none other than an abortion.

The woman accepts all this in exchange for carefree sex, but — what an irony! — she loses interest in sex. Why? Because, in women, the desire for sex is also governed by testosterone, and the pill suppresses testosterone production.

This leads to subtle changes in courtship behavior. Anthropologist Lionel Tiger researched changes in apes' sexual behavior under the effects of hormonal contraceptives.[25] It turned out that the male apes lost their sexual interest in females who were on hormonal contraceptives. They became disoriented, and the group's social structure became chaotic. As soon as the contraceptives were gone, normal attraction between males and females came back.

Coupling behavior of people also seems to change when women's fertility is hormonally deactivated. The pill reduces women's sexual attraction signal to men. Exposed cleavage and a short skirt have less attraction for men than intact fertility.[26] The pill changes the body odor, which can result in the partner being "unable to smell" the woman. This changes the woman's choice of partner,[27] and even her ability to interpret her partner's facial expression correctly.[28]

The pharmaceutical industry kept all this quiet for a long time, because no other product makes them so much money. And strangely enough, there seems to be no concern in the WHO or EU to protect women from the serious physical and mental damage. When it comes to unbridled enjoyment of the sex drive, then all warning systems fail and all lights switch to green.

Are the bad effects on the bodies and minds of women any surprise, then? Artificial hormones simulate in the woman's body exactly what she doesn't want: pregnancy. The extremely complex, delicate interaction of hormones is thrown out of whack — and that's expected to have no effect on the organism or the woman's intricate psyche? Instead of receiving the scientific findings on the miraculous operation of the body with awe and amazement, eugenicists and population control advocates, radical feminists, and pharmaceutical corporations use them to put women in the crosshairs, to rob them of their fertility, and to severely damage their health. And what's the win? Constant availability of carefree, sterile sex.

After half a century of the pill, even its co-inventor, Prof. Carl Djerassi (died 2015), thought the end of its era was in sight. On May 13, 2008, on a German talk show, he met a 51-year-old prostitute and brothel operator who used an egg donation from a foreign woman (forbidden in Germany) and her husband's sperm to bear a child, a lesbian psychoanalyst who had brought a child into the world through an anonymous sperm donor, and Catholic gynecologist Dr. Gabriele Marx, who refused to prescribe the pill.

Gabriele Marx and Carl Djerassi agreed on one point — that the pill era is ending — but for very different reasons. Marx considered it irresponsible to subject women to the massive health risks. Djerassi had a different vision: Between the ages of 18 and 20, the woman would have her fertilizable eggs removed, frozen, and kept in a bank for reproductive material. Then she would have herself sterilized to devote herself to her career and to freely satisfy her sexual needs. This is called *social freezing*, a costly process that Apple and Facebook finance for their female employees.

Then when they are 40, they get the feeling that one last thing is missing from their accomplishments. A child will be the cherry on top. The eggs can be thawed in the hope that some of them will still be usable. They can be fertilized by the sperm of the current partner or an anonymous donor, prenatal diagnosis can make sure that the fertilized eggs have no defects, and a surrogate can carry one of them in her womb. Perfect happiness in life! But is it that sure a thing? Will the child one yearns for fulfill all wishes?

Djcrassi was a clear-sighted man: Up to now it has been the era of "sex without children," and now we were to enter into the era of "children without sex," thus into the Brave New World that Aldous Huxley had already envisioned in 1932.

Don't we consider ourselves rational beings who can weigh risks and avoid the ones that complicate our lives? When it comes to sex, all safeguards go off the rails. We know from experience that this can easily happen. Cultures have therefore developed social and moral safety mechanisms that have domesticated the sex drive. In his work *Sex and Culture,* J. D. Unwin has shown that high culture comes only at the price of strict sexual morality. When a culture gives up confining sexuality to marriage, after a few generations it falls off the stage of history.[29]

There is a 100 percent effective safety device for the dignity and health of men and women: Sex only within marriage. Impossible! Unrealistic! Medieval! "It's retrograde!" is what people shout at those who consider this alternative reasonable and practicable. "No," is what the "family planners," population controllers, sex education teachers, and all those who have been carried away by the zeitgeist: People are like animals, who cannot govern their sex drive. But that's not true. Children can and must be raised to become reliable spouses and responsible parents, and to experience sexuality as an exhilarating expression of steadfast love.

A prophetic encyclical

One lone voice rose against the false promise of "sexual liberation," that of Pope Paul VI. In 1968, against the torrential current of the time, he published his encyclical *Humanae Vitae* (On Human Life).

He held to the existing teaching of the Church, that man must not autonomously do away with the two purposes of the marital act — loving unity and procreation (Art. 11 and 12). At the same time, it must not be ruled out that parents may "for serious reasons and with due respect to moral precepts, decide not to have additional children for either a certain or an indefinite period of time" (Art. 10).

A storm of indignation arose, not only outside, but even inside the Church. Theologians composed public declarations against the pope. Many bishops' conferences refused obedience to the magisterium (the Königstein

Declaration in Germany, the Mariatroster Declaration in Austria), and Catholic laypeople organized into resistance groups (a petition for a people's referendum in Austria). They could all count on the wind of the media powerfully blowing their sails.

The resistance was understandable. There was huge promise in the air from the pill, which had become available just a few years before: People's love life was no longer affected by worries of pregnancy. Parents could now plan and determine the number and spacing of the children they had (thus the name *International Planned Parenthood Federation*). The number of abortions would be reduced (but the opposite happened). In fact, considering the threat of "the population bomb," the need to prevent conception had become a truism for all humanity.

And here the pope had the guts to rain on the whole parade with his serious warnings! If the sex act were systematically severed from fertility, there would be a break in the dam with devastating consequences. Paul VI foresaw that:

- There would be a "wide way for marital infidelity and a general lowering of moral standards."
- Men "may forget the reverence due to a woman, and, disregarding her physical and emotional equilibrium, reduce her to being a mere instrument for the satisfaction of his own desires, no longer considering her as his partner whom he should surround with care and affection."
- The pope was also aware of the "dangerous power" this could give to authorities to ignore moral principles when trying to overcome their nations' difficulties. "Who will prevent public authorities from favoring those contraceptive methods which they consider more effective? Should they regard this as necessary, they may even impose their use on everyone" (Art. 17).

Half a century later, it is clear that the Holy Father's fears were prophetic. Contraception has become an assumed part of sexual behavior, and children are taught about it as early as elementary school. The "natural law" that was still supported by custom, civil law, and society in the middle of the last century was torn from its moorings in the hearts and minds of people.

However, there was one thing Pope Paul did not foresee in 1968: The demographic change and its threat to the survival of European, Christian, and Western culture.[30]

With nature and not against it — Natural Family Planning

Natural Family Planning, which Pope Paul VI recommended to the people, was still in its infancy back then. With the growing understanding of the woman's fertility cycle, it has now become a reliable method of regulating conception.

We've already seen where contraception leads: Damage to health, damage to the soul, destruction of the family, and creeping demographic suicide. Wouldn't it be great if there were a way to decide on the number and spacing of children responsibly — without all that harm to health, the soul, and the family? There is a way, but it comes at a price: A capacity for self-control and willingness for self-denial — both marks of human maturity. The method is called Natural Family Planning, or NFP.[31]

People have never known as much about the woman's hormonally controlled fertility cycle as we do now. It can be read from symptoms, particularly a change in vaginal mucus and the body temperature. The egg can only be fertilized within a 12-hour window. There is a generous margin of eight days outside of which a woman knows she cannot conceive. For this, she has to monitor her body for an extended time and keep charts in which to enter the varying numbers corresponding to these symptoms. Through knowledge and integration into the woman's natural cycle, the married couple can either aid conception of a child, or for reasons of parental responsibility avoid fertilization. It only takes a couple minutes a day. But the change in attitude is a revolution.

The woman and man no longer see themselves as the rulers of nature. They could evade natural law using chemicals or other measures to block fertility, but instead they subordinate themselves to nature. The sex act is not systematically severed from its goal of creating new life. The man and woman always give themselves to one another as an expression of their love. The man honors the woman, and together they subordinate themselves to nature in an act of humility. They become aware of the gravity of their human vocation through an act of love to conceive a child with unfathomable potential and an eternal soul. They accept one another as the mother and father of a child in common.

The sympto-thermal method

- is reliable
- does not block the woman's or man's fertility
- has no side effects
- does not damage the woman's organism through hormonal interference
- requires no manipulation before sexual intercourse
- introduces no barrier between the man and woman
- deepens the partnership through open communication about sexuality
- keeps sexual attraction alive through periodic abstinence
- does not damage the environment through hormonal contamination of waste water.

Are there also disadvantages? Sure, there are a few, such as these: One spouse was out of town. They yearn for each other, fall into each other's arms, but now can't give free reign to their attraction, because the fertility traffic light is still on green, and having another child simply wouldn't be responsible right now. Women report that right at the time of ovulation they feel a great deal of lust and find it hard to hold back. The man and woman don't want to be constantly caught up in the cycle. Their life is stressful, and they seldom have a chance to get together in a relaxed, spontaneous way. They don't want to get carried away.

These difficulties exist. People have crosses to bear in life, and no matter how hard we try, we will never get rid of them. Temptation says with a sneaky grin: Do what you want, "You won't die," (Genesis 3:4) and conceals the sorrowful consequences. The voice that calls us to the good makes no secret of the cross. It shows a way for people to grow in love: through erotic attraction, the *eros*, deep friendship, *philia*, and surrendering, sacrificial love, *agape*. It brings the profound happiness of fulfilling the meaning of life.

3.
Women reigning over life and death

> *The greatest destroyer of peace today is the cry of the innocent unborn child.*
> Mother Teresa of Calcutta upon accepting the 1979 Nobel Peace Prize

And if contraception doesn't work? No chemical or technical method is certain. Despite all technical refinements, our body and nature still have the last word. They are more powerful. Despite condoms, despite IUDs, and despite the pill women become pregnant nonetheless. And then?

People give lots of reasons for abortion:

I'm still way too young.
What on earth am I going to tell my parents?
I need to finish high school, college, and get a job first.
Can I live with this guy all my life? Out of the question!
That was just an adventure.
I don't want to raise my child alone.
He can't find out that I cheated on him. She can't find out that I cheated on her.
We can't handle another kid.

There are thousands of situations that seem like catastrophes when the sexual act works as designed — when it produces a child. Bitter tears, despair, suddenly being delivered to the harsh hand of fate. The hardship of an unwanted conception can be overwhelming. A woman in such hardship needs help, and she can find it.[32]

In a culture of extreme individualism, in which everything revolves around one's own rights and desires, there is an oversized temptation to look for a way out: Just get rid of it, it's just a clump of cells, medical insurance will pay for it, after a few days it's all over, and life can go on as normal.

Really?

Here are the statistics:

Every year, worldwide, more than 50 million women decide to have a child in their womb killed. In Germany, according to the Federal Statistical Office, 101,000 did that in 2018. Evidently, abortions have continuously decreased since 2000.

But this information is highly suspect. For years, the Federal Statistical Office has added a clarification to its charts: "The results and their trends must be viewed with caution," which means that there is actually a considerable number of unreported cases. Christian Fiala, gynecologist and head of two abortion clinics in Vienna and Salzburg, is convinced that, "the annual number of aborted pregnancies in Germany should be corrected by 200,000 to 300,000.... The [abortionists'] data are anonymized and are not traceable. Moreover, patient data are subject to strict medical confidentiality. No one can check whether they are completely reported."[33] Prof. Manfred Spieker uses very meticulous calculations to arrive at similar numbers of unreported cases.[34]

In Germany, in 2018, about 785,000 children were born (officially) and 101,000 aborted. It varies considerably among the federal states. The most abortions happen in Berlin and Bremen.[35] Killing of unborn children is a constant reality in medical facilities that deal with pregnancy.

Almost three-quarters of all women who have abortions are in the prime childbearing years, between 18 and 34 years old. Three percent are under 18, and the rest are over 35, when the chance of conceiving considerably diminishes. About 47,000 have had one or two children and don't want a larger family; 9,000 abort after the third child. Almost 60,000 are single, and almost 40,000 are married. Ninety-six percent of women who have had abortions had previously gone for "open-ended counseling," which is required by law. The other 3.8% have medical indications.[36]

Just a clump of cells?

Actually, the mother's womb should be the safest place for a person. In fact, though, it's the most dangerous location. Abortion is by far the most common cause of death. In 2008, about 3 million people in the EU died from abortion, followed by approximately 2 million from cardiac and circulatory illnesses.

Isn't it a woman's right to have control over her own body? To take her fate into her own hands, to plan her life at her own discretion, and decide over life and death when reality conflicts with her own wishes?

It all depends on the question of whether the "something" growing in the mother's womb is a person or not. There is no doubt that the state must respect a person's dignity and protect his right to life.

The first sentence of the constitution of the German Federal Republic is:

"Human dignity is inviolable." For a person's dignity to be preserved, he must live. That is why the state has the unconditional obligation to protect its citizens' lives. Article 2 of the constitution says: "Everyone has the right to life and bodily integrity."

Is that "something" in the mother's womb, which came about through the merging of egg and sperm cell, a person or not?

Could it be anything else? People create people, animals create animals, plants reproduce as plants. (Let's leave aside the fact that scientists plan to break these barriers through "transhumanism.".)

Could it be a person *anyway?* Not until implantation, not until the heart beats, not until the baby is *completely* born, not until consciousness is there? What is it before that, and what causes the complete ontological change from a "clump of cells" to a human being?

German case law has formulated clear, unambiguous answers to these questions. One year before the German parliament legalized abortion, in 1974, the country's federal constitutional court declared that:

> Where human life exists, it has human dignity; it is not decisive whether the bearer is aware of this dignity and knows how to defend it himself. The potential capabilities inherent to human existence are sufficient to establish human dignity.

On May 28, 1993, the federal constitutional court again declared that:

> The embryo develops as a person, not into a person.

But recognition of the embryo's human dignity and therefore its right to life did not prevent the court from using legal acrobatics to sacrifice the life of the unborn child to the mother's right to self-determination.

Thirty-six years later, after many countries had legalized abortion, the European Court of Human Rights made a similar decision. The motive for the lawsuit (Brüstle versus Greenpeace)[37] was not abortion, but a scientist's access to the embryo's stem cells. Undreamed-of possibilities for financial gain were emerging on the horizon, because there was talk of new medical cures. The judgment says: *"Every human egg cell, from the time of its fertilization, is a human embryo..., because the fertilization is enough to set the process of developing a human being into action."*[38]

Your life, my life, everyone's life started that way. An egg cell and a sperm cell merge. A new human being is formed. The genetic program, eternally unique in the universe, has been set off and will continuously unfold as long as the growth conditions are suitable — before and beyond birth.

New scientific findings on development of the embryo, and photographs of its progress inside the womb, are astounding. What a miracle the formation of a human being is! Starting with the third week of life, when the embryo is just 1.5 millimeters, the heart starts to beat, and when the fourth week comes, it reaches 113 beats per minute. At six weeks, the embryo is 14 millimeters, and the head, spine, hands, and brain hemispheres start to form. At seven weeks, a girl's ovaries and a boy's testicles develop. During the eighth week, the atrium of the heart forms. The embryo starts to grasp, move its fingers to its mouth, and one can already see whether a baby is right- or left-handed. Ninety percent of the physical structures present in adults have already formed and taken on their function. In the 10th week, the embryo — now called a fetus — already has fingernails and even fingerprints that are unique in the world.[39]

> Up to the 12th week of pregnancy, the child in the womb is allowed to be killed — and until birth, if it has a disability.

The child starts to hear at 17 weeks. By the time it is born, it recognizes its mother's and father's voices and songs that had been sung to it. It is accustomed to household sounds, such as noisy children and dogs barking. Starting with the 18th week, the fetus displays stress reactions that are perceived in children and adults as expressions of pain. Scientists variously estimate the ability to feel pain as starting between the 15th and 24th week.[40] From the 22nd week, the brain develops very quickly. The baby can smile or look serious, suck its thumb, distinguish high and low tones, and it reacts to its mother's movements. At this point, with a birth weight of just over a pound, the baby can survive outside the mother's womb. During the 28th week it opens its eyes. In the 38th week, the baby finds it too cramped in the womb, contractions set in, and the child is ready for the big step into the brilliant world. A human being is born.

How can it be that in Germany and many other countries in the world, abortion is legal if the mother perceives the child as an unreasonable burden, and if it's disabled right up until birth?

The German federal constitutional court declared abortion "unlawful" in 1993, but exempted it from penalty. With this, they squared the circle or, as medical law expert Rainer Beckmann puts it, did "a constitutional rollover crash completed by repeated new reforms to abortion law between 1974 and 1993." There were two casualties, the child and the rule of law. Under rule of law, the state must protect the life of all its citizens, without regard to the specific person, sex, or age. It has sacrificed the weakest, the smallest, those who have no voice, to the mother's "right to self-determination." But the mother who kills her unborn child is not determining only for herself, but also for another person who will need its mother before and long after birth, until it can take care of itself. It has its own soul, its own heart, its own body, its own capabilities, its own destiny and its own dignity.

I can feel joy and suffering.
I can speak and dance.
I can give and receive.
I can love and hate.
I can forgive or take revenge.
I can do good or evil.

I can worship God or myself.
I am a person,
not a stone, not a tree, not an animal.

The "illegal but exempt from consequences" judgment hollows out the rule of law. It's like convicting a shoplifter and letting him keep what he stole. What will the consequences be? The sense of right and wrong will weaken, more and more people will commit the same crime because they know they can't be penalized, until eventually there is no longer a sense that the crime is wrong. Rule of law has crashed.

With pretty but sophistic rationalizations, courts all over the world justify abandonment of the absolute obligation of the state to protect its citizens' lives.

In Germany, there is an obligatory consultation with the woman before she is allowed to abort her child. Originally, the federal constitutional court mandated this as *consultation for life.* The court had the idea that the lives of unborn children could be better protected through counseling than by the threat of punishment.

This sacrificed the individual's absolute right to life to the (highly uncertain) objective of possibly saving a larger number of children through counseling.[41] It may in fact have been the court's intention in 1993, which states in its judgment:

> II. 3. (1) Counseling serves to protect unborn life. It must be guided by the effort to encourage the woman to continue the pregnancy and to open her perspective to life with the child. It should help her make a responsible, conscientious decision. At the same time, the woman must be aware that the unborn child also has its own right to life in addition to hers, and that therefore, under the legal system, abortion can be considered only in exceptional situations when the burden of carrying the child ... is so difficult and extraordinary that it exceeds the reasonable limits of sacrifice.[42]

This opened the door to abortion on demand, clothed in euphemistic words. The same tactical principle is always used when it comes to large societal changes: The existing value system is confirmed verbally, but a gap is opened for hardship cases that evoke sympathy. The exceptions gradually become so broadly interpreted that they become general practice. The moral awareness of injustice shrivels until it finally disappears.

The same method was used to move from allowing contraception in exceptional cases (Lambeth Conference 1930) to universal use of the pill, from legalization of same-sex unions to homosexual "marriage," from suicide as an exception to organized, generally available commercial euthanasia (German federal constitutional court judgment of February 26, 2020). It went straight from allowing abortion in exceptional situations to an alleged "human right" to an abortion.

Counseling of women intending to have an abortion must be "open-ended." The woman does not need to explain why she wants to stop the beating heart of the living child in her womb. How can counseling be possible if the person seeking it does not reveal her motivation? Why, in such counseling, is everything not done to raise the woman's awareness that a new human being is growing inside her, which despite any temporary distress may become her greatest joy? Why are abortion-seeking women not told about the severe mental and physical problems they may suffer due to the killing of their child? How free is the woman's choice? Is she being pressured by her boyfriend, her husband, or her family? How much "self-determination" is in play here, and how much external control?

The counseling requirement became a mockery when Pro Familia was approved as a counseling organization. Pro Familia is the largest commercial abortion provider in Germany, whose worldwide umbrella organization is the International Planned Parenthood Federation. Can such an organization credibly offer "open-ended" counseling when a woman who has decided for abortion is a new paying customer?

The so-called "simple laws" that accompany fundamental decisions of the constitutional court pave the way to the abortion clinic: The health insurance companies pay for the preliminary and follow-up examinations. For the poor, the costs are fully assumed by the health insurance companies and reimbursed to them by the government. The federal states are required to offer comprehensive abortion facilities. The employer is required to continue paying wages. Doctors are allowed to make abortion their main source of income. Rainer Beckmann says:

> There is no longer any doubt that legislation and the legal precedent by the federal constitutional court have completely destroyed awareness that killing children before birth is wrong.[43]

This is shown by an award given to abortion doctors Friedrich Stapf (Munich) and Kristina Hänel (Giessen), who make their living killing unborn children and have been fighting for lifting of a ban on advertising abortion services, so far without success. On International Women's Day 2019, they were honored by a social democratic women's organization for their "special accomplishments toward equality." On June 7, 2019, the two abortion doctors were allowed to bring their lethal views on freedom of choice to the podium at the Münchner Kammerspiele, the most renowned theater in Munich.

The most important tool for mental and moral confusion is systematic distortion of the language to manipulate people's consciousness.

An example is the word "equality." Among whom does abortion promote equality? Between the woman and the man, who cannot bear children? The child certainly doesn't get equality, because the human right to life has been taken from it.

And "abortion" — what a strange word! It works like a mental tranquilizer to fog the reality that a child is being killed in the womb. Something is "removed," the pregnancy is "interrupted" as if it could be started back up again, or it is "terminated," quickly and painlessly and with no consequences — or so the woman is made to believe. Termination of the pregnancy is only half the truth. It is terminated by violently ending the life of the child.

"Pregnancy tissue" or a "clump of cells" is done away with. For parents who want a child, the "clump of cells" is a child right from the beginning. They celebrate when the pregnancy test comes out positive. They happily tell their family and friends that a *child* is on the way. And watch the ecstatic reactions of the baby's older siblings when they get the news — there are dozens of videos showing this on YouTube. They excitedly show the first ultrasound image of their *baby*. They may put it on the door of the fridge, where their children can view their new sibling every day. It never occurs to them to speak of "pregnancy tissue." And how intense is everyone's pain when this baby is lost to a miscarriage!

The organization in Germany that profitably kills these babies in the womb, and with government support, is called Pro Familia, although it actually destroys families.

Germany's court decisions releasing the state from its primary task of protecting it citizens' life and limb are called "pregnancy and family assistance laws" (1992, 1995), even though abortion does not help pregnant women or families.

In communication psychology, this technique is called "reframing." If something is placed into a new framework, people evaluate it differently. What is negative suddenly looks positive, for example: A deed that burden's someone's conscience with guilt is placed in the framework of the "right to self-determination" and "pro-choice." But that only lasts until the deed is done. What happens after that was described well by Goethe in his book *Wilhelm Meister's Apprenticeship and Travels:* "You lay guilt on the unfortunate person and then let him suffer the pain." This characterizes post-abortion syndrome (PAS), the severe consequences of abortion (see below).

Abortion methods

Let's take a look at the various methods by which embryos are killed in the womb. Even describing these methods in words is taboo. No one wants to know about it. No one wants to be aware of the horrifying barbarism. Even organizers of church congresses claim this shouldn't be brought up to people, because it is too gruesome. The image is too gruesome, but not the murder — strange for a society that has no problem entertaining itself with blood-soaked horror films and computer games.

Isn't it better to know the reality than to reinterpret or deny it? But reality is stronger than the denial. Sooner or later, it will mercilessly confront us. It increases our freedom when we know what we're doing. But beware! It may horrify you.

Menstrual extraction

The home suction method at the early stages of pregnancy is a risky do-it-yourself method used where abortion is forbidden by law. The International Planned Parenthood foundation distributes such handy suction devices in countries with high birth rates and delivers plans for making them oneself. If the woman fears she is pregnant, this device is used to suck away the uterine lining. The risk to women is very high — from a punctured uterus or an infection to an incomplete abortion.

Curettage

This is the method of choice up to the 12th week of pregnancy.
The uterus is dilated, and a curette with a sharp tip is inserted into the cervix. The baby is cut up with this blade, and the uterus is scraped out. The abortionist or assisting nurse checks whether all body parts are present in the bloody mass, because if anything is left in the uterus, serious complications can follow.

The suction method

A suction tube is inserted into the uterus and connected to a vacuum device that cuts the baby's body into pieces and sucks it up. Then the uterus is scraped out. Here also, the cut-up body parts must then be checked for completeness.

From the fourth to the sixth month of pregnancy, this process gets more difficult. The baby's tissue is now stiff enough that it can't be cut up. The cervix has to be spread wider, because larger instruments must be inserted. This is done over one to three days through insertion of rods made of laminaria algae which absorb fluid and swell. During this time, the woman can still decide against abortion. The cervix can also be spread in a few minutes using steel rods. The baby's arms and legs are cut off with a long, curved pair of scissors and are pulled out individually. The abortionist waits until the child has bled to death and then removes the torso. With larger babies, the head must be crushed, so that it can be pulled from the cervix in pieces. In contrast to other methods, such as burning with salt solution, this method gives the baby no chance of survival.

Saline abortions

This method is used from the second trimester to the start of the third trimester. The risks for the mother are very high, because the salt solution can get into one of the mother's blood vessels.

About half a pint (200 milliliters) of amniotic fluid is sucked out and replaced with salt solution. The baby swallows and inhales this solution. Over hours, it suffers an agonizing death through salt poisoning, dehydration, brain bleeds, and cramps. Within 24 to 48 hours, the baby is born through induced contractions. The child is either burnt or deep red. Mothers report that they can feel the baby's wild movements during its hours-long battle with death.

This method's "dreaded complication" is that the baby might survive. One famous case is Gianna Jessen. Her 17-year-old mother had a saline abortion in the 30th week of pregnancy, but it failed. The child came into the world with severe damage and was adopted. It was claimed she would never walk. Now she is a marathon runner and a right-to-life advocate who has spoken before the British House of Commons and the US Congress. Her life is recounted in the film *October Baby.*

Prostaglandin injection

At the end of the second trimester and in the third trimester of pregnancy, a large dose of the hormone prostaglandin is injected, which triggers extremely severe early contractions that can last as long as 20 hours. From 22 weeks, children can survive this form of abortion, and they usually suffer severe damage from it. The best-known example is Tim, the "Oldenburger baby." The doctor gave him only a year, but he actually died at age 21 on January 4, 2019. Surviving children are a problem that can cause a crisis for the doctor, because he can be sued for damages if an abortion fails.

Abortion with Rivanol disinfectant

The disinfectant Rivanol contains alcohol and is injected through the abdominal wall to mix with the amniotic fluid. Rivanol penetrates the tender, unprotected skin of the child in the uterus and destroys the cells. The high percentage of alcohol is very poisonous to the child, stops the heart relatively quickly and triggers contractions. This results in the stillbirth of a yellow-colored child.

Fetal homicide

The child is murdered with an injection of poison to the heart. Viewing the baby through ultrasound, the abortionist sticks a long needle through the mother's abdominal wall, seeks out the child's heart, inserts the needle and injects a potassium chloride solution into the heart. The poison prevents muscle contraction, causing the heart to stop. The dead child is delivered by cervical dilation and expulsion using hormone injections. This method is used with in vitro fertilization if more than one fertilized egg has been implanted and multiple births are to be prevented.

Late-term abortion or partial birth abortion (dilation and extraction methods)

These methods are mainly used in the United States to kill the child from the 24th week up until birth, or more precisely during actual birth. The abortionist uses ultrasound to determine the child's position. He guides tongs into the uterus, grabs one of the child's legs, and pulls the child out of the birth canal — all except its head. The child is alive and punches and kicks around. The abortionist places his fingers around the baby's shoulders, shoves a dull pair of scissors into the lower part of the head, spreads the scissors to enlarge the hole, pulls the scissors out and inserts a suction catheter to suck out the brain. The skull collapses. Now the child can be pulled from the uterus.

Legal regulations differ from one state to another. In Germany, late-term abortions are legally allowed up to the date of birth if they are "medically indicated," which means if they are considered a hazard to the physical *or mental* health of the mother. A late-term abortion due to a child's disability has been prohibited in Germany since 1995. However, if a disabled child may endanger the mother's health in the present *or the future*, such abortions are allowed. In Austria, abortion goes unpunished up to the time of birth if "there is a danger that the child is severely damaged mentally or physically." Eugenic selection can therefore be made without any obfuscation or rationalization through the horrid murder of a viable child.

Chemical abortion using the pill RU-486 (Mifepristone)

Swallowing pills seems less brutal than surgical methods. RU-486 can be taken until the end of the second month of pregnancy. An extremely high dose of the synthetic hormone RU-486 blocks the hormone progesterone required for pregnancy. The uterus recedes, which strangles the child to death. The uterine lining dies, and the dead child is expelled. The child's agony lasts many hours, during which it slowly dies of hunger, thirst, and suffocation. There is a discharge, and the fetus usually ends up in the toilet.

The risks to the woman are far higher than with chemical contraceptives.

Thrombosis, embolism, breast cancer, impaired fertility, heavy bleeding, heart attack, and cardiac arrhythmia can all result from a chemical abortion.

What happens to aborted children?

Once the abortionist or the nurse has checked the bloody pile of tiny bones and organs for completeness, it is disposed of as biological waste, burned on site, released for research purposes, or sold for profit.

In pathology, the tiny person has finally become usable material. A lot can be done with it: vaccine development, anti-aging cell treatment through injection of fetal germ cells, processing as a cosmetic for wrinkle reduction, use of embryonic stem cells in medicine for developing therapies and breeding replacement organs, "although within the past 20 years none of the cures researchers expected from embryonic stem cells have come about" (Stefan Rehder).[44]

In the United States, a young man made undercover videos bringing to light Planned Parenthood's profitable sales of the organs of aborted children. His name is David Daleiden, born 1989. He dared to singlehandedly expose the criminal activities of abortion giant Planned Parenthood. He founded the Center for Medical Progress and negotiated over lunch with Planned Parenthood representatives on the cost and condition of body parts from aborted children. In 2015, one video after another was made public and brought the global abortion organization under massive pressure.[45] The campaign *Defund Planned Parenthood* gained new impetus: Some US states stopped financing the International Planned Parenthood Federation with tax money, which led to sharp conflict with the Obama administration, but President Trump supported the campaign. Instead of Planned Parenthood being sued for trafficking in the organs of aborted children, Daleiden himself was sued, because he tricked IPPF into exposing themselves. He is threatened with 20 years in prison because he operated with false identity documents. The court case is still pending.[46]

A young man dared to take on the largest nongovernmental organization backing the culture of death, the International Planned Parenthood Federation, financed to the tune of billions by the world's most powerful. Truly a battle of David and Goliath. David Daleiden is a hero of our time, but the wheel of history must turn from death to life before he will be praised for it.

How was it possible to make the term "abortion" lose its association with the gruesome reality? We have seen what abortion means: The child is torn apart in the womb, dismembered, poisoned, burnt, suffocated; it must drink brine, a heart attack is induced; it is allowed to die of hunger and starvation within the womb; it is expelled, left to lie alone until it dies or inconspicuously suffocates. During birth, his head is bored into and the brain is sucked out.

When reading statistics, who thinks about how many children in his own country are killed in this way year after year? According to Germany's federal statistical office, by the end of 2019, a total of 6,175,000 children have been murdered — that's six million, one hundred seventy-five thousand! Who thinks about this when seeing a report that in one country the battle is on to legalize abortion, or to completely ban it, as in Poland in 2016? Abortionists who earn their money by killing unborn children do not need to hide — they ply their trade fully within the law, out in public, and are even honored for it.

How does a person's heart turn to stone that way? If the child were allowed to live, in a few months it would delight its parents with a smile.

Regret never comes too late

It's over. The child is dead. Linda is alone again. Relief comes first: My life can continue normally again. But there are shadows over it.

> *I'd better not think about it. They said it was no big deal. I'd have some pain for two or three days, and then it would all be over. I had a right to make my own decisions. I won't tell anyone about it. Best not to think about it. Tom and I don't talk at dinner. Nobody wants to talk about it. We're both irritable. Somehow, I'm angry at him, although he said it was my decision. I work a lot and that distracts me. Yesterday my coworker showed around photos of her sister's baby. I acted as if I was happy for her, but my heart tightened. Then this pressure in my head again that I never knew before. I haven't slept well for some time. I wake up at 3 a.m. filled with anxiety, although there's no reason for it. Sometimes images suddenly emerge of how I was lying there in surrender, the doctor with rubber*

> *gloves and tongs in his hand. My relationship with Tom gets worse all the time. He never touches me anymore. He talks about separation. Good that I didn't have a kid with him — he'd have left me sooner or later anyway. Men are basically worthless. I get along better with Stephanie. I used to wake up and look forward to the day. Now I'd rather stay in bed. I often start crying over nothing. No wonder people stay away from me. Am I even worth anything? But I'll pull myself together and go jogging. Then I can get through the day.*

Linda is groping in the dark, trapped in a dense fog. She doesn't know what's wrong with her. She doesn't realize she is suffering from what is called *post-abortion syndrome*, the negative impact of abortion on the woman, which is largely kept under wraps.[47] In a society in which abortion is just an extension of contraception by other means, the woman who has aborted is not allowed to have problems. Those who persuaded her, those who gave her "open-ended" counseling, without opening her eyes and heart to the reality of the child, those who performed the bloody act to make money, and all those who take the murder of an unborn child as a right and an act of women's liberation — none of them want to know that an abortion not only kills a child, but also mentally and physically injures the woman. This woman said no to her original essence, to her ability to give life. She has killed her child, and with it her motherhood, a part of herself. Does anyone really believe that this won't have consequences?

There are acts — ours and others' — that set the course. They often occur in no time, without awareness of their scope, without responsibility for the consequences of temptation and seduction, false information, and conscious manipulation. They lead to knots in the thread of life that reduce freedom.

Despite all the brainwashing through perversion of terminology, there is still the writing on the wall (Daniel 5:25) that anyone can read in his heart — and that's called *guilt.*

In our time, people no longer want to know anything about guilt, but the possibility of taking on guilt is a vital condition of human freedom. People have a free will and can choose good or evil. A lion feels no guilt when it tears up an animal. But a person feels guilty when he or she kills a child. To those whom he has harmed through the evil deed, he owes self-knowledge, regret, a request for forgiveness, and the will to redemption.

Today one can capitalize on victim status. It's other people's fault, others need to change, others must reform themselves, other must guarantee "safe spaces," others are muzzled and punished if they espouse opinions that someone finds "offensive." Whatever someone feels as stressful is perceived as inflicted misery that confers victim status, which can be exploited.

Why is it like that? Because a society that has fallen away from God has not only separated from the "vengeful God," but has also lost the merciful God. God's mercy can only be experienced by those who are aware of their sins before God.

The bad deed damages three relationships: with the victim, with oneself, and with God.

If the victim is dead, he cannot be brought to life again. But healing is possible, healing of the relationship with the deceased child, reconciliation of the perpetrator with herself and with God.

Healing begins with acknowledging reality. This process takes place in several stages, and it is advisable to seek help for it.

The first step is to allow the pain. This takes courage. Up to now, Linda has suppressed her pain, justified herself, and blamed others. The results were depression, self-debasement, mental and physical disturbances of all types. Linda needs to rise from this fog if she wants to find healing. The flood of tears will move aside the debris that previously obscured the cause of the mental disturbances. *At the beginning,* this will cause her to feel guilty and helpless. *The child is dead. I have killed it. I can never make it right.*

But it can be made up for![48] Other women have made the journey before Linda and were able to enjoy their lives again. She is not the first, and she won't be the last. There is a cleansing spring that will give her full life back if she bathes in it: It is filled with tears and regret.

Linda gives in to her regret, she cries and cries and cries from the bottom of her heart, and then the miracle happens. The child can take life in her mind. Linda gives the child a name. She speaks with it and recounts the distress that led her to have it killed. And what to do with the guilt? Linda suddenly feels the need to go to church. The tears come again, but now mild and tender. Linda remembers her First Communion, and the confession she made then as a child. She finds a priest to whom she opens her heart, and hears the healing words: *Ego te absolvo — I absolve you.* A new life can begin. Linda has found her child and has found herself again as a woman and mother. She knows that she can give life.

4.
From gift to product

Progress is the scourge that God has selected for us.
Nicolás Gómez Dávila

Modern humans have walked the earth for a couple hundred thousand years. Man begat man in the mysterious darkness of the female womb. *Four decades* ago, a mystery was unveiled: Science succeeded in fertilizing a woman's egg with a man's sperm in a test tube. The act of love was replaced with technical manipulation in a laboratory. *In vitro fertilization* (IVF) was invented. The first child created in a laboratory, Louise Joy Brown, came into the world in 1978. Later, in 2015,[49] more than 20,000 test tube babies were born in Germany. It's a rising trend.

Modern contraception methods had systematically separated the sex act from procreation, and now procreation has been separated from the sex act.

This opened the door to production of children and set humanity on the slippery slope to ever greater hubris regarding life and death. Egg and sperm cells are now put at the disposal of reproduction technicians. They can "harvest," freeze, select, "improve" (i.e., edit) and duplicate (clone) genetic material. They can freeze an embryo, plant it in a rented uterus, use it as research material, throw it away, kill it — all for money from the growing market for reproductive medicine. Man can now tinker with God's creation of the human being. Is this welcome progress, or is it overstepping boundaries to the detriment of humanity? Philosopher Dietrich Hildebrand is convinced of the latter:

> Reverence for the miracle of new life from two people's most intimate bond of love is the basis for disgust at every wicked, artificial, insolent destruction of this mysterious context of love and the emergence of a new person.[50]

Artificially fertile

The motives for using artificial methods of reproduction can vary a great deal. It ranges from the pain of an infertile couple who yearn for nothing more than to be good parents to a child, to single or same-sex people who are willing to buy the missing genetic material and rob the child of his natural heritage.

If a man and a woman have stated their sincere "I do," then the child they have together is the manifestation of their love. Think of the pain when one of the two is infertile and it turns out that their love cannot culminate in a child! They are gripped by a feeling of helplessness, and their plan for life collapses. It can be as sorrowful as if a child had died.

Becoming parents means that self-centeredness breaks away. In one fell swoop, their own ego is pushed aside to make room for a helpless little being, their child. A mother doesn't ask about the meaning of life when she has an infant in her arms. But that is not the only way to overcome egocentrism and be of service to others. The soul wants to do good, and in that it makes peace with its own existence. After a time of sorrow that the yearning for life and love and bond and caring cannot be fulfilled with a child of one's own, other possibilities for meaning and fulfillment will arise.

However, there can also be intentional bypassing of nature at the expense of the child. Disembodiment of human procreation results in its depersonalization. Biological parentage can now be "diversified." Up to this point, the old legal principle applied: *Mater semper certa est,* the mother is always sure. Even if the father occasionally wasn't sure, it was the most obvious thing in the world that a person had a father and a mother. It was always a hard blow of fate to lose one's father or mother. Fairy tales resound with it.

With the discovery of in vitro fertilization, it became technically possible and legally authorized to voluntarily and intentionally rob a person of his heritage. Everyone wants to know where he comes from, whose genetic material he has inherited, and what "startup capital" defines his identity. Membership in a family system gave the person a social identity. Adoptive children often go in search of their biological parents after learning that their mom or dad — no matter how loving they were — are not their "real" parents. Children created with anonymous genetic material also do this. Their family tree is replaced with a receipt from a gene bank.[51] The child becomes a product with a number and a price tag. This is the greatest imaginable blow to his dignity.

A person's dignity rests on his personal uniqueness: Anyone who has ever loved has been affected in their innermost being by the person they have loved, and no one else in the world could have replaced them. This is what parents feel with their newborn baby, even though his identity is still a total mystery. In contrast, a commercial product is selected based on quality criteria and is interchangeable.

We modern humans, who consider ourselves to have reached previously unattained heights of humaneness, feel disgust when people are bought and sold, both at the slave markets of the past and in human trafficking today. No one wants to be sold as a product. No one wants to find out someday that his genetic components were purchased, that he grew in a rented uterus and was borne by a person who was not his mother. Abolition of the right to life through legalization of abortion followed abolition of the second basic human right: the right of a child to its biological parents. The helpless child is sacrificed to the selfish desires of adults. Some kill the child that is not wanted, while others do violence to nature to gain ownership of a child. To modern-day people, the self has replaced God. This blocks the path for them to accept fate, submit to what is given, and to find new meaning for their life in it.

Today the average age of a first-time mother is 30 years and is therefore double the time from birth to sexual maturity. For a decade and a half, the greatest concern of women who have had sex since their youth is: *No kid!* It must be prevented!

When a woman decides to give up the pill, when her professional education is completed, when she has found a man who wants to become a father, when their income is adequate, their house is big enough, and the couple finally says "yes" to procreation, it happens ever more often that one of the partners finds out he or she is infertile. What a shock! What misfortune!

Suddenly the curtain is torn and life itself speaks in their own soul. Life wants to continue, life wants to create life, always start anew — but what if it can't? Throughout the years of contraception, the man and woman felt they were the masters over life and death. Now suddenly life is in charge, and it is not cooperating. Sorrow. Helplessness.

Or, the couple wonders, maybe we're not all that helpless. Can their desire for a child still be fulfilled? The parents on the websites for reproduction clinics look so happy. Could we have fertilization done in a laboratory? Bring the semen and egg together in a petri dish and then implant the embryo? Buy semen at a sperm bank? Or the egg of some other woman? We want a child so much! The child will have a good life with us.

More and more couples are getting into this situation, because infertility is growing among men and women. In Germany, as in the United States, every fifth woman is childless, some because they don't want kids, and others because they can't have a child anymore.

In just a few decades, the unfulfilled yearning for children has driven a billion-dollar business. In Germany, the 150 clinics for artificial reproduction are doing a land office business. The demand for carryout babies is increasing.

Who needs artificial reproduction? Those battling infertility, those missing eggs and/or sperm and/or a uterus for creating a child?

- A man and woman who want to become parents but can't because fertilization isn't working and the embryo is not implanting: As long as the egg and semen are intact, there is nothing they need to buy. Rather, they hand the egg and/or semen to the laboratory and hope for technical help with fertilization and implantation. The child, if one is born, will be related to both its parents (homologous fertilization).
- A man and woman, one of whom is infertile: They have to buy either the egg or semen from another person (heterologous fertilization). The child will never know either its biological mother or biological father.
- A woman who has not yet found the right man or who wants a career first before becoming a mother: She knows that her stock of eggs is limited, dramatically reduces after age 35, and loses vitality. For that reason, when she is young, she has eggs removed and frozen at minus 196°C to have them thawed out and fertilized in the laboratory *(social freezing)* when she is 40. If the right partner still hasn't appeared, she has to buy some anonymous man's sperm.
- A single woman who has no partner but still wants a child: She has to buy the sperm. The child will never know its biological father and will grow up without any father.[52]

- Two homosexual men who will become Parent 1 and Parent 2: They have to buy the egg and rent a uterus. The child will never know its genetic mother or the woman whose womb it lived in until birth. It will never have a maternal relationship, but there will be up to six adults who can claim parental rights: the genetic mother, the surrogate mother, her husband (in most legal situations), the biological father (if the semen was purchased), and two legal fathers.
- Two lesbians who will become Parent 1 and Parent 2: They have to buy the sperm. The child will never know its father and will grow up without any father. The two women can share motherhood: One woman delivers the egg, and the other her uterus for carrying the child.

There is a battle for legalization of all these scenarios all over the world. Those with the biggest stake in it are in the multi-billion-dollar business of reproductive medicine, as well as scientists who consume "excess embryos" from artificial reproduction for research purposes, and all those who want to fulfill their desire for a child whatever the cost.

And it costs a lot. Only the wealthy can afford artificial reproduction. They have to consider the $50,000 cost, depending on the quality of eggs, sperm, and clinic. In poor countries of Eastern Europe and Asia, there are cheap, all-inclusive packages: flight, hotel, and three cycles of IVF starting at $40,000.

Artificial reproduction doesn't just cost money. It comes with serious health risks to the mother, the surrogate mother, and the child; it costs millions of embryos their lives; it costs the child its right to its biological parents; and it costs human beings their dignity.

The risks of artificial fertilization

There are various methods of artificial fertilization. The two most common are fertilization in a petri dish and ICSI.

In classical in vitro fertilization (IVF), sperm cells and egg cells are mixed in a test tube. As in natural procreation, the egg has the choice of which sperm to accept. Because semen quality generally undergoes continuous degradation, test tube fertilization often doesn't work. Then *intracytoplasmic sperm injection* (ICSI) is used. In the glaring light of the laboratory, the doctor selects through the microscope a sperm cell that seems to him especially energetic, sticks a hypodermic needle into the egg cell, and injects the sperm cell.

Sixty to eighty percent of the embryos created in this way show chromosomal damage and cannot develop.

Excess embryos are cryopreserved at minus 196°C in liquid nitrogen — that is to say deep frozen — by the hundreds of thousands every year. These embryos are produced because three egg cells are typically fertilized, but only one or two are implanted. Most of these cryopreserved embryos are "orphaned" and eventually thrown away. If the parents donate the excess embryos for research, many reproduction clinics give them a discount.

It is very rare for pregnancy to take place at the first attempt, and in over 80% of the cases, it doesn't even happen after the last attempt. Only 15% to 17% of artificial fertilizations actually lead to a child being born. The older the woman is, the lower the probability. On average, around 20 embryos are needed for successful implantation to happen. This means that nearly all of them must die in the first stage of their existence, so that the "wanted child" can be born at great risk.

Naturally, people who want a child want a healthy one. Obviously, then, the artificially created embryo undergoes quality control to check whether it shows any signs of hereditary diseases or disabilities before it is implanted into the woman. This is called *preimplantation diagnosis* (PID). For a PID, about seven embryos are needed. The embryos are examined for genetic defects and disabilities, and if necessary, separated out. Thus, the doctor becomes a selective eugenicist, deciding at the early stage who is worthy of living and who is not.

At this point, still other choices present themselves: Should it be a boy or a girl? Should it have blue or brown eyes, black or blond hair? Can it be considered a tissue or organ donor for an already living sibling who is ill? That can also be a motive for artificial reproduction. In Germany, which has a very restrictive embryo protection law, that isn't possible, but parents can travel to the United States and for $140,000 acquire a healthy designer baby.[53]

Rollercoaster ride between hope and fear

The woman, or the couple, that takes advantage of artificial reproduction methods sets off on what may be a yearlong rollercoaster ride of hope, anxiety, humiliation, joy, and fear that four out of five cases end in deep disappointment. If all attempts to be the master of life and death fall flat, nothing is left but forced acceptance of helplessness. For those who take the path of artificial fertilization to force nature to fulfill their own wishes, nothing can be worse than failure.

The website of Germany's *Federal Center for Health Education* makes no secret of the risks to the couple. The organization cannot be suspected of rejecting artificial reproduction. It unapologetically discusses the risks and stresses to body and soul — all the way to "serious complications." It says:

> Elective fertility treatments can severely stress the woman, the man and their relationship to one another. The examinations, side effects of medication and procedures can be exhausting. Moreover, during this time the couple must coordinate a good deal of their time with the demands of the therapy — sometimes over several years. The appointments for checkups and treatments are often hard to reconcile with work obligations. This is especially true when the couple wishes to keep the treatment secret from their employer and/or coworkers. The financial burden can also be heavy.[54]

Anxiety phase 1 — Harvesting eggs

The hormonal stimulation is extremely stressful for the woman. In nature, only one egg is typically ready for fertilization during each cycle. For artificial fertilization, the woman must release as many eggs as possible, because the wear is considerable. Many eggs — both fertilized and unfertilized — go dead sooner or later.

Because the woman's body is forced by the hormone supplements to bring out more than one egg, "overstimulation syndrome" can result. Possible side effects are persistent nausea, fluid in the abdomen, blood clotting disorders, shortness of breath, hot flashes, dizziness, vision disorders, and depression. There is also the risk of bacterial infection of the ovaries and injury to the bladder and intestines during egg retrieval.

Purchased eggs and semen from donors must usually be frozen and thawed back out. Only a small portion of them survive.

Anxiety phase 2 — Implantation

If fertilization succeeds, two or three embryos are transferred to the uterus. The next round of fearful waiting begins. It takes two weeks of daily examinations and more hormone injections until the doctor can say whether pregnancy has occurred or whether the embryo has died.

And if it hasn't worked — which is highly probable — there is still a greater ordeal in store. Insurance pays for three cycles, but the doctors who profit from every new cycle may recommend persisting. The difficult decision can become a heavy burden on the couple, whose scheduling and intimate life take a back seat to months of treatment and directives from the doctor. For most couples, this disrupts their partnership and sexuality.[55]

Anxiety phase 3 — Pregnancy

It even happens that one, two, maybe three of the artificially produced embryos have implanted in the uterus, and then the big anxiety starts: Will the child remain to term? A lot of women have this worry in pregnancy even from natural procreation, because miscarriages are nothing unusual. With artificial procreation, the risk of miscarriage is drastically higher: More than half of all artificially induced pregnancies end in miscarriage or in an ectopic pregnancy.[56] For months, if not years, the couple has made their desire for a child the main theme of their lives: The woman has undergone several cycles of extremely exhausting treatment, she has finally received the news that she is pregnant, only to find out later that she has lost another child. Anger, grief, pain, shame, self-doubt. Many couples break up from it.

There is still another special dilemma the woman certainly didn't consider when she longingly wished for a child. Because implantation often goes wrong, several embryos are usually "transferred" to the uterus. What to do if two or even three actually take hold? Twins or triplets weren't part of the plan. Thus "embryonic reduction" is conducted. The woman has made enormous sacrifices to become pregnant. Now the hearts of multiple children beat in her womb, and if she just wants one, she has to decide which ones should be killed.

The smallest? The weakest? Should the boy stay, or the girl? Who decides? The doctor or the mother? They wanted a child — they did not want to kill a child — but twins or triplets? Out of the question!

Excess babies are killed with a calcium chloride injection through the abdominal wall and uterus into the child's heart. The surviving child then remains in the mother's womb next to her dead sibling until delivery. If the dead sibling has not been "absorbed," it is expelled at birth. What might be the effects of a child having grown next to the corpse of its own sibling?

Anxiety phase 4 — Prenatal diagnostics

A child should be healthy and intelligent, one that makes his parents proud.

The chances are high that an artificially created child will display anomalies.

Screening before implantation does not adequately rule out that the child will be disabled. Therefore, the mother usually also undergoes prenatal diagnosis (PND).

Up to 2012, this was only possible by removing amniotic fluid, which greatly increased the danger of losing the child. Still another dilemma for the woman is when she has to decide on life or death: To have a disabled child aborted, she must risk losing a healthy child. Ninety-five percent of all children diagnosed with Down syndrome are aborted. Soon we'll never see any.

Since 2012, there has been a simple blood test that with a high level of certainty tells whether a child has Down syndrome.[57] Many insurance companies pay for these tests because they save the cost associated with a disabled child. But here too, a positive result could be wrong. Imagine that the woman finds *after the abortion* that she has had a healthy child killed. How happy will she be in life?

Anxiety phase 5 — Birth

Most IVF children come into the world too early and too small and have to be removed by caesarean section. They usually start life in an incubator. IVF children are twice as likely to be born weighing less than six pounds — even when just one is born — which triples the risk of development problems.[58]

Birth is risky for any mother. Thanks to medical progress, the death of mother or child during delivery is ever rarer. For women who want to force nature through artificial reproduction, the risks are considerably higher: severe vaginal tears, lacerations to the uterus, unplanned hysterectomy, blood transfusions, removal to intensive care. If the egg of another woman was used, and the fertilized egg cell was inserted, 30% of all pregnancies involve severe complications.[59] A woman's fear for herself and the child is justified.

Anxiety phase 6 — Long-term damage to IVF children?

The yearning was enormous to hold a healthy child in her arms and to find meaning in life through caring for it. But will the child be healthy and develop normally? Will nature cope with all the interventions in the extremely complex, finely tuned process of human procreation? Heavy hormone supplements, invasive fertilization by piercing the egg, cultivation of the eggs and sperm in nutrient solution, freezing and thawing of the egg, semen, or embryo, and then massive hormone stimulation for implantation and reception, low birth weight and premature birth — not to mention the psychological and spiritual factors of the beginning of life.

Since the first test-tube baby in 1978, more than 4 million IVF children have been born around the world. Most of them are healthy, thank God. The few studies of artificially created humans have not yet been able to follow them for their entire lives, but they show that the people are at high risk of birth defects, long-term damage due to low birth weight and premature birth,[60] high blood pressure, and premature aging of the arteries.[61]

And what are the long-term mental consequences? The first major study on this topic was conducted at the University of Copenhagen and reaches this distressing conclusion:

> For ART children [artificial reproductive technology], the risk of schizophrenia and psychosis was 27% higher, of anxiety and other neurotic disturbances such as anorexia 37% higher, for behavioral disorders, such as ADHD 40% and for mental development disorders, such as autism, 22% compared to children created by natural means.[62]

The sperm donor

The sperm donor is not a donor, but a seller of his own sperm. It is difficult to empathize with the motivations of a man who sells his sperm, thus becoming father to countless children that he will never know, with whom he will have no relationship, and to whom he will never be a real father. Is a side job like that just about making a few extra bucks or is there a personal satisfaction in siring many children without any bond or responsibility?

The sperm donor injures his own dignity, sells a part of himself that is intended to create sons and daughters who will enrich and fulfill his life. But between the father and his sons and daughters, an impenetrable wall is inserted: instead of love, responsibility, and fullness of life — money, disconnection, and loneliness.

A woman who buys a stranger's sperm to create her own child wants to be sure that the goods are of high quality. She wants them to be vigorous and have the desired genetic properties, good health, an attractive appearance, intelligence, a specific skin color (white is still the most preferred), and perhaps a specific hair and eye color. The sperm banks publish donor profiles for the customers to choose from.

For the sperm bank to guarantee quality to the purchasers, the sperm donor is screened in detail. He must fill out a questionnaire spanning pages and provide information about his health status, the health status of three generations of his family, his social status, education, profession, and interests. The better and more precise the screening, the higher a price the sperm fetches.

If the man has made it through all the screenings, he can deliver his sample in the bank's masturbation room, supplied with pornography for stimulation. The sperm count per ejaculation is checked. In recent decades, this has dropped by half, on average, and moreover is considerably lower during masturbation than during sexual intercourse.

Once his sperm is accepted, he is offered an annual contract with default clauses: He must deliver at least every two weeks. His health status is constantly checked. So that he won't lose interest in paid masturbation, the bank pays only part of his fee upon contract signing. If health risks arise, the contract is void.

If he is willing to reveal his identity to the purchaser, the price rises.

It is possible that in the area near the sperm bank, there are many children running around who look strangely like him and each other. They are half siblings without knowing it. If fate so wills it, they may fall in love with each other without knowing they are engaging in incest.

In 2017, the German parliament stopped the complete dissolution of lineage with the "Act on regulating the right to knowledge of family lineage when heterologous semen is used." A nationwide sperm donor register was set up, in which children created from July 2018 on, and over 16 years old, can query the name, birth date, national citizenship, and address (at the time) of their genetic father.[63] All children created before that have a black hole in their identity instead of a father. They will never be able to find out who their father is.

The surrogate mother

As long as science has not succeeded in developing an artificial uterus, some people will only be able to satisfy their yearning for a child by renting another woman's uterus. That is another quantum leap in artificial reproduction. After the separation of sexuality from procreation, the separation of procreation from the sex act, the separation of the child from its genetic mother or father, now the child is also separated from his biological mother, and the mother from the child who for so many months grew close to her heart.

Various configurations are possible for getting a surrogate mother involved. The scenarios range from a married couple who for medical reasons cannot have a child, to homosexual couples who for natural reasons cannot create a child, to Hollywood stars who want to spare their bodies from the hardship of pregnancy.

If the embryo is made of genetic material produced by the customer, it is still related to its parents. Maybe it will never know that it was created in a laboratory, implanted in an unrelated woman and was carried by her until birth. (However, from psychology we know that family secrets only keep for so long.)

If both components of the embryo are purchased and the womb rented, the child has no relationship to its client parents, but has many invisible connections to "parents" it will never come to know and whose names it will never learn: the egg donor, the sperm donor,[64] the surrogate mother, and — depending on the legal situation — her husband.

A child carried by a surrogate mother grows alone and unloved in a rented uterus. Previously, a woman's uterus was an idyllic place of security that imprints in the human heart an unquenchable longing for perfect unity. For the child carried by a surrogate mother, the womb is a dark dungeon into which not a single ray of love or anticipation enters, because the mother knows that she must hand over the child to strangers immediately after birth. She must force herself to have no relationship with the child that stirs within her. She must refrain from joyful affection, because this would inevitably change to great pain after birth.

Children who grow in a rented womb mostly leave this dark, lonely place before maturity, through caesarean section, so they begin their lives in an incubator — abandoned by the mother's heart.

A naturally created child knows its mother's heartbeat, her scent, her voice, the songs she has sung to it, the taste of her milk. This provides security after the shock of birth. The child is welcomed by a smiling face. The happiness hormone, oxytocin, floods through the mother, the baby finds her breast, presses its nose into the soft flesh, and sucks from the mother's body what it needs for life, finally to descend into deep, satisfied sleep. The child of a surrogate mother will never experience this.

One knows all along: From the very beginning, the unborn child is designed to be dependent on relationships, bonding, and learning.[65] Embryos can hear, taste, smell, and feel. Prenatal researcher Peter Fedor-Freybergh writes:

> The preborn child drinks, smokes, loves and hates with the mother, it rejoices and suffers with her. It feels her heart sounds, is scared when she is scared.... Its life depends on her and her life.[66]

What might it be like for a child whose mother suppresses emotional contact during pregnancy? What underlying sentiment will he be imprinted with? The isolation in the womb becomes forsakenness when nothing is familiar to him after birth.

How will it go for the client mother who has not carried her child herself? Pregnancy is supposed to be a time to prepare for being a mother —

that means a completely new direction for her existence, whose center can no longer be herself, but the helpless infant. Now, however, mother and child are strangers. The happiness hormone, oxytocin, is not secreted and the mother's breasts produce no milk. How happy will the mother be to get up at night to calm the crying child? Will the foster mother have that rapport with the child — the hypersensitive perception of all its expressions? Will all the sacrifices a mother must make be balanced out by profound joy?

Maybe the child will no longer remain with the purchaser who contracted for it, because in their country of origin surrogate motherhood is prohibited and they are prevented at the border from entering with the child — that happened to an Italian couple who had a child produced with purchased sperm. The European Court of Human Rights decided that the state had custody, upon which the child was taken into care and put up for adoption.[67] The legal chaos is every bit as great as the lineage chaos the hapless child falls into.

The coronavirus pandemic has brought a completely new problem: Children were ordered but not picked up, because the borders were closed. In May 2020, hundreds of babies from surrogate mothers were waiting to be picked up by their buyers.[68]

How does it go for the surrogate mother? Generally these are women from poor countries whom financial stress drives to sell their ability to carry a child, nourish it with her own physical substance, and finally undergo the pain of delivery.

In addition to the physical stress, the surrogate mother is subject to higher than average health risks, including:

- High blood pressure with risk of stroke during the pregnancy, and after that
- Gestational diabetes
- Preeclampsia with premature termination of pregnancy by caesarean section
- Life-threatening birth complications, blood transfusions and transfer of mother and child to the ICU
- Severe vaginal tears
- Unplanned hysterectomy

What might a woman do if she is in Ukraine with an average annual income of €3,000, lives in bitter poverty, and in the subway sees an advertisement to rent her womb for a promised €16,000?

Customers from rich countries will buy her services. India, once the baby factory of the world with 3,000 reproduction clinics, banned commercial surrogate motherhood in 2019, and Thailand in 2015. But business is booming in Ukraine and the Czech Republic.

Surrogate mother contract[69]

The woman must have reached the age of legal adulthood and have already borne children of her own. With her signature, she agrees to follow the agency's directives and give them total control of her life during the pregnancy. She agrees to an abortion if the doctors deem this necessary or the potential parents want it. She agrees to "embryonic reduction," but must carry the multiple children to term if the doctors order it. If she herself is responsible for an abortion or refuses to have an abortion, she must pay 200% of the sum of the contract.

She must provide the client parents very precise information on her social and health status and can be contacted and examined by them at any time. She herself is subject to penalty if she obtains any information on the customers.

She is not to smoke or drink alcohol, and must have any medication, including herbal teas and alternative medicine, approved by the agency doctors, and follow their dietary specifications. During the period of the contract, she is not allowed to leave her town or use public transportation without approval. She must avoid physical and mental stress and have physical activity approved. She is not to color her hair. Pets must be removed. Failure to comply results in drastic monetary penalties.

At the beginning of the seventh month, she must move into a room assigned by the agency and is not to take care of her own children.

She must hand over the child to the client parents or hospital personnel immediately after birth and must never again have contact with it.

She receives the first half of the remuneration at contract signing, and the second half when the child's birth certificate and passport are issued. If there is a miscarriage within the first 6 weeks, she receives 3% of the contractual amount, 10% between the 22nd and 30th week, and 50% in the case of a stillbirth. If her uterus must be removed, she gets an additional 20%. Her uterus is therefore worth €3,200. The customer must pay for medical treatment up to one month after birth.

She is informed of the risks, but it is questionable to what degree women who mostly have little education understand what they are agreeing to. The potential parents are obligated to accept children who show anomalies, are too small or weigh too little, and have genetic damage, hereditary illnesses, or other developmental disorders.

If the surrogate mother reveals any information on the content of this contract, she must pay a penalty of 200% of the sum of the contract and can be legally prosecuted.

Surrogate motherhood as a "labor of love"

The brutal degradation of the surrogate mother and child seems diminished if a woman is willing to assist an infertile couple out of the goodness of her heart.[70]

Nick's sister — let's call her Susan — is herself the mother of two children, but she can no longer watch how much her brother suffers because his wife Jane, who has brought two children into the marriage, cannot conceive children with him. For a whole year, the refrigerator was full of pills and injections, and the only topic of conversation was failed IVF attempts and miscarriages that have repeatedly thrown the couple into a dark sea of dashed hopes and ever deeper depression. Susan wanted to help.

Another woman's egg was purchased, fertilized by Nick, and implanted into Susan. She kept a diary:

Week 3

I feel sick all the time — I have headaches and I'm tired. I have to down hormones, antibiotics, aspirin and folic acid. The worst is the depression. Normally I'm a happy person.

Week 8

I'm having twins.

Week 11
I'd like to set up the nursery, buy baby things, a stroller, but they're not my children. I'd better not get attached. I need to maintain a distance.

Week 15
I tell my children what's going on. My daughter asks, "You're not going to give me away, are you?" My son is belligerent and unapproachable. The teacher is asking what's wrong. We don't say what is going on.

Week 19
I see little hands and feet in the ultrasound and am shaken with sobs. It's unbearable to imagine going home from the clinic with no children.

Week 25
Nick asks me, "How are my kids doing?" It stabs me in the heart. They're setting up the nursery and buying the kids' going-home clothes. Jane is hiring a nanny, because she wants to go to back to work soon.

Week 30
I have to legally transfer parentage to Nick and Jane. Everything in me is resisting, but I have to.

Week 33
My blood pressure is way too high. A pregnancy poisoning is looming, and therefore a caesarean section. A huge delivery team is standing all around me. It looks serious.

Birth
The children are very small, have to go into the incubator and be artificially nourished. I have to stay in the hospital for 10 days. I'm exhausted and very sad. Nick takes me home by subway. I can't stop crying. It feels as if I've had a miscarriage and both children are dead.

Pros and cons
As human beings with free will, whenever we make decisions, we try to weigh the pros and cons. Let's imagine a scale. On one side are the costs of artificial reproduction, and on the other side the benefits.

Costs

- Debasement of the child
- Erasing the family lineage
- Debasement of the sellers of the the biological components
- Debasement of the surrogate mother
- Risks to the mother's mental and physical health during egg harvesting, implantation, birth
- Long-term risks to the child's mental and physical health
- Risks to the surrogate mother's mental and physical health
- Selection of genetic material
- Consumption of embryos
- Orphaning of embryos
- Freezing of embryos
- Relationship chaos
- Costs of approximately $50,000

Benefit

- Fulfillment of the desire for a child in fewer than 20% of the case

Which side is the scale tilting toward? On the one side there is a mountain of damage, risk, and degradation, and on the other side only the adult's wish to have a child. Yes, it is very sad if a couple cannot have a child even though they meet the conditions for parenthood and want to give the child everything he needs. May the love they wish to give to a child prevent them from taking the child's natural lineage away from him.

Have couples who have succeeded in producing a child with other people's genetic material or even a surrogate mother also bought happiness? What will the parents tell the child when it asks about its father and mother and later finds out the whole truth?

- Why don't I have a father?
- Why don't I have a mother?
- Who is my dad?
- Who is my mom?

- Why do I have two fathers? Which one is the real one?
- Why do I have three mothers? Which one is "mine"?
- How was I created?
- Why was I born in Prague, or Kiev?
- Why am I sad so often?
- Why am I sick so often?

Prof. Ulrich Kutschera, who describes himself as an "atheist evolution researcher," says:

> Over the course of the evolution of mammals, over 150 million years, the mother-child bond has developed into the strongest bond there is. If the child is thus deliberately deprived of its mother as a primary relationship (as with homosexual men) or one tries to replace the biological father with a woman, this violates the most elemental human right that exists.[71]

The desire for children must not become an obsession, so that the rights and dignity of the child (and the genetic supplier) are disregarded. No person has a right to a child, but the child has a right to his biological parents. Those who produce children artificially with other people's genetic material negate this human right and with it the "human ecology." On September 22, 2011, Pope Benedict XVI reminded the German parliament of this. He said:

> There is also an ecology of humanity. Man too has a nature that he must respect and that he cannot manipulate at will. Man is not merely self-creating freedom. Man does not create himself. He is intellect and will, but he is also nature, and his will is rightly ordered if he respects his nature, listens to it and accepts himself for who he is, as one who did not create himself. In this way, and in no other, is true human freedom fulfilled.

5.
Becoming parents

Children are a puzzle from God and the hardest of all to solve, but love can do it, if it puts itself to it.
Friedrich Hebbel

Simona recounts: We so longed for a child. I made room in my soul for a child, I made room in my professional life, and I decided: Not still *more* responsibility! Don't take it any higher! I want a family, and I want children. We want a family. We want children.

I already knew it before the test: I'm pregnant!

We looked at each other for a long time and said not a word, knowing that nothing would be the same as before. Our first flash of joy — mixed with angst. Will everything go okay?

For awhile it remained our secret. My breasts became sensitive. I can't bear the smell of brown rice! I got cravings for salmon rolls and chocolate mousse! Every morning I'm sick, and I'm losing weight. I don't drink alcohol anymore, and smoking is far in my past. I work as usual, but my drive is diminishing. It doesn't seem as important anymore.

The people in my environment notice the change and I come out with the news: There's a baby on the way. Everyone I tell I'm pregnant radiates with joy.

We look at books and movies about the emergence of life. The images of the first months are a bit disturbing, because when I think of a "child," I see a baby before me, not a strange being with a giant head and large eye sockets. But I want to know what's happening down in there.

During the fourth week, the heart starts to beat, and in the second month the brain starts to develop. All the organs are there and start doing their job.

The child is now about an inch and a half big but already has toes and fingers and can move its arms and legs. On the ultrasound, I can see it sucking its thumb. It brings me to tears. It's really a baby in my womb.

The major ultrasound examinations are scheduled, the first between 9 and 12 weeks, the second between 19 and 22 weeks, and the last one near the end. Mother and baby are examined to see if everything is going according to plan.

If you read the many flyers laid out in the waiting room, you could get really upset at everything that can go wrong. I could get preeclampsia, a poisoning during pregnancy "that poses a fatal threat to mother and fetus," or gestational diabetes, toxoplasmosis — or I could get a parasite that causes premature or still birth. It seems as if a monster is lurking around every corner and can swallow up my child. Someone advises me not to eat raw dairy products anymore, because they may contain listeria, which can cause meningitis and blood poisoning in newborns. I look up the risks: According to the Robert Koch Institute, there are 300 infections per year, 8 percent of which are in babies, that's 24 a year. In 2015, Germany saw the birth of 737,575 children. About 0.003% had a listeria infection. So I eat all kinds of cheese.

Do I really have to know everything?

After three months, I gradually stop feeling sick. Slowly I get a baby bump.

The doctor asks us if we want to know the sex. We think it over: Should it stay a secret until the day comes? Or would it be nice to know ahead of time whether it will be a girl or boy, whether we should buy baby things for one or the other ... less mystery, more relationship?

No, we don't want to know. We want to be excited and don't want to spoil the surprise.

The doctor keeps going.

Do I want an extended screening? It's for early detection of defects and hereditary illnesses. If there is evidence of that, the amniotic fluid can be examined. The amniotic fluid holds genetic information about the child.

To remove the amniotic fluid, the baby's secure amniotic sac must be punctured with a hollow needle. In 1% of cases, this causes a miscarriage — in Germany about 700 children die from this examination.[72] Both the positive and negative diagnosis can be wrong.

To detect Down syndrome early, there is now a prenatal test. This involves taking a blood sample, no need to puncture the amniotic sac. The test can determine with greater accuracy whether the child has Down syndrome, but this test is also not 100% reliable.

And if the result is positive, what then? The doctor says that in that case I don't have to carry the child to term.

Huh? I should abort it?

We need time.

This is an awful decision to make. If only they hadn't asked us! If only tests like that didn't exist! Kill the child that I have at long last conceived? And what if after all that it turned out to be healthy? A horrible thought.

And if the test shows the child has Down syndrome?

Suddenly, we're confronted with a question that is much too big for us: Should the child live or die? We read and ask around. At the bus stop, we notice a mother with a Down syndrome child. The two talk and laugh together. Would it really be such a disaster?

We go to the Internet and run across Catherine MacMillan, a young woman who became pregnant at 18, when she had just started music school. She didn't feel ready for motherhood at all, her relationship to the father was iffy, and she thought about abortion. Then, in the 26th week, came the diagnosis: Dandy-Walker syndrome — three-quarters of the brain was not normally developed.

For the doctors, there was no question: "pregnancy termination," as they call it — kill the child. Catherine should not ruin her life!

But once she felt the child in her body, there was no longer any question: The child should live. This meant Catherine had to run the gauntlet — she constantly had to justify this decision.

On March 31, 2010, Sara was born. She was severely disabled. But her heart was not disabled. Sara was capable of love. Sara couldn't speak, but she could engage with the ducks at the pond. She couldn't sing, but she could take irrepressible joy in music. Her overflowing joy in life overcame everyone who met her.

Catherine began publicly advocating for children's right to life. She also held lectures, showed photos of her beloved and so exceedingly loving daughter Sara. "Heart lost to heart" was how Catherine's father described his daughter's relationship to her child.[73]

One morning, when Sara was 6, Catherine found her deceased in her bed one morning. It was completely unexpected. A sword pierced her heart.

The pain just strengthened Catherine's resolve to fight so that disabled children would be allowed to live.

We looked around more and also found testimonies from parents who had reached their absolute mental and physical limits with a disabled child. What should we do?

We talk for a long time, go silent, place our hands on my belly.

Suddenly, it was clear to us: Despite it all, we want no tests. We do not want to be the lords of life and death. That's too much for us. We will not abort the child under any circumstances. If the child is disabled, we will accept it. Making this decision took a big load off us.

Aren't the train stations being converted to barrier-free? Don't public places have lavatories for the disabled? Aren't we amazed at the incredible achievements of people with disabilities at the Paralympics? Isn't discrimination against the disabled banned by law? But killing disabled children before they are born, that's allowed. What hypocrisy!

The doctor's question has also brought something good: If the baby really is disabled, we'll be ready.

We are waiting and hopeful. Was that really the child that pressed its little feet against my abdominal wall? Soon there's no longer any doubt — the baby kicks and turns. My belly gets larger and larger. I'm carrying a child in my body, a person, a great mystery. A strange pride grips me when I'm walking down the street. I don't hide my belly. Look! I'm carrying life in me!

We get the child's room ready, set up the crib that my mother once laid me in.

A friend presses a book into my hand: Louann Brizendine, *The Female Brain.*[74] "Read this! Then you'll know what's happening to you!" I'm amazed: All the changes I'm perceiving — both the physical and mental — have to do with changes in the brain and hormonal balance. New circuits are forming in the brain for maternal behavior. "These changes result in a motivated, highly attentive, and aggressively protective brain that forces the new mother to alter her responses and priorities in life." The strange cravings during pregnancy, the oversensitivity to sound, the need for sleep, the lack of motivation, the forgetfulness — I used to be so well-organized! — that is all triggered by new hormones that are produced by the fetus and the placenta and flood the brain. I learn that starting in the sixth month of pregnancy, my brain — temporarily — shrinks. Two weeks before delivery, it goes back to normal size. The brain shuts down for conversion to a "mommy brain."

My belly grows and grows. I can finally stop working. I clean out the basement, sew curtains for the baby's room, order little shirts, pants, and diapers on the Internet. We shop for a stroller together. Often, I just sit there, put a hand on my belly, hum a tune, and tell my child about the family it will be born into.

Mark is working a lot, as always, but he has taken two weeks off for the birth. The abdominal wall gets tenser and more and more often hard as a board — a preliminary exercise for the contractions. Can this belly get any bigger? It gets hard to climb the stairs, put on shoes, or carry shopping bags. The clock is ticking.

Birth

Strange: I have no fear of the birth. It is coming, and it's inevitable. I give in. The child barely has any room left to move, and we're two days past the due date. Now the time is here. The contractions come at regular intervals. We drive to the hospital — we know the way. They had an introductory night for the parents.

A minute and a half, a pause, a minute and a half, a pause.... The next contraction and the next, rolling over me like waves in the ocean. The cervix opens. The amniotic sac bursts. There's just one thing to do: complete surrender to what is happening, and at the same time cooperate with all my might. Passivity and activity merge. Push, breathe, and push again, and push again.... It is like a hurricane, the elemental force of life that I'm surrendering to. The midwife says the head is already visible. Push again with all my might, and in the next moment the baby works itself out with a spiral movement, and is caught by two hands.

"It's a boy!" — the first declaration of his future identity. The newborn screams and is immediately placed in warm water. He relaxes and opens his eyes. Gradually the umbilical cord stops pulsing. The doctor hands Mark scissors, and he cuts the cord that linked child to mother. We look deep into each other's soul. The child is laid naked on my breast. *My child!* Has anything ever belonged to me more than this child?

Mark stays the first night with me, with us, in the clinic. Amazed, we look at our great mystery. Who are you? What will your path in life be? The midwife comes and lays the baby on me. It can suck, and the first drops of thick yellow milk come. The child sleeps in the crook of my arm, and I with him. Sometime at night, the nurse comes and lays him in the crib next to me. I awake to every little sound. I look and look, sniff his little head, and take in the fragrance.

The child in the making

A child has come into the world. The world has become one person richer. In one fell swoop, two independent people become parents — father and mother. Their life has a new focus, a tiny, helpless child, who is completely dependent on their care, so that now their life is dependent on the child. Life has catapulted them into a new stage. Until the pregnancy, everything revolved around themselves. With the moment of birth, the father and mother revolve around the newborn child.

There is no question: It is stressful to bring an infant into the world. One of the most common side effects is lack of sleep. Fortunate is the woman whose husband stands behind her, giving her space and time, recognition and love, so that she feels secure and can fully devote herself to the child. From month to month, the father takes a greater role in the child's life. He also strives to make room in his professional life for his family.

With the first child, the mother cannot imagine how she would cope with two children, but once the second has arrived, she is more relaxed, and with the third, it's all routine for the parents.

With every fiber of their being, the parents hope for the child to thrive. Even though the child's unique individuality has not yet unfolded, they perceive a limitless treasure when they look at the child, and the thought of any misfortune is a look into the abyss.

The child is unique. Uniqueness is a principle of creation. No two snowflakes are alike! But the child is more than just unique: It is a person. A person differs from all other creatures in that it has dignity and is equipped with intelligence, self-reflection, and free will — it can decide whether to do good or evil. A small child's spiritual endowments, the examples set for him, and his upbringing, play a major role in what use he will put his free will to in life. What unspeakable responsibility is placed in the parents' hands!

Small children can't talk yet, but they can radiantly smile, blissfully fall asleep, or cry and scream, not go to sleep and not eat. They can be a profound joy to their parents or a burden that brings the parents' nerves to their limits. They can discover the world with effervescent joy, or become belligerent, sad, and apathetic. In their first years of life, they can develop an inherent sense of trust, or they can start their life with deep distrust of themselves, other people, and the world. Not everything lies in the parents' hands, but a lot does.

A person starts the journey from conception to death in idyllic security, floats in amniotic fluid, gets everything he needs through the umbilical cord, is rocked incessantly, hears the mother's voice and shares her feelings. If the mother is filled with hope, joy, and anticipation, the baby's soul is imprinted with a sunny undertone. If she is full of worry, anxiety, and stress, this throws a shadow on the child's soul.

Birth is a shock. Suddenly and painfully, the baby is catapulted into a world that is bright and loud, and in which its basic needs take time to meet. It experiences its body as a source of pain. The newborn child can suck and can grasp a finger with its tiny hands. It can cry and scream. In a few weeks it will be able to smile. It is dependent on loving care round the clock. The child has been released into the world and needs nothing more urgently than a physical and emotional bond to its mother. What makes a newborn child feel secure? The soft, warm skin of its mother, her breast, from which milk flows, her trusted voice, her comforting look, her loving glance, to be carried and rocked in her arms, sleeping in her palpable proximity. In all this, the child learns through its senses: Mommy is there. I'm safe. Everything is fine.

Is there anything more moving than a baby's smile? In this small creature lives a loving soul that radiates from the child's eyes and shines from its face. A human being! A great mystery. What will become of him? Mother and infant are a uniquely fine-tuned symbiotic duo.

The outer need and dependence of the infant corresponds to the biological, hormonally triggered love of the mother. The happiness and bonding hormone oxytocin floods mother and child at birth and during nursing. Full of love, the mother looks into the face of the little one and sees the most beautiful child in the world. She hears every sound and reacts immediately. A lioness has emerged, ready to rescue her child from flames, if need be.

The child receives everything within this secure bond. The baby wants to and must be lovingly cared for 24 hours a day, seven days a week, and its expressions of life and need call for an immediate, sensitive reaction. If the baby does not receive a reassuring reaction to its cries within minutes, it falls into existential anxiety. The volume, pitch, and urgency of the cry increase from minute to minute until panic sets in. The mother can divine her child's emotional state and usually knows what's wrong: hunger, a stomach ache, a need for mother's presence, sleep. There is nothing else for her but to aid the child as fast as possible and calm it. If she doesn't succeed, it is massive stress for her. The mother does all this on her own if she is not damaged herself, and the child learns and learns on its own. No one has to teach this to the mother or the child.

The need for existential security is not specific to babies, but is a basic drive of people until their final breath. What wouldn't we do, what compromises wouldn't we make for material security and social acceptance? The unknown evokes fear, the known provides security. The baby needs the mother as a place of safety, which in a family environment soon expands to father, siblings, and grandparents.

The more secure the bond, the more curiosity, courage, and joy the child explores the world with, and it dares on its own to venture farther and farther from its mother. It needs an unwinding "leash" that stays connected to the mother during its playful explorations and whose length it can determine itself. Then he doesn't have to expend any energy to reassure himself of the mother's presence and learns on the fly.

Never again does a person learn so much in so little time as in the first year of life. The brain's weight increases by 500 grams. Mental structures are indelibly imprinted on the brain.

Learning is driven by feedback. Between mother and child, there is a constant flow of micro-communication, which the child takes in with its fine-tuned sensors. Approval, joy, laughter, delight, — head shaking, sighs, annoyance — the child's activities receive nonstop feedback through the mother's reactions. The famous pediatrician Prof. Theodor Hellbrügge has observed:

> Every change in the mother's face — even the most subtle — is perceived and imitated by the infant.... One can almost say that the first language occurs in the visual communication between mother and child.[75]

The child needs constant feedback from the mother and sensitive reaction to his overwhelming emotions, which the child itself can't control yet. Regulation of emotions occurs through the mother's comforting reaction. This comfort gives security, confidence, courage, help and protection, from which the secure foundation of basic trust then emerges.

This security and constant communication with the mother sprouts synapses in the brain. The infant's brain gradually develops firm structures and modes of operation through early childhood experiences. If love is lacking, there are actual voids in the brain, as science has shown through imaging processes.[76]

No one shows the child how to turn over, crawl, or walk. No one demands that it make the effort to grasp an object or exert itself to climb the stairs. Every milestone is celebrated, not only by the parents, but by everyone with whom joy in the child's progress can be so easily shared by smartphone. Grandparents, aunts, uncles, godparents, and friends delight in the photos and videos: Yay! She can crawl! She can stand! Good for her! The first little tooth has poked through! Finally, around the first birthday, the first step. What an achievement!

Life is blazing its trail. Life itself is a work in progress, and we can see it firsthand in the small child. When a child receives what it needs, it delights those around it with its smile, its untamed joy of life, its creativity, the light in its eyes, the radiance of its sleeping face, its complete, nonjudgmental acceptance of people and the world, the miracle of its awakening intelligence, the words it creates and the love it declares. Having in one's lap a child who completely relaxes in physical closeness is soothing to the soul. When the mother's heart is near to the child, then the world is new to her as well. No one accepts her as completely as her own child. This can be a path to healing for the mother.

Soon the first word comes. During exhalation, the lips come together twice, and the word "Mama" sounds. And when the air is pushed out with a bit more strength, then comes "Papa". At age 2, the child begins to talk, girls sooner than boys, and at 3, entire sentences are forming. A child's creativity in forming words is so much fun for the family!

Only gradually does a feel for time develop. In the first year, the child only knows the here and now. If someone goes away, he's gone forever. Only gradually does the child form an idea of what it sees, and not until sometime in the second year of life is this idea stored in the brain so that it can be recognized again. It then knows that Mother, who has left the room, will come back.

The child now discovers that it can act on something — turn on the light, start a musical toy or build a tower. It learns to orient itself in space, control its body more and more, experience itself as its own person, who can say yes or no to things that come his way. A feeling of self-efficacy arises. If, during its learning stages, a child is not constantly positively affirmed — normally by happiness radiating from its mother's face — then its motivation slackens, it doesn't experience the exhilarating feeling of, "I can!" but develops a basic feeling of inadequacy.

Just as standing on his own two feet is a quantum leap in development, so is the first "I" in the third year of life. The child starts to give validity to its free will. The child must say "no" to exist in the world as a separate person with a self of his own, so the defiant phase often called "the terrible twos" sets in. Just as the child has learned *on its own* to crawl, walk and talk, it must dissolve the symbiosis with its mother to perceive itself as a separate person. Then the child is suddenly able to poop and tinkle in the potty. Parents need patience — a great deal of patience — instead of giving in to the temptation to exercise power. *Having time* is the indispensable precondition to love, just as water must flow through a pipe, love flows through the medium of time.

Parents forever

Once the woman has grown into motherhood for a couple of years, soon and unexpectedly the first signals come that the woman must reel in her protective instinct a little, not to hover over the child, but to hear and hearken to what is unfolding in the child. Let the father take on his big, strong presence in the life of the child; do not close the child off from external influences, but do not hand the defenseless child to them — an extremely difficult balancing act. Being a parent is a constant, ever more profound exercise in letting go — it never ends. It means letting go of one's emotional needs, of one's own preconceptions of what the child should do and not do, of the seemingly self-evident demands for closeness, of the conviction that one knows what is good for the child and the demand that the child do it — a never-ending process of refining one's love.

There are constantly decisions to make: vaccinations, daycare, kindergarten, whether to go back to work, which school, which friends, which media, a smartphone or not. It is all difficult in an overreaching society that increasingly tramples on parental rights.

Before you know it, puberty arrives. Now the detachment process gets serious. All the big mistakes one has made, all breaches of the child's trust, such as through parental exercise of power, take their revenge now.

But even if the parents haven't made any major errors, it can still be tough. Vehement and unclouded by wisdom, the child seeks his own way. The young person — no longer a child — leaves the house for college and then the world of work. The child becomes an adult. Romantic relationships begin — disordered as they may be these days.

The focus of the mother's existence must be shifted again, away from the children and back to herself. It is good when the mother can seize on the new phase of life with joy and energy. Nonetheless, her antennas are still set to the child's transmitter.

Small children, small worries; big children, big worries. At some point, parents must realize that the upbringing is over, once and for all. And the worrying doesn't do the children any good. What they need is trust and the confidence that they will do well. Fortunate are the parents who can transform their worries into prayers!

Finally, perhaps, comes the marriage. The son or daughter "leave father and mother and become one flesh." Even if the wedding comes after years of love and romance, now everything will be different. The new "we" made up of son and daughter-in-law or daughter and son-in-law now have a firm shell. The parents recede to the periphery.

And what happiness if a grandchild is born! This lets love loose in the extended family, the enormous joy as life begins anew. The child is like a magnet in the heart of the family; it draws the outward-directed forces back inward. Pictures and messages about the child's achievements are sent around and continuously feed the joy of life. For grandparents — especially the grandmother — the next phase of letting go begins. She must learn to be sparing in her advice. Transfer of maternal wisdom over the generations is no longer in demand. Young mothers get information from books, doctors and the Internet. Experienced grandmothers keep quiet, hold back and give presents.

Those are all lessons of love that everyone has to learn in life's college of parenting. If the bond has anchored deep and permanently in the heart, there is no way out: Either grow in love, selflessness and forgiveness, or grow in sadness and depression. The battleground is the family. There is no model that can release us from this battle. There is just the ever-repeating decision to love.

6.
Daycare — Socialism 2.0

The devaluation of motherhood is discrimination against the most important, most inalienable task for survival of the community and hope for the future. It is destruction of its central core and thereby a plan for suicide.
Christa Meves

In June 2019, UNICEF, the child welfare organization of the United Nations, published a list ranking the "child friendliness" of the 31 richest countries. Their criteria for child friendliness were: Length of parental leave at full salary and affordable childcare "from birth until school begins." Between the end of parental leave (UNICEF calls for six months) and the start of affordable childcare ("from birth"), there should be no gaps, so that "children can best develop." UNICEF's executive director Henrietta Fore says:

> There is no time more critical to children's brain development — and therefore their futures — than the earliest years of life. We need governments to help provide parents with the support they need to create a nurturing environment for their young children. And we need the support and influence of the private sector to make this happen.[77]

How true! No time is more formative for the rest of a person's life than the first three years. Therefore, we need governments that support parents in creating an environment in which children can develop well.

But can children develop well when their mother returns to work in the first year of her child's life and infants enter collective care at the age of six months? To the United Nations' child welfare agency, availability of daycare centers is the crucial criterion for a country's "family friendliness." The UN, the EU, and the governments of the wealthiest countries agree:

Starting in infancy, children belong in the care of strangers. This is contradicted by attachment researchers, brain researchers, pediatricians, child psychologists, and social scientists. They substantiate that children can be permanently damaged psychologically and physically when external care starts too early.

Until the globally orchestrated daycare offensive in politics, collective external care of children under three years old was considered by the Western countries to be a failed communist path for creating the socialist man. He was to obediently get into line with the collective and thereby help bring about the communist revolution. A strong bond to the family was the greatest obstacle to this. As early as 1848, in the *Communist Manifesto*, destruction of the family was promoted as a condition for creating the classless society. Integration of women into the production process and the earliest possible collectivization of children was the key to bringing about the socialist utopia.

A hundred and fifty years later, the Western countries have jumped on the bandwagon. But the vocabulary has changed. It is no longer about the "classless society" of the totalitarian worker state, but about "compatibility of work and family," "early childhood education," and "equal opportunity." And the word "crèche" was put to use in some English-speaking countries — an ingenious move by those who see the family as the greatest obstacle to the postmodern paradise of equality, because even in a de-Christianized culture the word "crèche" still evokes Christmassy feelings of family security.

The daycare offensive

In Germany, it was Ursula von der Leyen, Minister of Family Affairs from 2005 to 2009, since 2019 president of the European Commission, who implemented the comprehensive establishment of daycare centers with support from the Social Democrats, the Left, the Greens, and the trade associations — with no resistance from the churches.

The project was peddled as "freedom of choice" for the mother. Sure, if there are no daycare centers, mothers can't choose to put their children in one. But if a place in daycare is subsidized to the tune of €1,000 per child per month, and mothers who care for children at home get nothing, then the freedom of choice is just a sham. Freedom of choice would only exist if mothers who care for their children at home also received suitable state support. But the care subsidy was defamed as a "barefoot and in the kitchen" subsidy and was never established by the federal government. The powerless voices that warned of this large-scale experiment conducted on the next generation were shunned and ridiculed.

In a few years, hundreds of thousands of daycares sprang up. To force communities to establish daycare centers, in 2013 Ursula von der Leyen conjured up a legal right of parents to a daycare slot.

This "legal right" is the trump card for implementing measures that will penetrate deep into the social order. In any village, just *one* mother has to demand daycare, and the village is forced to build a daycare center. To make it financially viable, they then have to make sure the daycare center fills up.

The result: In 2007, 15% of children under 3 were in daycare, which means 320,000. In 2017, the number was 33%, which was 760,000 children. (The rate varies between the former West and East Germany by up to 30%.) In 2018 the number of children reached 790,000.[78] In just 10 years, the concentrated political and media powers have convinced more than a third of all mothers to take the child they have carried in their womb for nine months — on whose physical and mental wellbeing they are focused with every fiber of their being — drop him off at a door, and after four, six, or even eight hours pick him back up again.

How was that possible? Two factors must especially be emphasized: the feminist devaluation of motherhood and the labor shortage in the economy.

Mothers naturally protect their small children when danger threatens. This isn't a matter of courage, but of instinct. Weakening the instinct to protect life is the result of a decades-long feminist barrage against mothers. Radical feminism, brought to life by Simone de Beauvoir ("Put an end to the slavery of motherhood!"), fights against men, against mothers, against children, and for the "human right" to abortion. The unmarried, childless, sexually promiscuous woman, who desperately strives to get to the executive suites, speaks of equality but wants power. This doesn't go together with pregnancy, nursing, caring for a small child — a task that the biological mother is equipped for by nature as no one else.

Women can thank "women's liberation" for the fact that they're only worth what their job pays them. Caring for children doesn't count as work.

The woman who does it receives no recognition, no financial relief, and no appropriate retirement pension, even though she's doing the most important job of all. She gives life to children who will not only support the pensions of an ever-aging population, but on whom the future of the whole society depends: on their sheer existence, on development of their skills, and on their character.

This feminist-plowed field is fertile ground for the seeds of daycare propaganda:

- You deserve your own self-fulfillment.
- A paid job is what gives you value.
- Childrearing and profession are compatible if you put your child in daycare.
- Small children need schooling.
- Professional caregivers can do a better job than you.

Really? Let's look closer.[79] The central existential crisis of most Western countries is a demographic one. Too few children are born to replace the existing population. The age pyramid is changing to a mushroom — the portion of old people keeps growing, and the portion of young people is shrinking. The Berlin Institute for Population and Development depicts the change in drastic language: "In some districts, in the year 2035, there may be one birth for every four funerals. In many places, residents will be more likely to meet at a funeral feast than at their grandchildren's first day of school."[80]

The demographic change leads to a labor shortage in the economy, which cannot be remedied by mass immigration of inadequately qualified workers — not to mention dissolution of the cultural heritage. In a much-noticed article in the Frankfurter Allgemeine Zeitung *Die dunkle Seite der Kindheit* (The Dark Side of Childhood) pediatrician Dr. Rainer Böhm explains the interests of the economy:

> The German "daycare offensive" is largely due to the massive political lobbying and public relations work of the trade associations, who, due to demographic developments, are trying to mobilize labor reserves even among young parents. Thus, publications of

> business-related institutes largely try to define the term "family friendliness" through availability of daycare slots.[81]

It is expensive to let women leave productive work for a few years and hold their jobs for them. So they have to be convinced to do something contrary to their nature: tear themselves away from the small child they carried and gave birth to, hand him over to strangers, and go back to work as quickly as possible. That plugs a demographic hole, saves the employer money, and is positive for tax revenues and social security contributions. How can that be made palatable to the mother?

1. They devalue the mother and the work of motherhood and tell her that professional "self-actualization" brings the greatest happiness. "Why aren't you working?" or, "What do you do for a living?" are the usual questions asked a mother who gives her all for her children round the clock. She needs a lot of mental stamina not to feel inferior when asked such questions.

2. They suggest that "work and family can be combined" if she sends the children to daycare as soon as possible after birth. In truth, this establishes a system of hyper-stress that makes masses of women sick. According to daycare propaganda, this supposedly even increases the birth rate — strange logic: If you can separate from your child as fast as possible after birth, that will be an incentive for you to have more children. Demographer Herwig Birg jokes: "The statistical correlation between the birth rate and the number of storks is probably higher than the alleged relationship with the employment rate for women."[82]

3. They put parents who decide against the state's early childcare under financial pressure: The daycares are subsidized with about €1,000 of tax money every month. If the woman is employed outside the home, she receives pension entitlements. If she cares for her own toddler herself, she gets absolutely nothing after a year of parental allowance.[83] With or without daycare, most families have to rely on two incomes, because statistically, in wealthy Germany, families with three or more children are threatened with poverty. A full 25% of all families with three or more children and 42% of single parents must make do with less than 60% of the national average income.[84]

Collective external care for small children allegedly creates "equal opportunity." The ministry of families says:

> All children should have an equal chance to discover what lies in them and to develop their talents. Early support for children in daycare significantly contributes to equal opportunity. And it should contribute to equal living conditions: In the East and West, in the country and cities, in rich and poor regions.[85]

The federal statistical office blows the same horn:

> Good childcare and therefore an early boost for all children are among the central tasks for Germany's future. They are important factors for children's development and equal opportunity. Nationwide, high-quality daycare slots are to be created — especially for children under 3. It is a goal shared by the federal government, the states and the local communities.

"Good childcare," "an early boost," "central task for the future," "equal opportunity," "high-quality" — who can resist this cornucopia of promises the state empties onto parents?

Franziska Giffey, the German Minister of Families (2018–2021), who wants to impose a statutory *daycare obligation* starting at age 3, introduced the "Good Daycare Act." The states will get €5.5 billion from the federal government up to 2022 and can use it as needed. This won't result in much quality improvement, because the billions are also to be used to completely free families on social assistance from paying daycare fees. The ministry says that this will be available to 1.2 million children. This alone creates a need that exceeds that €5.5 billion several times over.

No quality standards are established for the child-to-worker ratio or the length of time in daycare. The lack of personnel will be balanced out with assistants and interns — but frequently a caregiver will have to deal with 10 small children. Physical closeness, eye contact, talking, and immediate reaction to the infant's needs are impossible even with the best of intentions.

The "Good Daycare Act" is supposed to expand the number of daycare facilities and create a "needs-based offering for parents working shifts, through longer daycare hours" — daycare should therefore also become nightcare. Measures like this don't make any daycare center good but drive forward the damage done to children by government care of small children.

Collective care of small children by strangers does not produce equal opportunity, but an existentially unequal opportunity between children who grow up amidst the security of family with the loving attention of mother and father, and those who must do without their mother from earliest childhood.

Bonding instead of schooling

What do children need in order to learn well? Anyone can answer this question from their own experience — without going deep into psychological learning theory. We need to feel safe, secure, and accepted. No one can convey this feeling in the first three years better than the mother: the same face, the same voice, the same smell, the tender touch, her constant presence, and her immediate reaction — to put it briefly: *The bond to one person.*

If, God forbid, the child loses his mother, it can also be another person, as long as she is stable and present with love.

Renowned education researchers Sir Richard Bowlby (UK), Allan Shore (US), and Steve Biddulph (Australia) and many others scientifically confirm it: The more secure the child feels, the more curiously and courageously he explores the world and the earlier his circle of trusted people expands. A secure bond in early childhood creates basic trust. Without a secure bond, there is no basic trust, and without basic trust, there is a deep, lifelong fragility at the basis of one's personality.

SMALL CHILDREN NEED BONDING, NOT SCHOOLING

Education and childrearing are not fully possible anyway until, in the fourth year of life, the brain has reached a certain level of maturity (formation of the prefrontal cortex), and this maturity is best reached when the child knows he is secure and loved. If that is not the case, even the brain's physical composition changes: The hippocampus, which governs the processes of learning and thinking, is smaller in teenagers who were placed early in all-day daycare than in children whose parents cared for them.[86] Psychiatrist

Hans-Joachim Maaz, who grew up in communist East Germany, knows the devastating psychological effects of early, all-day, collective daycare from experience and writes:

> Developmental psychology, educational research, infant research, brain research agree in one central finding — that the quality of the early creation of relationships with the child is crucial to personality development. This allows one to state with confidence that early childcare is not about schooling but about the relationship. Children under 3 years old cannot be schooled.[87]

They also cannot form a relationship to other children their own age. If, according to UNICEF recommendations, a child lands in daycare at 6 months old, he has still not yet developed self-perception, a feel for time, and cannot yet speak or even say "I." So how can he form a relationship to another child? A small child needs a fixed reference person, normally the mother, a trusted environment, people who react to his expressions of pain, talk with him, and perceive and applaud his achievements.

To cushion the transition from a safe home, within view, hearing, reaching, and touching distance of the mother (and the father, and the siblings, and the grandparents and the cat), the child is granted an acclimation period that may last from a few days to a few weeks. With the mother, the child is supposed to get to know the new environment and "bond" as fast as possible to a daycare worker. But very few small children do that. They scream, cry, cling and whimper. "The child just has to work through it," is the sentence used to suggest to parents that it's all completely normal and will let up. But it doesn't let up, other than that the child becomes resigned to it because no one is reacting to his suffering. Every morning, the child has to go through the pain of separation again.

He has to compete with other children for attention and physical contact with the daycare worker, the contact on which he depends. Is he a cute, likable child who gets what he needs, or an introverted one who quickly gives up? Is there any constant reference person for the child? There is turnover among daycare workers. They go on vacation, and like the children, they often get sick. For a small child, who doesn't even develop a feeling for time until age 2, that means that not only is Mommy gone, but so is her replacement. The child can fall into feelings of hopeless abandonment.

Small children don't get what they need if they are put into collective external care before age 3. Their basic trust takes a hit. How hard and deep the hit will be depends on many factors, including the child's "resilience." What is certain is that no child between 0 and 3 years of age would leave his mother of his own accord and replace her with unknown daycare workers and a group of strangers his own age, if you could ask him. But no one asks him, and he can't step in on behalf of his own existential needs. He can only cry, scream, refuse to sleep, refuse to eat, refuse to play, punch, bite, become apathetic, stare into space with sad, empty eyes, or get sick.

Sound scientific studies[88] on the long-term effects of early daycare show results that no one would wish on anybody:

- Children cared for outside the family have more behavioral issues in their teen years.
- The longer a child is in daycare per day, the more aggressive he becomes. The quality of care largely doesn't matter. At 15, the children tend toward more risky, impulsive behavior.[89]
- In their teens, daycare kids
    - have a higher incidence of criminal behavior
    - are sick more often
    - are less satisfied with life
    - are marked by aggression, disobedience, poor self-control, and violence if their daycare lasts many hours.[90]
- Children who are bonded to no one turn indiscriminately to grownups to get a little bit of physical security. The child's natural protective impulse against adults transgressing limits are overridden — an alarming symptom in times of rampant sexual abuse.[91]

On the other hand, safely bonded children have big advantages in life:

- They have better self-control, do not panic right away in the face of adversity, and can handle sad situations better.
- They can pursue long-term objectives, which means they can forego immediate gratification in order to reach a higher goal.

- They are less prone to drug abuse.
- They reach a higher level of education.
- They tend less toward obesity.
- They are more adaptable and resilient in overcoming interpersonal problems.
- They can maintain relationships longer.[92]

Language development depends on bonding. Only humans are capable of symbolizing the world in terminology and communicating with others in highly complex, ever-evolving language. Anyone who accompanies a child through his language development marvels at this miracle.

The child learns to speak from his mother. In the very first weeks, the baby starts to form sounds, and to read these sounds from his mother's lips. The baby feels secure when it recognizes her voice after birth and is constantly connected to her by the lifeline of her baby talk. (The rich nuance of expression in one's *native language* can almost never be achieved in a foreign language.)

Learning expressive nuance requires that the mother be there and speak with him. In daycare, direct attention through physical and eye contact totals at most 30 minutes a day. The child is in a group his own age who also can't talk, missing their mother, and deafening noise reigns.

It is therefore not surprising that more and more children are showing up in kindergarten with speech disorders. Sixteen percent of all boys and girls between 0 and 17 years old have language and speech disorders, and among 5-year-olds, 42% of boys and 30% of girls are affected.[93] Social causes — above all screen time (see Chapter 11) — are far more common than medical ones. Over the past 10 years, according to data from German health insurance company AOK, the number of diagnosed developmental disorders in children between 5 and 7 has increased by 26.5%. Of those, 82% involve speech and language disorders.[94] Almost every fourth first-grader gets speech therapy.[95]

Brain researcher Prof. Manfred Spreng warns:

> After birth, if the vital communicative bond between mother and child is not established and maintained well enough and long enough, the infant's and toddler's imitation abilities don't

fully come into their own, and failures of early childhood learning processes can lead to apathy (this learned helplessness is a type of early childhood resignation or even depression).[96]

Constant stress and cortisol

Daycare children suffer from persistent stress that can make them physically and mentally ill. There is a highly complex stress hormone system that starts in the hypothalamus and the pituitary gland in the adrenal cortex to produce the stress hormone cortisol. An acute level of cortisol can easily be tested through saliva samples (the long-term ones through hair samples). Rat experiments have shown that when high levels of cortisol are chronically secreted during continuous stress, memory performance and learning capability decrease, because the brain has no periods to relax and regenerate. It's no different with people.

The normal pattern with cortisol shows an increase upon waking, a continuous drop during the day, until it declines all the way at night and comes to rest. In daycare, this normal profile is reversed: The cortisol level is lowest in the morning and rises during the day. Then it doesn't even go into rest mode at night.

This is not a temporary disturbance that subsides during days off from daycare or on vacation. Daycare children continue to have a high level of cortisol into their teens, and the longer they were cared for outside the family as small children, the higher the cortisol level is.

The constant hyperactivity of the stress hormone system can cause permanent changes in the brain that decrease learning and memory performance and lead to a depressive state. But it can also lead to a trauma-like condition: Then the cortisol level is permanently too low. Prof. Serge Sulz, head of the Center for Integrated Psychotherapy (CIP), says in a lecture entitled *Kinderkrippe als toxischer Dauerstress für Kinder* (Daycare as toxic continuous stress for children):

> This is the result of complete surrender of the self, the experience of inescapability and the absence of opportunities to take any action. Stress is experienced, but the (normal) fight or flight response is no longer triggered by cortisol.[97]

These are then the "easy to care for" children who have "settled in well." The *Wiener Krippenstudie* (Vienna Daycare Study) has shown: After five months, children placed in daycare at age 2 showed a qualitatively average daily cortisol profile in daycare that was comparable to the values measured in 2-year-old children in Romanian orphanages in the 1990s.[98]

The child is subjected to a timed daily routine in daycare. At specified times, the children must eat simultaneously, play, go out for fresh air, sleep, or have their diapers changed in a one-minute cycle. What caregiver has the time to deal with the needs of the individual child, much as she wishes she could? The fact that she can't saps her strength and makes her discontented. A study of the basic situation in daycare centers shows:

> "Maladaptive" behavior, which includes crying, screaming or defiance, deadpan facial expressions, seclusion, aimless wandering, avoidance of eye contact, inability to play, lack of interest in play, fun and other daily offerings, as well as driving away or injuring other children and even themselves, represents an attempt to build contact with the caregiver. The child tries by all available means to get attention, to satisfy his genetically programmed need for a secure bond. However, this type of relationship search often ends abruptly. Because day-to-day operation of the daycare would be impaired, and the size of the groups simply does not allow intensive interaction with the individual child, the caregivers must intervene and try to suppress the child's "disruptive" behavior as fast as possible. At the same time, it is overlooked that the child's behavior is a reaction to the lack of care from the caregiver and expresses an absolute existential need.[99]

How strongly a child reacts to the "continuous toxic stress" in daycare (and kindergarten, see Chapter 8) depends on many factors. The most important are: the family situation (bonding, childrearing behavior, neglect); the age of the child at separation from the mother; the child-to-worker ratio; availability of a person to consistently bond within the daycare, and the length of care.[100]

Many children are in daycare all day. In the morning they are torn from their sleep, and in the evening they wait — completely exhausted — for their mothers. They have been through more than one shift of caregivers. The pain of the children who are picked up last is heart-rending. When they sit alone on their little chair and wait and wait and wait, they fear that they've been forgotten forever. When their mother or father finally comes, they're completely exhausted, as are the parents after their day's work. Even at night, their cortisol level doesn't drop.

Daily life in daycare is not only stressful for the children, but also for the caregivers. Even with their best efforts, they cannot meet the demands of the children and their parents, and they themselves are under continuous stress. Any parent knows how hard it is to stand up to the crying, screaming, and defiance of small children. In a daycare, several children are usually crying at the same time, and the caregiver is completely unable to attend to every one of them. Will she be able to remain affectionate, or curse, threaten and punish?

The noise level in daycares is so high that the employer should provide ear protection to the caregivers, according to a report on *Health in Daycare Facilities*.[101] This is one cause of the numerous psychosomatic disorders among caregivers. They often lack the opportunity to remove themselves briefly from the noise-intensive group work. The usual symptoms of stress arise: tension, irritability, psychosomatic disorders (gastrointestinal and circulatory problems, headaches), and when the stress lasts longer, also dissatisfaction with work, depression, and burnout. "Conflicts with parents" and "too little recognition" are also mentioned as stressful.

This is how grownup, educated caregivers react to everyday life in daycare. That's not even to mention how the children fare — whose tender little ears still have to get used to the noisy world and who have no chance at all to withdraw from the "noise-intensive group work."

Any mother knows how much stress it is to care for just two preschool children, how it plays on the nerves when a child cries and screams, when he is unhappy, won't sleep, eats poorly or gets sick. How should a daycare worker, who does a poorly paid job and has no bond to the children, deal with five or more small children who have to be forced into a predetermined rhythm?

Caregivers complain that they suffer pressure from parents. If something goes wrong with their child, then the caregiver must be at fault.

Parents often don't want to know too much about how things are going in the daycare or with their child. Many caregivers would rather send a child who is having trouble home to his mother, but then she would come under pressure from management. They are encouraged to tell the parents something nice about the day, so as not to upset them.

Rearing children is a constant challenge to one's character. Even mothers and fathers are not always completely affectionate, patient, and sensitive, but normally they love their child, take joy in him and are willing to sacrifice. In the first years, the mother lives with the child in a delicate, symbiotic unit. Should a stranger really intrude in this most intimate of all relationships? What kind of character does the caregiver have? What wounds does her soul bear from her own childhood? In contact with the unfulfillable needs of small children, these wounds will tear open. Even a good education can't prevent that.

Is it any wonder that both children and caregivers constantly catch infectious illnesses? Continuous stress weakens the immune system. A Danish study of 140,000 children ages 0 to 5 showed that daycare children receive hospital treatment for about double as many acute respiratory infections as children raised at home.[102]

And how are the parents doing when they pick up their child after a day of work? The professional workday is no walk in the park. The mother (or father) is also stressed. What they actually need now is a relaxing evening. But they bring home a sad, exhausted child who expresses his dissatisfaction in all possible ways. Neither mother nor child is in good shape to spend their moments together as happy "quality time," because the small child needs *quantity* time — 24/7. How can you take joy in your child under so much stress? How does a mother who hardly sees her child most of the day really get to know her child and develop a sensitive feel for him? She and the child are overloaded. She can easily be haunted by doubts about her competence as a mother: Perhaps the trained caregiver is doing a better job than me?

Normally, no one knows her own child as well as the mother. But for that, she needs time and space, and spiritual and material security. Not to give her this time to devote to her children's early years and instead subsidize the socialist external care system to the tune of billions is a political decision that damages the whole society.

Professor Sulz's institute has developed 38 criteria for estimating the daycare risk for children and indicates this risk with a traffic light: Red: Damages children. Yellow: Questionable. Green: Good.[103] The bottom line: Ninety-three percent of daycare centers damage children.

Many factors determine the degree of privation that the child must suffer in the forced time among strangers. Each month's delay in arriving at daycare reduces the probability of mental harm. Each hour less at daycare also reduces the harm.[104]

The authors advise: No daycare in the first two years of life. No all-day daycare in the first three years of life. No daycare with more than two, or a maximum of three children per caregiver! No changing of reference people. This means that if the normal family situation — mother and one or two siblings — can be simulated, the child suffers no damage. Under "optimal" conditions, he may call his caregiver "Mom." Would a mother want that?

Besides: If a child has bonded to the caregiver under favorable circumstances, he will have to separate from her anyway when kindergarten comes. A 5-year-old child has therefore already suffered two separations from his most important reference person, which will leave scars on his subconscious. *Can I trust anybody? Will I be abandoned whenever I get close to somebody? Will you also abandon me?* Basic trust has been damaged.

The negative consequences of early childhood external care hits the children of single parents especially hard. About 60% of them are welfare recipients. Naturally, they have to work and put their child in daycare. Consider this: A single mother has usually separated from her partner shortly after the child's birth, if not before — a traumatic event for her and the child. Now the child must also separate from his mother, often for the whole day, because his mother needs to earn money. The risk of mental disorders among children of single mothers is — as one would expect — significantly higher than for children who grow up in intact families. One study says that there is a danger "that the increased risk of mental problems among children of single parents and the risks of early childcare outside the family may not just add up, but actually multiply."[105]

Daycare is an institutionalized hyper-stress system for children, caregivers, and parents that hurts everybody. Michael Hüter, childhood researcher and author, says:

> If we consider the scientific research findings from neurobiology, psychology, anthropology and sociology — from all the research on childhood that we currently have — and take them seriously, every daycare center would have to be closed immediately.[106]

Collective early childhood care is a system that dulls the heart: the hearts of the children whose pain is not heard, the heart of the mother who cannot act according to her finely tuned radar system, and the heart of the caregiver who can't replace the mother no matter how much she may wish she could. This means the experience of being loved at the beginning of life — indispensable for the development of a healthy personality — is flawed. The child develops deep doubts as to whether he is welcome in this world, whether he can trust people, and whether he can trust anything at all.

Children grow into youth and adults. What will the child use to fill the hole in his soul when adolescence comes? The world offers him booze, drugs, computer games, the Internet, smartphones and sex. Will he be strong enough not to be seduced by them and to set his own goals? How will he behave as an adult? Will a deep feeling of inner weakness and privation drive him into radical politics? Will the adult want to and be able to bond in marriage and become a good father or mother?

Weakening of personality in a large portion of the young generation has societal consequences. For the first time, an international work group headed by German researcher Christian Bachmann has looked into the potential cost to the overall society when children have no solid bond to their parents and skid into antisocial behavior. The study's English title is: *The cost of love: financial consequences of insecure attachment in antisocial youth.* It should actually be called: The cost of *lacking* love, because the study shows the enormous costs to the economy and society from insecure attachment among antisocial youth.[107]

And think about this, too: Parents get old. Then they're the ones in need of loving attention. Then it is up to the children to sacrifice themselves to soothe the loneliness, illness, or dementia of their aged parents. Why should they do that when the bond of love was torn in early childhood? Will they hand their parents over to strangers who, like the daycare workers, are paid by the state?

Let's have no illusions: In a post-Christian society, euthanasia and assisted suicide — as already practiced in Belgium, the Netherlands, Luxembourg, Switzerland, and Germany — are passing as normal and even coming to be considered acts of "charity." On Ash Wednesday 2020, the Federal Constitutional Court of Germany cleared all the legal hurdles for a new line of business — suicide assistance.[108] Who is there to protect parents from this, other than their own children?

If in childhood — especially in the first three years — a solid bond forms between parents and children, there is the chance that the children will hold up under the tests of stamina and character that life inevitably brings.

Daycare is an institutionalized hyper-stress system that damages everyone: the children, the parents, the family, and the whole society. Therefore:

DO AWAY WITH DAYCARE!

Is that a completely unrealistic demand? Yes! But that should be no obstacle to making the demand. All major cultural achievements have begun with completely unrealistic demands. There is no future in destroying families. Strong families create the future.

7.
Stress and sex in kindergarten

There was a hill, where in the grass,
I loved to let my summers pass,
As a happy child — alone.
All around, the meadow's dew,
And high above the clearest blue,
From which the golden sunrays shone.
Julius Sturm, 1816–1896

What a beautiful name: *kindergarten.* Some English speakers call it "kiddie garden." A garden is a place of peace and growth, where a gardener ensures that plants receive all they need to bloom and delight people.

Kindergarten and preschool should be for children what a garden is for flowers. At least that's what the inventor of kindergarten, Friedrich Fröbel (1782–1852), had in mind. He was a student of the great pedagogue Johann Heinrich Pestalozzi. To them it was about natural rearing of the child, so that "the power of the head (intellectual power), of the heart (moral and religious power) and the hands (craftsmanship powers) unfold in harmony." Long before modern-day research on familial bonding, Fröbel recognized the special meaning of the vital unity between mother and child "in the mother's arms and on the mother's lap." He wrote special maternal songs so that love might flow in the most intimate of all human relationships. Even today they are still a rich source for kindergarten teachers.

Play was at the center of his pedagogy, because Fröbel knew that:

> A child who plays thoroughly and perseveringly, until physical fatigue forbids, will be a determined adult, capable of self-sacrifice both for his own welfare and that of others.[109]

The child learns by playing. With very few props, children play according to their imagination, what they experience — what the grownups do, what plays out in the family, what they long for, what scares them — play is how a child assimilates to the world. Effortlessly, children create symbols for the reality that is important to them. A child who feels secure and loved can play alone for a long time and burst into tears when they are torn from their self-created world for mealtimes or bedtime.

If you watch a child playing in the security of the household environment, you can see what it means for someone to be internally directed.[110]

The child follows his own impulses, lingers with whatever evokes his interest, and plunges into the world of his imagination. If he's lucky, and the radio or TV aren't going all the time, external distractions are reduced. The mentally healthy child is an inner-directed person, a free spirit, who moves sovereignly through his world. For the grownups around, who are constrained by duties, adaptation, and external direction, a child is a vital breath of freedom.

At the end of the third year of life, a certain plateau is reached: Both brain hemispheres are fully operating. The child says "I," thereby signaling the first stage of personal self-awareness. She can therefore perceive other people as separate and initiate communication with them. She can usually control her excretory organs. She has developed a certain feel for time, so that she can put hours of separation from her primary reference person into proportion and accept them. In short, the child is ready for preschool, provided that in the first three years she has had enough parental closeness in the domestic environment.

At this point, children really do need other children to play with — especially the 30% of children who grow up as the only child in their family. Once the youngest child has reached this point, the mother can go back to work half days, and the parents can hope that the child can bloom and be ready for primary school at age 6. Will preschool give the child the leeway to further develop her capability for play? This is a crucial precondition for school readiness.

Stress — the enemy of play

Complaints are getting ever louder about the deficiencies of children entering school, and children's ability to play is ever reducing. (For the disastrous effects of media consumption, see Chapter 11.) Research into play shows that children who play intensively can deal with their feelings better (emotional control), communicate better with children and adults (social competence), have better motor skills, can concentrate better and learn better.

The motto, "Children need schooling," which is used to suggest to parents that they do not have adequate competence to raise their toddler, determines the preschool day to an ever-greater extent. Public educational institutions react to the developmental deficits of children entering school with schooling requirements. This creates stress. And there is no greater enemy of play than stress.

Growing up in an environment with several siblings (only 12% of families have three children now and only 4% have four or more), romping in nature, playing on the street with neighbor kids, unplanned time, quiet, chances to withdraw from the group for a while, eating and sleeping according to the child's own rhythm — that world has gone.

Do today's preschools and kindergartens still reflect the ideal of a protected garden in which the fragile bud of a child of 3 to 6 years old can bloom and thrive? The stress on daycare kids under 3 is traumatic to them, but stress can also be toxic for children between 3 and 6. It decreases learning ability and the child's joy in life, and causes psychological disturbances. "Stressed children don't learn," says pediatrician Herbert Renz-Polster, who would like to post this sentence above every preschool and elementary school.[111] They don't learn because they lack the leisure to play on their own.

Stress appears in children as behavioral disorders and physical symptoms. A German insurance fund has determined that "small children are now more than ever under deadline and performance pressure. Pedagogues report almost unanimously that children today are more agitated, more aggressive and altogether behave more strangely than just a few years ago."[112]

Experienced caregiver Ilona Böhnke says:

> What kindergarten children have to accomplish every week would be forbidden for adults. Children's day is perfectly clocked, despite enormous noise and mayhem, which is the permanent situation in a group of 25 children. The children have to function and perform in the various "educational areas."

> When they get picked up, they're either completely worn out, or totally wound up. Childhood as we imagine it no longer exists.[113]

One of the main stress factors is the noise. "Quiet nourishes and noise consumes," is a saying by Reinhold Schneider that the association Nestbau e.V. puts on its home page. It says:

> Even if all the children in a group are peacefully playing, the noise level can never be compared to that in the household environment. Children are never quiet. In addition, there are admonitions and explanations from the caregivers, loud shouts and often screaming and crying. It is very stressful and also influences language development: The actually important language stimuli and suggestions can only be inadequately filtered from the noisy environment, or not at all. As a result, children's speech is very unclear and wishy-washy or sparse.[114]

How can children there meet their sleep needs and follow their sleep rhythm? Adequate, deep, undisturbed sleep is indispensable to the child's healthy development. Without it, stress cannot be relieved, and production of growth hormones can decrease, with considerable consequences to physical development and brain maturity, says brain researcher Dr. Manfred Spreng.[115]

A right to sex?

Children's needs revolve around eating, sleeping, playing, and loving care — they don't revolve around sex. Why does that even need to be said? Because in the process of "sexual liberation," which has been driven forward since its outbreak around 1967, a child's right to sexuality has been proclaimed, which parents and caregivers evidently are to fulfill.

The sexually liberated students of the late 1960s in Germany also wanted to free children for sex and promoted and practiced sex in front of children, sex with children, sex among children. In the 1980s, the Green Party advocated legalization of sex between adults and children.[116] Nothing came of it, but compulsory government regulation did a lot to promote sexualization of children starting in kindergarten.

The European sexual revolutionaries of the late '60s had carte blanche. Other than farsighted Christa Meves, barely anyone opposed it. She unmasked the sexual revolutionaries early and warned tirelessly of the calamitous consequences.[117] The churches should have proclaimed the doctrine of holistic love and chosen to mount a resistance, but they didn't do it and still do nothing to this day.

One of the most prominent champions of sexualization of children was Helmut Kentler (1928–2008), whose 1970 book *Sexualerziehung*[118] (Sex Education) recommends for preschool children:

- Masturbation starting in toddlerhood
- Eliminating the incest taboo between parents and children
- Support for sexual play at the preschool and elementary school age

Kentler served as an expert witness at court trials. For "rehabilitation," he transferred boys guilty of criminal offenses to the supervision of pedophile men, who then abused them for years. Kentler publicly advocated the opinion that this was helpful to their personality development.

Kentler was no solo perp but operated in a wide political and social network that reached deep into Germany's elites and was supported by the influential Humanistic Union. The pederastic swamp at the elite boarding school Odenwaldschule was a result of this.

From 1976 to his assumption of emeritus status in 1996, Kentler was professor at the Technical University of Hanover. Twenty-three years later, in 2019, that institution published a research report on his effects. In his introduction, Professor Epping, president of the university, spoke of the "guilt that weighs particularly heavily on the institutions involved and possible accomplices. Leibniz University Hanover distances itself from minimization of sexual violence against children under the mask of science, and sharply condemns this wrongdoing."[119]

In June 2020, the University of Hildesheim published another study on Kentler's activity at Berlin child and youth welfare services.[120] The researchers came to the conclusion that Kentler shaped three decades of child and youth welfare services in Berlin.

Officially organized homosexual abuse of children therefore extended into the third millennium and was in no way limited to Berlin, but with the cooperation of people like Gerold Becker, director of Max Planck Institute for education research, extended throughout Germany.

A docile student of Helmut Kentler is Uwe Sielert, professor of sex education at Christian Albrecht University in Kiel from 1992 to 2017. In Wikipedia, Helmut Kentler is described as a "father figure" of Uwe Sielert.[121] In a festschrift for Uwe Sielert by Frank Herrath with the title *How to till an educational field,*[122] the first sentence reads:

"Sexual education in Germany was shaped by Helmut Kentler and Uwe Sielert."[123]

Herrath is coauthor of the book *Lisa & Jan* (Lisa and John's Sex Education Book for Children and Their Parents), put out by Beltz Verlag publishers and on the market for a quarter century.[124] Frank Ruprecht Illustrated the book in color. The pictures show:

> During play, a girl spreads her vagina before the gaze of another girl who has her hand on her genitals. A boy masturbates with a teddy bear in his arm. Six adults and four children frolic naked at the swimming pool. A boy looks at a girl's exposed vagina. Two naked children embrace. A boy has his hand on another boy's penis. A mother smiles as she watches her son and daughter masturbate in the shower. A child observes his parents having intercourse.

So far, this decades-long collaboration between Uwe Sielert, Germany's "pope" of sex education, with a proponent and organizer of (homo)sexual abuse of children hasn't seemed to bother any figures in politics or the media — the entanglements go too deep. Right out in the open, Frank Herrath describes the sex education network Sielert built: founding of the Institute for Sex Education in Dortmund and the Society for Sex Education (the GSP), long-term employee of the Federal Centre for Health Education (1989 to 1992), for which he created countless brochures that still flood the educational institutions of the country.

This network extends far beyond Germany. In 2009, the Sex Education Alliance was founded, a merger of related professional associations in

Germany (the GSP), Austria (Platform for Sexual, Rearing and Education in Hofen Castle, Vorarlberg), Switzerland (Sedes), and South Tirol (Platform for Sex Education).

Uwe Sielert succeeded in affecting the content of sex education in K-12 schools and the training of sex educators according to the principles of his mentor Kentler. Enveloped in the aura of advanced "science," this state-supported, ubiquitously pervasive network drives the sexual revolution through government-forced sexualization of children.[125]

Antje Elsbeck is an experienced caregiver and has long headed a preschool for the worker's welfare organization in North Rhine-Westphalia, Germany. She is a graduate of the Institute for Sexual Education. In an interview published in *Das Kita-Handbuch* (The Daycare Handbook), she says:

> Sexuality is part of [children's play]. Children undress when they play doctor.... We tell them that no objects should be inserted into the vagina or penis, because the children can hurt themselves. This is a concern of the parents ... If children are playing in the hallway and want to undress, we make sure they don't do it at times when visitors might be present ... I tell parents that we don't forbid the children to change clothes or play naked in the role play corner.[126]

Antje Elsbeck thinks sex education in kindergarten is part of social education and personality formation. Children should be aware of and accept their own bodies and set aside anxieties and inhibitions.

> With our room layout, we provide children the possibility to play undisturbed. We offer a secure environment (cuddle corners, blankets, niches, dimmed light). The children have many materials available that are conducive to sex education (costume items, medical bags, massage balls, rollers, sponges, feathers, music, mirrors, sensory materials, etc.).

Wherever you look, whether at organizations like Pro Familia (the German branch of Planned Parenthood), the worker's welfare association, Catholic Women's Social Services, Donum Vitae, Caritas or Diakonie — they all work based on a hedonistic concept of sexuality. They reduce sexuality to physical lust, destroy the natural boundaries of modesty, and thereby break up the integrity of the person, who not only has a body, but also a heart that yearns for love, loyalty, and family. This demoralized and demoralizing concept of sexuality, as taught by the Institute for Sex Education in Germany, Switzerland, Austria and Italy for 40 years, was established with close cooperation from the government for the basis of sex education in preschools and elementary schools.

- Whatever lust wants is allowed.
- Children have a "right to sexuality" from birth.
- Children must be familiarized with "sexual diversity" (LGBTIQ) in word and deed.

That means, as explained by Uwe Sielert in the parental information supplement to the *Lisa & Jan* book: "Naturally, children discover this pleasure on their own if they are positively caressed ahead of time by their parents [!]. If they don't know at all what lust is, there will also be no sex play."

"Sexual games" easily lead to sexual violation of children by children. In a church preschool in a large city in Germany, a mother happened to discover that her daughter's preschool had a room for children to strip naked.[127] The parents were never informed of it. When she asked, the mother was told that this was part of the educational concept.

- It was supposedly important to respond to the children's natural desire to strip naked and discover each other sexually.
- The area was intentionally left unsupervised for a certain time so that children could feel undisturbed (the curtains could also be drawn).
- The children were allowed to look at "what they have," but were not to touch each other.
- It was better for this to go on in a protected room than in the lavatory.
- This way, children would learn to say "no," which is part of prevention work.

The mother who happened on two naked boys in one of the preschool's rooms spoke to the mother of the younger child. It came out that he was talked by the older child into undressing, because he wanted to "kiss his butt" and "suck his penis."[128]

This is the practice of "emancipatory sex education" or "diversity sex education" that has become established in Germany and most Western countries.

With sexualization of children beginning in preschool, a new problem comes up — how to practically distinguish between "playing doctor" and sexual assault. There shouldn't be any assaults, because "many girls and boys experience sexual violence not only from adults, but from children their own age or older as helplessness." Therefore rules are agreed to with the children, such as these:

- Each girl or boy determines him- or herself who he or she would like to play doctor with.
- Girls and boys caress and explore each other only as long as it is pleasant for themselves and the other children.
- No one inserts anything into another child's anus, vagina, penis, mouth, nose or ear.

The obligation to hold to these rules doesn't work with children. Statutory restraint of the sex drive doesn't work well with adults either, as shown by rampant sexual abuse of children.

In a Catholic Montessori preschool in Cologne, Germany, in February 2019, there were repeated assaults by a 5-year-old girl and boy on smaller children: They inserted sticks into the toddlers' vaginas and anuses. Twelve children from eight families were affected and — understandably — the parents lost faith in the caregivers. There were fierce conflicts that resulted in the 12 victims having to leave the preschool, while the 5-year-old perpetrators were transferred to another group.[129]

Most parents are likely to send their children to preschool in anticipation of the children being offered a variety of age-appropriate activities there. Most of the children are likely to come from families that enable them to grow up unburdened by the sexuality of adults, that respect their feelings of shame, and that answer their children's questions on where babies come from in an age-appropriate manner. It is an intolerable attack on the rights of parents when the child then has to discuss "rules for playing doctor" and is given the opportunity to act out in these cuddle corners with soft music and dim lights.

It sounds especially cynical when this is described as "prevention." The systematic destruction of the feeling of shame prepares children for pedophile abuse. Masses of children are suffering from a lack of care and security in broken families. Sexualized toddlers can no longer distinguish between an adult's touch of benevolent affection or an insidious attempt at grooming for sexual abuse.

A new gateway for sex abuse is the concept of *original play*. Because children so often do without a father who romps, wrestles, and tickles, now men from the outside offer to make up for this by rolling around with them, letting the children ride them, cuddling and otherwise getting physically active.[130] In some German states *original play* has been banned, because it can be used as an opportunity for sexual assault.[131]

Not long ago, people spoke of "innocent children." This was intended to mean that they had not entered the realm of sexuality, in which a person can so easily bear guilt if he has not learned to control his sex drive and ensure that sexuality becomes a holistic expression of love between two people. Earlier, before "sexual liberation," children's environment was protected from sexual words, images, and jokes, so that the child could grow up carefree. Today an adult's sense of shame is violated when he hears what kinds of images, words, and sounds children are confronted with as early as preschool.

Inclusion

Inclusion is a wonderful idea: Everyone should belong, no one should be left behind, and everyone should receive justice through creation of equality (of opportunity).

Life provides a place for inclusion — that is the family. Grownups and children live under one roof, perhaps with grandparents not far away. The family lives with and from the differences in gender, age, character, abilities, interests and opinions, and can tolerate them, because their belonging is not brought into question. Within the family, the balance of multifold relationships is always in flux and must always be sought anew, which requires inner growth from all involved.

With the overall society in decline, the family's cohesiveness is often lost forever. But the yearning for inclusion, for belonging, remains. Now the state steps in to ensure inclusion: inclusion of mentally and physically disabled children in regular school, and of migrant children who have not learned the language yet. The possible human benefit of inclusion has a high price: One group experiences little but failure, and the learning level of the others decreases.[132]

In preschools and elementary schools, however, it's not just about inclusion of disabled and migrant children, but also inclusion of "diversity of sexual identities." What the "inclusion" ticket gets you can be seen in the efforts of Germany's red-green government in Berlin to "remove barriers in relation to the diversity of genders and family structures" in preschool.

In spring 2018, Berlin's senate committee for education, youth and family published a 140-page "handout for education staff in preschool care." Its title is: *Murat plays princess, Alex has two mothers, and Sophie's name is Ben now*; the author is listed as "Queer Format." The title makes it clear what children are supposed to learn: It is proper, normal and OK if a (Muslim) boy likes to put on princess clothes, Alex has two lesbian mothers, and Sophie has changed her gender. This should be supported by the LGBTIQ educational staff to promote the "colorful diversity" of "gender-varied children" aged 3 to 6 — even if the children have no interest in it — because it may well be that they will "later identify as lesbian, gay or bisexual."[133]

It's not only under the red-green government in Berlin that preschool children are introduced to the diverse "sexual orientations" — gay, lesbian, bisexual and transsexual — and raised to accept them. All over they are receiving picture books in which the prince marries the prince, and in which families with two fathers or two mothers are shown as completely normal, whereas the normal family with a father, mother and children are depicted as an outdated model. The split family (single parents), the stepfamily (patchwork) and the "family" with two same-sex "parents" (rainbow family) are in reality broken families in which rifts have occurred that cause pain for all involved, most of all the children. If the broken families the children must live in are represented as "normal," then their pain no longer has its place and can no longer be expressed — other than as mental and physical symptoms. This is what the statistics at the beginning of this book are talking about.

Destabilizing the gender identity of boys and girls at the age when they are just about to identify with their natural gender — at which the girl wants to be like Mom and the boy wants to be like Dad — is a grave offense to the children.

Picture books show "androgynous" children, and the child looking at them doesn't know if it's a boy or a girl. A fairy floats down from the sky and says, "Only you know what you are." (The Internet contains a rich selection of *transgender picture books for little ones.*)

Participation

The preferred means of inclusion is *participation.* Daycare and preschool children are supposed to be involved in all decisions at the facility: buying food, hygiene, clothing, furniture, and establishing rules.

The powerful Bertelsmann foundation is committed to this. Daycare is supposed to be the nursery of democracy.[134] Here children from 0 to 6 years are supposed to learn to assert their "right" against adults to participation in decisions. Because: "Democracy is created in daycare when children have the right and the power (and are supported in them) to negotiate and participate in the decisions that affect them."[135] The adults are called on to surrender power to the children by clarifying children's rights to them, introducing reliable participation committees, and allowing and challenging complaints. The author is a social educator named Rüdiger Hansen from the Institute of Participation and Education, which, like the Society for Sex Education, is also in Kiel.

At the Congress on Children's Rights in Munich on February 2019,[136] Dr. Elke Möller-Nehring, a child and youth psychiatrist, and Ms. Elisabeth Suntinger, a preschool director — both mothers of three children — report on the new regulations that government authorities have created for children. The "right to participation and complaint" must be anchored in the daycare's constitution, or else it won't receive funds. "Procedural routes and responsibilities for complaint stimulation [!], complaint acceptance and complaint analysis, and monitoring of the results should be transparently represented at the facility." The rules and constitutions should be drawn up with the children. There should be children's parliaments, group councils, general assemblies, votes, and election of delegates.[137]

A daycare constitution means: "Children should be able to decide for themselves whether, when and by whom their diapers are changed. The educational staff reserve the right to determine when a child's diaper will be changed if in their point of view the health of the child or others will be acutely threatened by the child's elimination."[138]

Small children are torn from their family environment before they can control their sphincter, and are then allowed to decide if, when, and by whom they want their diaper changed at daycare or preschool, where there are usually too few caregivers seeing to too many children. Can this ideological insanity be surpassed?

A child in diapers wants to be changed by his mommy or daddy, and when the diaper is full, accompanied by tender caresses and little jokes that make him laugh. But nobody asks about the child's basic needs. What he really needs is taken from him, and instead he is offered "co-decision-making" as a substitute, which is neither desirable nor practicable.

The child psychiatrist and preschool director explained that children are completely overwhelmed by this. With the fiction of democratic decision processes, the caregivers are in violation of their duty of care. The child learns that his own will trumps all, that everything revolves around his own wishes, so that normal childish selfishness solidifies in his character. This does not bring about personalities that can sustain democracy, but quite the contrary: It is a breeding ground for totalitarian characters who will use any available power to ensure that their own will is done.

Children need to be raised to function in community and to know that delayed gratification is necessary to a successful life. This is possible only in a stable, trusting relationship with a reliable reference person who is finely tuned to the needs of the child, but also demands that he learn to restrain his impulses, submit when necessary, take on services to the community, and to be considerate and respectful of others.

The participation model is nothing more than a new "democratic" mantle for anti-authoritarian childrearing, which was practiced in the '60s generation's alternative kindergartens and permanently damaged the children. It is an education in rebelliousness and hostility that the children, their teachers, their parents, and the entire society will have to pay the price for as long as they live. Aldous Huxley, who prophetically envisioned the *Brave New World*, said:

> To give children too much freedom and responsibility is to impose a strain which many of them find distressing and even exhausting. Exceptional cases apart, children like to have security, like to feel the support of a firm framework of moral laws and even of rules of polite conduct.[139]

Adults can't yield their power at all, because children have no power over grownups other than to become rebellious tyrants who make life miserable for their parents and themselves. They are driven to such destructive behavior by uprooting, stress, sexualization, and premature participation.

Of course, parents and caregivers must not abuse their own power through punishments that harm the dignity of the child and make him fear all-powerful adults, being locked in the closet, or verbal and physical humiliation. If the parents and caregivers have not themselves learned the virtue of self-control and loving care of small, dependent, fragile people, no children's parliament will teach it to them.

What a joy it is to experience well-brought-up children, who are bonded to their parents, who look up to them, listen to them, say please and thank you, can remain in the background when grownups speak to each other, who have table manners, and can communicate with adults with an inner freedom.

Parents who do not want their child to be under stress constantly, to be sexualized in word, image and deed, to be raised for rebelliousness, should take an accurate look at any preschool they are considering and not be afraid to ask concretely what its stand is about "playing doctor," disrobing, cuddle corners, masturbation, transgenderism, inclusion of sexual identities and participation models. Maybe the parents will be lucky and find a child-friendly preschool nearby, possibly a private or parochial one, if they can afford it. But be careful there too: A preschool that calls itself "Christian" — whether Catholic or Protestant — may not have been Christian for a long time, when it comes to sex education. The label means nothing. Parents must ask the unpleasant questions even if they think they are exaggerated or unnecessary. It's best for the father to do this, instead of the mother, because his task is to protect his family.

Preschool at home

There is another possibility: Don't send the child to preschool, as long as preschool is not government mandated.

A group of parents who have opted for that are the basis for a "life without preschool."[140]

- No stress! Live peacefully with the children
- Immediate response to the children's needs
- Be able to console the children
- Observe the children's biorhythm. No fights about getting up
- Retreat options for the child, rest periods as needed
- Home as a protected place for carefree play and learning
- Self-directed play, promotion of concentration ability
- Lots of time outdoors, experiencing nature throughout the seasons
- Taking on age-appropriate chores at home
- No fighting for recognition in a large group of peers
- Developing social skills through the example of older siblings
- Age-appropriate response to questions about sexuality
- No indoctrination in gender ideology
- No seduction into sexual behavior
- Individual development without judgmental comparisons
- Loving, stable relationships, instead of changing paid caregivers
- Imparting of the family's values, customs, traditions and beliefs

Often circumstances and finances don't allow this solution. But parents often never even think about it, because the child needs "schooling" after all, because trained caregivers can do it better than Mom and Dad, and because the child "needs other children." Parents who have recognized that their small children need *them* above all, their loving father and mother, are not alone. They will find other parents with whom they can build a social network for their own support and for creating a social environment for the children. In exchange for the sacrifice the parents make for the good of their children, they will be rewarded with a lively, loving, lifelong relationship to their children.

Childrearing and persistence

According to the philosopher Immanuel Kant, human beings are the only creatures who need to be brought up. At the beginning, the child knows only his own needs: hunger, thirst, sleep, closeness to his mother. He is entirely "selfish." For at least a year, the baby's needs must be met immediately, around the clock, if he isn't to fall into existential fear. But in the second year, the child starts to run into his parents' "No" and now has to learn to accept boundaries, which he initially does willingly. Around the time the child is 2, to the chagrin of inexperienced parents, the Terrible Twos arrive: The child says "No" nonsensically, noisily, and nonstop.

Responsible parents are forever balancing between meeting needs and drawing boundaries. Fortunate is the child whose parents (or caregivers) don't succumb to the temptation to exert power, but instead give the child *time* to submit to their demands. A child who can develop basic trust loves his parents, expects good from them, and is fundamentally ready to follow them.

In his book *12 Rules for Life,* Jordan Peterson tells of how he struggled for a good hour to get his 2-year-old son to eat properly. The father won the battle by investing time and determination. The chapter is titled: "Do not let your children do anything that makes you dislike them."

Parents don't like children who throw themselves shrieking onto the supermarket floor, scream in a restaurant, pull off tablecloths, bite, punch and turn all everyday communication into a power struggle.

What should children be raised to be? The child should become a good person, right? "A determined adult, capable of self-sacrifice both for his own welfare and that of others" is what Fröbel said.

Fröbel uses a word that has gone completely out of style: *sacrifice.* Even for one's own *good* it is necessary to learn sacrifice, so that goals can be achieved. Is a person able to give up something small now to gain something greater in the future? Can he delay gratification to achieve a goal?

One of the most famous personality tests is the "Marshmallow Test": A piece of candy is placed in reach of a 4-year-old child, who is told that if he can hold back from eating it, he can get two of them later. Thirteen years later, the children, who are now young adults, were surveyed, and the results were astounding: The children who, at age 4, had the impulse control not to reach for the candy right away were more successful in their education, could concentrate better, were more intelligent and self-confident, had better social skills, could deal better with setbacks and stress, and were less likely to be dependent on drugs. At 25 and 30, they were less likely to be obese, had a high level of education, and could maintain better relationships.[141]

I'm sure that all parents want their children to be among those who can delay gratification, because they want their children to have all the attributes that this basic ability brings with it. They must start learning it when they're small, because you can't teach an old dog new tricks. Bonded children who feel secure and loved can do that much better, because they do not find themselves in a chronic state of need that compels them to grab for something in the vain hope of filling a gap in their soul.

Self-control is needed to practice the virtue of moderation. During adolescence, when the child proves impervious to parental directives, the worst temptations bang at the door: alcohol, tobacco, drugs, computer games, smartphones, sex, pornography. Fortunate is the youth who has learned moderation, self-denial, and the ability to say no. And fortunate is the father who has succeeded in remaining at this growing son's side as adviser.

Moderation is one of the four cardinal virtues, and the other three are wisdom, justice, and courage. The cardinal virtues are called that because they are the pivot points of a noble existence and allow virtuous decisions in everyday life. Wouldn't all parents be proud of their children (and themselves) if they were moderate, wise, just, and courageous?

8.
Sexual diversity in school

Destroying the sense of shame means dissolution of all sexual and conjugal order — in fact all social order.
Dietrich Bonhoeffer

What do young people want for their future? "A faithful relationship" and "a good family life." That is what 90% of those surveyed said in the most recent Shell Youth Study in 2019.[142] Almost 70% want children of their own, and more than half of them even prefer "the traditional breadwinner model" in which the mother stays home with her 2-year-old and the father works full-time. This once more confirms what all youth surveys show: The young generation yearns for stable marriage and family.

What do most parents want for their children? Son or daughter puts the pedal to the metal at school, gets to know the world, establishes good friendships, pursues passionate interests, marries, and delights their parents with grandchildren. This shows life to be sustainable in the long term, horizontally through the bond of two people and the networking of their families, and vertically through the connection of past, present, and future.

Parents don't want their son or daughter to stagger from one sexual relationship to the next starting at 14, to become a parent early or get an abortion, introduce them to a same-sex partner, or have an anonymous sperm donor father their grandchild. They also don't want their son to become a "woman," or their daughter a "man." Even if many of them cave in to the constant pounding of the media to accept "gender diversity," it's definitely not what they want for their own child's future.

"Liberation" of the sex drive from the social protection of marriage between one man and one woman results in the wishes of young people and their parents *not* being fulfilled. A decisive factor in this is the gender indoctrination and sexualization of children and youth which, as described, starts as early as preschool and continues throughout their entire school and college years.

A "trusting partnership" means a loyal bond. If a partner cheats, the trust is broken. If he or she says, "I'm faithful right now, but tomorrow I might not be," then doubt gnaws at the foundation and trust cannot grow. The ultimate "trusting partnership" comes about when both partners are all in for the long haul.

We stare at divorce rates and hardly believe that life-long marriage is possible. But more than 50% of married couples do keep their promises.

For the wishes of the young generation to be fulfilled, it is necessary that people learn to cultivate their sexuality such that it becomes a personal expression of love of heart and body — only then will they be capable of living the way their heart wants to: in a stable partnership and family. The ability to give oneself unconditionally to one person of the opposite sex requires a holistic upbringing and preparation for marriage, fatherhood, and motherhood. Only then will sexuality unfold its full joyful power. For this, society must maintain the vision of marriage and family as a worthy goal. Education in "sexual diversity" destroys this vision and makes the young generation incapable of reaching their own objective in life.

The adversity of diversity

Today the rainbow flag of gender ideology flutters over the world. Its message: There is such a thing as "social gender," which is separate from biological sex, allegedly "*assigned*" at birth. Between the two poles of man and woman there is *gender fluidity*, a fluid transition for those who don't feel like a man or a woman, which brings forth a "diversity of sexual identities." Anyone can freely choose his or her gender and change it at will. "Sexual orientation" — whether gay, lesbian, bisexual, transsexual, or queer — must be legally protected from discrimination. A "human right" for homosexuals and transsexuals to marriage and children is construed for the first time in human history. There are many types of families, and the father-mother-children family is sinking below the horizon of history.

In many Western countries, this novel concept of the human being has been legislated into societal reality. On October 10, 2017, the German federal constitutional court decided that in addition to "male" and "female," the category "diverse" must be entered into the register of births, deaths, and marriages.[143] This supreme court decision was the result of a game cooked up between constitutional judge Susanne Baer, former director of the Center for Gender Competence at Humboldt University, constitutional judge Gabriele Britz, and plaintiff attorney Friederike Wapler.[144] In subsequent years, the new option of "diverse" was taken by fewer than 200 people. Nonetheless, companies are now required to advertise open jobs as being for male, female, and "diverse" applicants.[145]

At German universities, 200 female professors teach fanciful gender theories that have become unmoored from science and reality. Their artificial linguistic usage has meanwhile entered the vocabulary of legal regulations. Thus, our progressive contemporaries no longer speak of women, but of "people with uteruses." This is because a bearded transgender man, i.e., a woman pumped full of testosterone, can have a pregnant belly and "he" would feel discriminated against if pregnancy were limited to women who have accepted their biological gender.

If a man-woman can choose and change his/her/diverse gender, then naturally he/she/diverse can freely choose his/her/diverse "sexual orientation," and whether he/she/diverse wants to satisfy his/her/diverse sexual desire with a man, a woman, or with both or with diverse genders.

These new freedoms and self-determination are part of the "values" that the UN and EU are enforcing, and resistant nations in places like Africa are forced by economic blackmail to accept them.[146] Anyone who holds to "traditional role models," the so-called "stereotypes," Christian sexual morality, and the father-mother-child family structure thinks "biologicistically" is a "homophobe" or a "transphobe," "discriminates" and spreads "hate." He can therefore be shunned, fired, harassed by the legal system, and sentenced to fines and prison.

Strangely enough, many courts and legislative bodies have made it their mission to protect the perceived interests of smaller and smaller minorities from "discrimination," even if it endangers the existential foundations of democratic society, specifically the family as the "natural fundamental group unit of society" (Universal Declaration of Human Rights, Art. 16.3).

To achieve dissolution of human gender identity and the societal structures founded on it, people have to be converted, and the younger they are, the more sustainable the intrusions into their mental and neuronal development. The method of choice is sexualization starting in preschool. "Heteronormativity" must be overcome, homo-, bi- and transsexual lifestyles must be promoted, the family with heterosexual parents and their own biological children must be "denaturalized" by targeted confusion of sex identity "stereotypes" in boys and girls.

With various levels of radicalism, schools are obligated to include sexuality and diversity in their curricula. These are often drawn up by lobbying groups from the LGBTIQ movement, who then also get access to the schools to teach children the "joy" of a non-heterosexual lifestyle, assist them in "coming out" and network them to the LGBTIQ community.

In all government sex education programs, children are taught to be contraception experts long before puberty. In mixed classes, it is part of the standard program to practice pulling condoms over plastic penises in class. The main purpose of such exercises is not to teach skills that young people will certainly master without school instruction should they need them, but to break down the boundaries of modesty and send the message: Sexual intercourse is okay and "safe" for teens. If not, there's always the morning-after pill or abortion — Planned Parenthood will discretely get rid of this "clump of cells."

The 2008 book *Sexualpädagogik der Vielfalt*, from the renowned publisher Juventa-Verlag, gives an overview of this "neo-emancipative sex education."[147] This is "deconstructive education," which, "since its establishment by Helmut Kentler in 1970, has striven for the liberation of people from their sexual immaturity." "Consistent thinking and naming of the diverse possibilities of sexual preferences (hetero-, homo-, bi-, poly- and pansexual) as well as the different lifestyles (couple, single, family, chosen family, roommates, etc.) should be practiced" (p. 19).

In mixed classes, instruction involves imaginative methods such as role plays and talk about sexual experiences with practices like oral and anal sex, the erogenous zones and how best to stimulate them, whether by using a vibrator, vagina balls, latex, a leather whip, sadomasochistic performance, and pornographic depictions. The book is subtitled: *Praxismethoden zu Identitäten, Beziehungen, Körper und Prävention für Schule und Jugendarbeit* (Practical Methods on Identities, Relationships, Body and Prevention for school and youth work). It should bear the title: Practical Methods for Seducing Children and Youth into All Types of Personally Destructive Activities in School and Youth Work.

The authors, Stefan Timmermanns, Elisabeth Tuider, Mario Müller, and Petra Bruns-Bachmann were or are on the board of the Society for Sex Education (GSP), founded by Uwe Sielert, which awards the quality seal "Q" (as in queer) as Europe-wide recognition for the professional designation "Sex Educator." At the same time, some of the authors are members of the Institute for Sex Education in Dortmund, and Dr. Timmermanns also belongs to the Global Alliance for LGBT Education. They cooperate closely with the Federal Center for Health Education.

In other words, these authors are not exotic bystanders who use "post-modern dissolution of boundaries" to make perversions palatable as optional ways of satisfying one's lust. They are among the strategists and activists of a sex education network who have succeeded in bringing school sex education under their power. They sail under the flag of "science": Their representatives hold professorships, create educational curricula and seals of approval, publish their works through recognized education publishers, and they are consulted by politicians as *the* experts. This is how they have succeeded in penetrating even parochial schools and preschools. When schools and educational institutions call themselves "Catholic," that is no longer a guarantee of a Christian education. The probability that children will be confronted with traumatizing content is lowest in schools with a high proportion of migrants, because nobody wants to get on the bad side of Muslims.

In a legal opinion on the constitutionality and legality of the education of school children to accept sexual diversity, Dr. Christian Winterhoff says:

> Especially in the area of sex education, the government is obligated to restraint and tolerance. The school must refrain from any attempt at indoctrinating students for the purpose of advocating or rejecting a specific sexual behavior. It must respect the children's natural sense of shame and must take into account the religious belief or worldview of the parents in regard to sexuality. Against this background, school instruction with the purpose of educating students to accept any type of sexual behavior is unconstitutional. Government guidelines for school sex education that profess hetero-, bi-, homo- and transsexuality as equal forms of sexual expression violate the constitutional

> prohibition against indoctrination. In the case of an indoctrinating and therefore constitutionally impermissible sex education concept, children and parents with differing values have a right to an exemption.

But who cares? Here and there, there is a tactical withdrawal in the face of public resistance — the start was a petition by high school teacher Gabriel Stängle in 2013 against the education plan from the Green administration of Baden-Württemberg, which was signed by 200,000 people in no time flat. Thousands of concerned parents took peacefully to the streets several times to protect their children against forced sexualization and had to be protected by hundreds of police from a hate-filled opposition ready for violence.[148] Every resistance to sexual indoctrination of schoolchildren is either hushed up by the media or attributed to the dark world of diehards who have missed the bus to postmodernism.

The sexual revolutionaries have the backing of governments, state institutions (such as the Federal Center for Health Education), the media, the political parties and their foundations, international organizations like the UN and the EU, and countless NGOs (the International Planned Parenthood Federation, ILGA).

The global attack on the integrity of youth

The basic assumption of the new sex education is the idea that a child is a sexual being, who from the very beginning has a right to sexual activity and lust experiences just as adults do. Whichever document on *comprehensive sexual education* (CSE) you pick up, they all advocate the same thing: a new sexualized person without gender or family identity. This person can change his gender. He/she/diverse reduces sexuality to physical lust, knows no moral boundaries to sexual activity, prevents procreation through contraception and abortion, and sees the marriage of one man and one woman as a worn-out relic of patriarchal rule.

The *Standards for Sexuality Education in Europe*, published in 2010 by the WHO's regional office and the Federal Center for Health Education,[149] are a "framework for policy makers, educational and health authorities and specialists." The publication dolls itself up with the names of powerful editors, but is in fact a nonbinding paper that has gained entry into such educational curricula and (appears to) legitimize them.[150] The end of it shows a long list of organizations, people, literature, and websites that support and propagate the *Standards,* and implement them in curricula.

The *Standards* show age-appropriate "sex education" in a table. A few excerpts:

- Age 0–4: Enjoyment and pleasure when touching one's own body, early childhood masturbation, discovery of one's body and genitals, enjoyment of physical closeness, the right to explore nakedness.
- Age 4–6: Enjoyment and pleasure when touching one's own body; early childhood masturbation. Appropriate sexual language. Sexual feelings (closeness, enjoyment, excitement) as a part of all human feelings. Same-sex relationships. Different kinds of (family) relationship. Turn to somebody you trust if in trouble. Awareness of rights and choices.
- Age 6–9: Body changes, menstruation, ejaculation. The basic idea of contraception. Enjoyment and pleasure when touching one's own body (masturbation/self-stimulation). Deal with sex in the media. Use sexual language in a non-offensive way. An understanding of "acceptable sex." Sexual rights of children.
- Age 9–12: First sexual experience. Pleasure, masturbation, orgasm. Differences between gender identity and biological sex. Acceptance, respect, and understanding of diversity in sexuality and sexual orientation. Sexually transmitted infections (STI), HIV, unintended pregnancy. Sexual rights.
- Age 10–15: Ineffective contraception. Pregnancy (also in same-sex relationships). Abortion. Gender-identity and sexual orientation, including coming out/homosexuality. Pleasure, masturbation, orgasm.
- Age 15: A critical view of cultural norms related to the human body. Transactional sex (prostitution), acceptance of different sexual orientations and identities. Sexual rights. Right to abortion.

The word "marriage" never appears in the whole document. "Fatherhood" and "motherhood" only once in the context of contraception and abortion for preventing parenthood.

It gives just one principle for limiting sexual activity: the consensus principle. Do only what your partner agrees to! The sexual abuse statistics show that the consensus principle doesn't take hold: According to the UN, 20% of women and 5% to 10% of men were sexually abused as children. Meanwhile, sexual assaults among children and teens have been rising dramatically. Haven't all these perpetrators heard that the sex act requires consent, or are they depraved slaves to their sex drives?

The document never mentions a prohibition of sex between adults and children. The child is just supposed to learn to say "no" when she doesn't like something. That is the content of the prevention programs that confront children with sexual degeneracy, from which both their minds and bodies should actually be protected. These programs have the opposite effect, however. A sexualized child whose sense of shame has been systematically broken down[151] has no warning system against sexual assault. In truth, the child could be no better groomed for pedophile abuse than through pleasure-fixated sex education — the stated goal of Helmut Kentler, the father of current sex education.

What empowers the World Health Organization (WHO) and the German state to shatter the foundation of marriage and family, and with them the entire society, and thereby destroy the conditions for the next generation's vision of life ("good family relationships")? Nothing empowers them to do it other than power itself. Those with power in this world, the United Nations, the European Union, global corporations, the Internet giants, the multi-billion-dollar foundations of Soros, Gates, and Rockefeller, and the worldwide NGOs such as the International Planned Parenthood Federation, all want to enforce "sexual and reproductive rights" for the world's youth.

While the *Standards* are aimed at Europe, the *International technical guidance on sexuality education* has its sights on all children and teens between 5 and 18 throughout the world.[152] Those responsible are UNESCO, together with UNICEF, UNAIDS, UN WOMEN and the WHO. The IPPF is not mentioned as a publisher but is quoted 20 times. The contents of the 140-page *Technical Guidance* are meant to be implemented in legislation, teacher education, schools, and youth-institutions other than schools. The word "technical" is meant to create the impression that this is value-neutral know-how on promoting health and wellbeing, with no judgment of sexual behavior, sexual orientation, gender identity, or health status — homo, bi, trans, anal and oral, the autonomous individual can choose anything without judgment. Actually, this is about dissolving the traditions, values, and social norms that form identity as they exist in all cultures as the foundation of the family and culture.

The contents of the *Technical Guidance* are the same as in the *Standards*: Children have a right to sexuality and "correct information." Starting at age 5, they should decide for themselves who can touch their bodies when and where, because everyone supposedly "deserves to make their own decisions." As preschool children, they should advocate for human rights and "identify unfair gender roles" before they are then recruited starting at age 15 for "peer education," that is, advising their peers on sexual matters. Pregnancy is depicted only as "unintended" in the context of sexually transmitted diseases and HIV; thus defense against sexually transmitted diseases is mentally associated with prevention of pregnancy.

Deceptive language

It is not easy to flip people's standards for good and evil so that they consider good what they used to call evil and vice versa. This requires sophisticated *social engineering* techniques.

The most important tool is the use of deceptive language. Terms are thrown out, emptied of meaning, perverted, outlawed, forbidden, and arbitrarily invented. Thus, language, with which human beings alone are endowed and that enables them to think and be aware of themselves, no longer serves to communicate truth, but becomes a means of misrepresentation and manipulation reminiscent of the old Marx brothers line, "Who are you going to believe — me or your own eyes?" The expressions become smoke bombs raising a fog of false virtue to veil the evil they are intended to achieve.

1. Terms that express traditional values are called into suspicion and discarded. Examples: virtue, loyalty, self-denial, sacrifice, chastity, purity.
2. Terms with positive connotations are given new content and then exploited. Examples: freedom, human rights, diversity.
3. New terms are invented for transmitting new ideologies. Examples: gender, sexual orientation, sexual identity, sexual expression, reproductive rights.

4. New terms are introduced to smear opponents. Examples: homophobia, transphobia, hate speech.

This sort of manipulative falsification of language can be seen in a third document, the *IPPF Framework for Comprehensive Sexuality Education (CSE) — From choice, a world of possibilities.*[153] The International Planned Parenthood Federation has 151 member organizations and representation in 180 countries, so it has immense power to implement its programs worldwide.

The word "comprehensive" is already a trick. We need exactly that — sex education that considers the whole person: body, mind and soul, the body's desire for sexual satisfaction, the heart's yearning for love, and the spirit as the seat of human reason and will. Human beings exist amidst this tension and can fulfill their yearning for lasting love only if their sexuality is guided by reason and will. The paradox of "sexual liberation" is that the body overpowers the soul and makes it a slave to the physical sex drive. The results: Pornography addiction, massive sexual abuse of children, human trafficking and prostitution.

"Choice" is the second bait used to reel the allegedly autonomous individual into a "world of possibilities." Everyone longs for freedom, because dignity comes from self-determined decision-making. But life constantly places obstacles in the way of the free will. A religious person recognizes that there is a divine order and that fitting into this order requires restraint but lastingly guides him to the fullness of life. The postmodern person who has made himself into God rams right into these obstacles. Wouldn't it be wonderful to live in a world of unlimited possibilities and, as Planned Parenthood promises, have "control over one's own body and destiny"? Planned Parenthood feeds this yearning into the grinder of its worldwide abortion network.

The "freedom of choice" to kill a baby in the womb is described to women and youth with another code term: "reproductive health and services." In the obfuscated jargon of the UN and EU, universal access to contraceptives, abortion, and sex education in the schools are described collectively as "the highest healthcare standards." But the promises again reveal themselves as snares for the strategies of the sexual revolutionaries who deliver the opposite of what they promise.

There's no such thing as safe sex. Promiscuous sex has led to an epidemic of sexually transmitted diseases — a quarter of all sexually active teenage girls in the US have contracted them.[154] Pregnancy can also not be reliably prevented as an undesired side effect of sex but produces new customers for the abortion industry.

An especially telling example of deceptive use of language are Olsson's "Stairs of Tolerance," shown in the *Framework for Comprehensive Sexuality Education* from Planned Parenthood. The stairs going upward lead from tolerance to acceptance to respect to mutual understanding, and finally to "celebration of diversity." The downward staircase leads from absence of tolerance to dislike to homophobia to discrimination to stigmatization and finally to hate and violence.

It appears that Mr. Olsson has never experienced a prolife demonstration, because then he would see that the protectors of life are peaceful and respectful, while their opponents bombard them with hateful cursing and must be prevented by a strong police presence from violent rioting.

Once the sexual revolutionaries have established themselves as "scientists" and gotten access to schools and preschools, then it's about forcing their way into the hearts of the children. In kindergarten, it's easy. Small children are putty in the hands of their caregivers, learn by example and imitation, and have no possibility of arriving at their own judgments. Contradictions between their parents' home and the kindergarten cause confusion and disorientation when storybooks or real life show them two women or two men as "parents" or they suddenly have to call Sophie by the name Ben.

Older children, who may have been raised in preschool through "participation" to assert their "rights," require a more clever approach. The sex educators usually arrive from outside and come off as "experts" who are more competent than the teachers or parents. At the same time, they present themselves to the students as friends, trusted individuals and advocates against strict parents and their old-fashioned moral ideas. They divert the children's and teens' prematurely stimulated sex drive for their counterrevolutionary purposes. Here are their methods:

- Representing permissive sexuality as normal and mainstream: "Everybody does it."

- Creating peer pressure in the group.
- Destroying the sense of shame by fooling around with plastic penises, plush vaginas, condoms, verbalization of sexual processes as a class, and sexually oriented role plays and physical exercises.
- Detailed representation of sexual behavior in words, images and movies.
- Representing sexually transmitted diseases together with pregnancy as unwanted side effects of sex.
- Failing to mention marriage and family.
- Representing decadent family structures as equal.
- Peer education: Training and use of teenagers of the same age for sex education.[155]

Let no one be fooled by the propaganda that represents this sex education as modern, enlightened, "scientific" and youth friendly and its opponents as diehard fundamentalists. Sexualization of children and destabilization of their gender identity is an attack on the moral foundations of the person, the family, and the society — with foreseeable and unforeseeable consequences. The children are robbed of their lighthearted, unburdened childhood by being plunged into the moral morass of the hyper-sexualized society. The parents' childrearing authority is undermined by puncturing the sense of shame and the incitement to demand "children's rights." Children's capabilities are weakened if they have to battle with relationship dramas and deep spiritual disappointments too early.[156] Mental indoctrination all the way to encouragement to "come out" and even undergo "sex change" thwarts their own vision of a future with a happy family.

Sex educators who like to present themselves as "scientists" would like to show studies that show that families are more stable, children happier, mental disorders fewer, capabilities greater, and the incidence of drug use and crime lower if children are programmed to experience sexual pleasure from babyhood. But they can't because there aren't any such studies.

The latest hype: transgenderism

Suddenly transgenderism is on everybody's lips. "Sex change" has become a hype among teenagers, especially adolescent girls. Dr. Alexander Korte, head of child psychiatry at Munich Municipal Hospital, says that cases of children who cannot identify with their biological sex have quintupled since 2013.[157] In the United Kingdom, 97 children and teens sought help from a relevant center in 2010, while in 2017–18 the number was 2,519. The professional term for this mental disorder is *gender dysphoria.* Twenty years ago, this word didn't exist, and the phenomenon barely existed at all. What happened?

As part of saturating the whole society with gender ideology, the UN and the EU have promoted dissolution of "gender stereotypes" for decades. Pink for girls and blue for boys was supposedly an inadmissible definition of the child's sex "assigned" at birth. They claim that a child does not come into the world as a boy or girl, but that those around the child assign gender as if with a peel-off sticker. As already shown, undermining gender identity starts in preschool. There are parents who give their children gender-neutral first names so that the child can decide later what he or she wants to be. This sows the seeds of identity confusion in the child's malleable, vulnerable little heart.

Political power elites in Western countries are promoting dissolution of gender identity: US president Barack Obama fired the next stage of the LGBTIQ rocket one day after the Supreme Court legalized same-sex "marriage" on June 26, 2015. He started the "bathroom battle" by ordering schools to allow transsexual students to use the lavatory or locker room of their choice. This meant that a boy who claimed to be a girl could get under the shower with the girls, by presidential decree.

In Scotland, the health ministry has demanded since 2016 that schools support children in changing their gender even without the knowledge or approval of the parents.[158] Long story short: Charlie leaves for school in boy's clothes, changes into girl's clothes at school, is called Rosie there, and then wears boy's clothes back home. In this way, Charlie is "protected" from his parents, who do not approve of his gender dysphoria.

In 2018, Canada's university sports organization adopted an "inclusive transgender policy"[159]: All athletes are allowed to compete on the team that represents the gender of their choice. Understandably, feminists are rebelling against this and are therefore being defamed as "transphobes."

In the interview with *Der Spiegel* quoted above, child psychiatrist Dr. Korte talks of a "zeitgeist phenomenon" that the media have played a large role in creating.

> The transgender issue is currently being heavily hyped, especially on YouTube and Instagram. There are a number of trans boys who are stars on these channels and act as influencers. Trans girls have participated in "Germany's Next Top Model." These people serve as role models. Adolescence is a phase of partial reinvention. For teenagers, identity can be an open question. Transgenderism gives them a new identity template.

The hype is understandable: In a society where the family is collapsing, there are masses of children and teens with severe psychological problems. Children are on the Internet very early and run into the message there: The reason for your problem is that you have the wrong gender. Change it, and you'll be fine. They can't change their family situation, so they fall for the lie that they can change their gender. These children and their families urgently need therapeutic help.

After their coming out, they immediately receive an overdose of attention — in the family, in school and on the Internet — and fall for the treacherous seduction: *Then* at one fell swoop, I'll become a happy person.

Schools, doctors, therapists, and the media turn themselves into collaborators because they don't want to be accused of "discrimination" and "transphobia." Parents are pressured to support their children in gender transformation — the child may even commit suicide if the parents don't agree to puberty-blocking hormones.

The problem: These hormones make young people infertile for a lifetime, they have numerous serious side effects, such as a high risk of heart and circulatory diseases, thrombosis, stroke, osteoporosis, growth disorders, and cancer. The person is turned into a lifelong patient, who must take hormones daily and whose vital energy is devoted to the futile battle to change his or her own gender. Before *and after* the transformation, the suicide rate for transgender people is eight times higher than the average for the population — 41% versus 5%.[160]

This decision has irreversible consequences and falls upon children at an age when the law deems them too immature to drive a car or buy alcohol. The American College of Pediatricians has warned emphatically against these experiments, which have no scientific basis.[161]

In the United Kingdom, over the past three years, 35 psychologists have left the Gender Identity Development Service (GIDS), the main institution that performs "gender reassignment" in children. They speak of a "medical scandal" and no longer want to bear any of the guilt. However, they shy away from the public, because they can expect persecution from the transgender lobby. In 2009, the GIDS treated 77 children, but in 2018/19 it was 2,590 with a waiting list of 3,000 children, overwhelmingly girls. Psychotherapy is not offered to them, although psychological trauma, including sexual abuse, leads to the child's rejection of her own gender.

There are victims of transgender ideology who are lifting their voices. One of them is Walt Heyer.[162] He lived through all the crises, twists, and turns of the transgender life until, after surgical change from man to "woman," he finally accepted his natural male gender again. Now he travels worldwide, with sorrowful compassion, to help people take charge of their lives again: *Take back your life. Others have. You can, too.*[163]

The good news is: More than 90% of young people who doubt their gender during adolescence stabilize all on their own in their immutable biological identity — as long as they don't get into the hands of a doctor or into a social environment that enables a life of destructive decisions.

... And as long as they don't have a mother who renames her son Luna at age 3, dresses him in girl's clothing and registers him at school as a girl. There is now talk of James, the son of a female pediatrician in Texas. The child is not related to his mother, because he was created through egg donation. His legal mother wanted to give her 7-year-old son puberty-blocking hormones, his divorced father stood in the way, and the case went to court in October 2019: Eleven of the 12 jurors decided that the mother has the right to initiate "sex change" in her son.

Outrage arose throughout the country. Within a few days, a petition to save James from chemical castration received 211,000 signatures.[164] Senator Ted Cruz got involved and demanded that government prevent James from being used as a guinea pig for the left's agenda. Soon after, an appellate court ruled that the "sex change" could not occur without the consent of the father.

James was lucky for a while, but still another judge reversed the appellate court's decision and gave full decision-making power back to the mother. His father is still fighting, but powerful officials are putting obstacles in the way. In an interview, he said:

> This case is going to wind up in the Texas Supreme Court, I would be surprised if it doesn't make it into federal courts and even go to the US Supreme Court, and I'm ready and willing to go there, because I would like to protect every child in the United States from these abhorrent practices by the medical community. We need to pass a law against this. This shouldn't happen to any other child.[165]

How is it possible that within just a few years the destruction of one's own gender identity — with severe lifelong consequences — has become a fashion among young people and supported by the government and media? How is it possible that neither the courts nor the medical authorities have stepped in and prevented the severe damage to children?

In a 65-page handbook created by one of the world's largest law firms together with the Thomson Reuters Foundation (media) and an LGBTIQ youth organization, strategies and tactics are laid out for changing the consciousness of the masses, the childrearing rights of parents, and the legislation. The document is called *Only Adults? Good Practices in Legal Gender Recognition of Youth*.[166]

One great obstacle to the right to free choice of gender for children and youth is the rights of parents who refuse their consent. The handbook explains proven tactics for lobbying groups to prevent resistance from emerging and on how laws can be implemented before the public even knows about them.

- Beat the government to it and publish progressive legislation proposals before the government does.
- Hide your campaign behind the smoke screen of another campaign that has widespread acceptance. For example: transgender rights for children as part of the campaign for same-sex marriage.
- Avoid media reports, and instead lobby individual politicians.

If debate among the affected interest groups is replaced with highly developed manipulation strategies, and politicians and judges are ready to play along, then democracy is hollowed out from within until there is finally no more right to difference of opinion or differing action.

This is about children and youth, their life, their future, and therefore the future of the entire society. They are being abused by transgender ideology activists who entirely lack conscience.[167] These people know that destroying gender identity gives them the hammer they need to smash the nuclear family. It is no longer the natural conditions of human existence that determine what man and woman, marriage, parenthood and family are, but the state presumes to override these conditions through arbitrary legislation. When the state raises itself above nature in service to an ideology, there is nothing that is not within its reach anymore.

The costs are immense. It comes at the cost of family stability, the mental and physical health of children, ever-increasing social funding, justice, and the rule of law.

9.

Children's rights — the ever-encroaching state

> *Without the traditional family consisting of a mother, father, and child(ren), there can be no state. Without the family, a community becomes an anthill of de-individualized beings. Without the family, there is no resistance to indoctrination by ideologues.*
> Josef Kraus, educator, commentator and psychologist

Who wouldn't want children to have a good life — for their wellbeing to be assured and for them to be protected from influences that work against their developing into mature, responsible people? According to the German constitution, this is the right and obligation of the parents until the children reach the legal age of majority and take over the power of decision-making for their own lives.

Because parents have created the child and normally love him, they have the greatest lifelong interest in the child's wellbeing. Nothing gives them a greater sense of accomplishment than seeing their children thrive.

Children's rights in the constitution?

These are the rights that the constitution of the Federal Republic of Germany sets forth for marriage, family, and children in article 6, paragraph 2:

(1) Marriage and family are under the special protection of the state.
(2) Care and rearing of children are the natural right of the parents and their first and foremost duty. The state community watches over their activity.
(3) Children can be legally separated from the family against the will of their legal guardians only if their legal guardians fail or if the children are threatened with neglect for other reasons.

(4) Every mother has the right to the protection and care of the community.

If the government held to this, we would have a society in which marriage, the family, mothers, and children are respected, promoted and supported — to the benefit of everyone. The government would create material and social conditions under which families could thrive — especially a social, tax, and pension system that suitably compensates work within the family. The government would respect the principle of subsidiarity and not take on tasks or responsibilities that the family itself can handle. The government would respect the right of parents to raise and protect their children according to their own ideals, because it would know: The family owes nothing to the state, but rather the state and society depend on the indispensable achievements of the family.

Instead of implementing the principles of the constitution, for years the left-wing parties have pressed to adopt special children's rights into the constitution. Do the left and the Greens have a special love for children? Are they committed to strengthening families consisting of father, mother, and children, which have been shown a thousand times over to be the best habitat for children? How do "children's rights" fit into the structure of parents' and children's lives?

Rights are based on value judgments. What values are to be enforced through children's rights? Rights of whom versus whom?

The source document for children's rights is the UN Convention for Children's Rights, which came into force in 1990 and was ratified by Germany in 1992. The convention reads like a child-friendly document, but if one looks closer, some questions jump out.

- The child should be protected from discrimination (Art. 1).
  Question: Isn't the child already protected from discrimination, like all other people?
- The welfare of the child must be given priority in all government measures (Art. 3.1).
  Question: Priority over whom?
- The child, "who is capable of forming his own opinion," has the right "to express this opinion in all matters affecting the child and must be

heard" (Art. 12).Question: How does a child form his own opinion, and who must hear it?

- The child "must have access to information and materials from a diversity of national and international sources" (Art. 17).
  Question: What if the parents limit access to the mass media?
- The child has a right to "the highest achievable level of health and access to health services." For this, the signatory countries must "develop family planning education and services" (Art. 24).
  Question: Does this mean sex education, contraception, and abortion?
- Educational goals and educational institutions must "meet the minimum standards set by the state" (Art. 29).
  Question: What educational goals does the state have? What if they clash with the parents' educational goals?

For such a convention to be accepted in the UN General Assembly by representatives of 193 countries, the wording must be chosen very carefully. This is why the wording looks harmless and worthy of consent at first glance. But the second look reveals what the fuzzy terminology can make possible: Minors of all ages get the right to enforce their wishes — formed by sex educators, peer groups, Facebook, and the media — against their parents through state intervention. The spongy terms used by the children's rights convention are really placeholders for revolutionary content that turns the basic values of society upside down.

In 2013[168] and 2016[169] a proposed law for adopting children's rights into the German constitution was presented at the Bundestag, but without success, because at the committee hearings, the experts expressed clear refusal to amend the constitution. They unanimously emphasized that the constitution contained no loopholes. Children are human, and the human rights apply unconditionally to all people — they don't need to be defined separately for individual groups. On June 26, 2013, constitutional expert Prof. Gregor Kirchhof expounded that the comprehensive constitutional protection for children would even be weakened by it and the parent-child relationship would be "incorporated into the law."[170]

The negative opinions of the legal experts seemed not to faze the children's rights promoters. For years, Germany's Christian Democratic Union (CDU) operated as a firewall against these red/green objectives, but the wall was finally breached, and children's rights were adopted into the CDU and SPD coalition agreement in 2017. In November 2019, justice minister Christine Lambrecht (SPD) made another attempt to "promote the fundamental rights of children." A new paragraph was to be inserted into Article 6 of the constitution:

> Every child has the right to respect, protection and promotion of his fundamental rights, including his right to develop his own autonomous personality in the social community.

Questions come up again: What does "autonomous" mean, and who is the "social community"? Isn't the child first and foremost responsible to the parents until reaching the legal adulthood? Their duty is to raise their children in collaboration with the school so that, as adults, they can take on autonomous responsibility in society.

Rights can be sued over. Exactly who will sue whom over children's rights? In the final report of the federal states working group "Children's Rights in the Constitution" of October 14, 2019, it says that "the minor who is already legally competent should be able to exercise the rights assigned to him autonomously [!]" and that in the event of "conflicts of interest between child and guardian, a supplementary guardian or other representative will be appointed, as otherwise provided for in trial law."[171]

Differences of opinion between children and parents over what the child should and is allowed to do, or should not and is not allowed to do, happen all the time. These are not "conflicts of interest," but the daily challenges of childrearing. A government-appointed "supplementary guardian" would undermine the parents' authority to raise their children without this being justified by abuse or neglect.

Parents are never perfect, and they make mistakes — often serious ones. Because people, unfortunately, are not good through and through, families are not only a place of strength and support, but also a place of privation and injury. Should that be a reason for the state to take over childrearing? Will state functionaries care for the child better than the parents? They may also be wounded people, but they differ from the parents in one important respect: Parents have given life to their children, they know and love their children. The state cannot love. Parents are concerned about their children's wellbeing their entire lives. The state acts through paid functionaries. It pretends to be an über-father that knows what is the right upbringing for the children and which values should be imparted to them.

How does it work in real life when a minor child is given a "supplementary guardian" for enforcement of his wishes? Something like this, for example: Karl, 12 years old, absolutely has to have a smartphone, because everyone else has one and because otherwise he'll be cut off from his pals' WhatsApp group. His parents don't want him to have a smartphone, among other reasons, because they want to protect him from pornography. They believe that pornography permanently damages a child's wellbeing, but they don't get any backing in protecting their child against pornography.

Karl has been told in school that the constitution guarantees him the right to access information. He demands that his parents grant him this right. His parents refuse. Karl goes to the youth welfare office, where he is assigned a "supplementary guardian" as legal counsel. The family court rules that Karl's parents must equip him with a smartphone. The relationship between the parents and child is shattered.

Or 13-year-old Sophie now wants to become Ben and take puberty-blocking hormones. Her parents do not go along. Sophie sues over her "right to development of an autonomous personality." The parents are forced to allow their pubescent daughter to do something that will probably leave her infertile and at an eightfold higher risk of suicide — consequences they want to protect their 13-year-old daughter from.

If the state really wanted to support the child's wellbeing, it would have to strengthen the family, because nothing hinders a child's welfare more than a broken family. Establishing "children's rights" into the constitution jams a wedge into the relationship between parents and children. Should parents "violate children's rights," the state takes custody as a last resort.

"Custody" of the state

In Article 6 (2) of the constitution, the state is the guardian of a child's wellbeing. Naturally, the state must step in when children are abused or neglected.[172] But the state tends to exercise its guardianship extensively and without control. In Germany, 25,664 children were taken into custody in 2005, 84,230 in 2016, and 52,590 in 2018.[173] The majority of the rise in

2016 is due to "minor refugees traveling alone," but even when this group is subtracted, the number of cases still rose. The costs run to more than €9 billion per year, a business that employs hundreds of thousands. There is little transparency or control, as a study by the German Economic Institute points out.[174] 41% of children and teens eventually return to their families. For 59%, the bond of family is torn forever.

The youth welfare offices operate in a gray area of state power. In fact, in Germany a legal decision must be made one day after the action is first initiated. Then the youth welfare offices do whatever they want in regard to visitation rights, assignment to one of the parents, or permanent separation, and even release for adoption. Parental appeal through the courts is lengthy and costly. There are no clear criteria and no higher court to advise and monitor the youth welfare offices.

A case that attracted international media attention and exposed the German state's arbitrariness is that of the Wunderlich family. The parents fought for years to be allowed to homeschool their children. Homeschooling is banned in Germany but allowed in almost all other European countries. (In the United States, there is a consistently growing homeschool movement that raises young people to learn independently and attain social competence, and they are especially sought after by elite universities.)

In August 2013, 30 police officers and social workers stormed the Wunderlich family's house and took their four children into custody — a traumatic event for the whole family. Not until months later did they get their children back, under the condition that they send them to public schools. The Wunderlichs had no other choice, but they continued to fight for the right to homeschooling. The case went all the way to the European Court of Human Rights (ECHR), which ruled against the family in January 2019, even though the children were judged to be well-educated and socially competent. Thus, the ECHR did not touch Germany's active ban on homeschooling. But that's not the last word in the Wunderlich case — it could go to the Grand Chamber of the European Court of Human Rights.[175]

In the face of ever greater intrusion of the state into parental rights, and the drastic drop in standards in the German educational system,[176] homeschooling would give parents the option — through great personal commitment and responsibility — to see to their own children's education. The coronavirus made its powerful, completely surprising contribution in the spring of 2020: In many countries around the world, the schools and daycare centers were closed for months, and all parents were forced to homeschool — alongside working from home, an unfulfillable task. Can the state ban of homeschooling continue after that?

There is probably no country where parental rights are as abused as in the democratic showcase of Norway.[177] The state agency for child welfare, called *Bernavernet*, defines a child's wellbeing arbitrarily. If Bernavernet concludes the bond between parents and child is lacking, or the mother's mental condition is not good enough to care for her baby, or the upbringing is too Christian, or moderate corporal punishment is incompatible with the child protection law, then Bernavernet removes the children from the family, puts them in homes or with foster families, limits parental visitation to a few hours per year, takes the parents' protest as refusal to cooperate, and may even release the child for adoption. Affected parents flee from Norway so that the state won't seize their children. A film from ARTE TV shows the incomprehensible breach of parental rights and children's welfare.[178] Every year, 44,000 families are exposed to Bernavernet's investigations; more than 2,000 children were taken into custody in 2015. Twenty-six cases are pending at the European Court of Human Rights.

The Bodnariu case attracted international attention. In 2015, agents in two black cars appeared in front of their farm, told the parents that their two daughters had already been picked up at school, took two sons with them, and the next day returned and took the 3-month-old baby. The parents' offense: bringing their children up in the Christian faith and setting occasional physical boundaries. But this time Bernavernet went too far: There was an international outcry and demonstrations before Norwegian embassies from Barcelona to Washington.

The ECHR had previously rejected suits against Bernavernet, but the wind was starting to change. In June 2018, the Council of Europe published a critical report on Bernavernet's attacks, which led to the ECHR taking up the case of Trude Strand Lobben again. During her pregnancy, the young mother had asked the youth welfare office for help and received an assisted living unit. A few weeks after her son was born, she wanted to live independently again. But that was prevented. The youth welfare office took her baby away, granted her only a few hours of visitation per week, and finally gave the child up for adoption. Eleven years later, the Grand Chamber of the ECHR found in favor of Ms. Strand Lobben. It was an important success, which didn't bring her son back, however, because he had already been adopted.[179]

No European country has gone as far as Scotland in its attempt to completely snuff out parental rights and establish state supervisory authority over every child. Scotland wanted to assign every child at birth to a "named person" designated by the state, who was to monitor the "welfare of the child." Lawsuits reached as high as the Supreme Court of the United Kingdom. In a remarkable judgment, the court rejected this atrocity with a justification fully outside the bounds of political correctness:

> Different people grow up differently. The first thing a totalitarian state tries to do is bring the children under its power, to remove them from the insubordinate and deviating influences of their families, and to indoctrinate them with the worldview of those who wield power. Within certain limits, family must be allowed to raise their children as they see fit.[180]

The demands raised by the leftist parties to strengthen children's rights and weaken parental rights have nothing to do with the welfare of the child, but a lot to do with the state's attempt to "bring the children under its power in order to indoctrinate them with the worldview of those who wield power."

Charter of the Rights of the Family

In 1983, the Pontifical Council for the Family presented the *Charter of the Rights of the Family* to the public and to governments. The charter explains the naturally endowed rights of the family, which always apply regardless of any government system or worldview.

> The rights promulgated in this charter are written on the conscience of people and in the overall values of humanity ... Ultimately, these rights belong to the law that the Creator has inscribed on the hearts of all human beings. Society is called on to defend these rights against all breaches and to respect and promote them in their entirety.[181]

The charter's most important statements:

- The family is based on marriage.
- The family, a natural society, exists prior to the State or any other community, and possesses inherent rights which are inalienable.
- The family constitutes, much more than a mere juridical, social and economic unit, a community of love and solidarity, which is uniquely suited to teach and transmit cultural, ethical, social, spiritual, and religious values essential for the development and well-being of its own members and of society.
- Human life must be respected and protected absolutely from the moment of conception.
- Respect of the dignity of the human being excludes all experimental manipulation or exploitation of the human embryo.
- Since they have conferred life on their children, parents have the original, primary, and inalienable right to educate them; hence they must be acknowledged as the first and foremost educators of their children.
- Families have the right to economic conditions which assure them a standard of living appropriate to their dignity and full development.

These are the inalienable rights of the family, which are focused on the welfare of both the child and family. Parents, who take responsibility for their children in a way that often border on heroic, are under pressure and must constantly fight to protect their family rights against intrusion by the state and a morally corrupt society. It is the most important war they can wage, because their first responsibility is to their children. However, there is one children's right that actually should be protected by international law and the constitution: the right of the child to his family lineage. Since artificial insemination has been possible (1960), the right of the child to his biological parents has been undermined more and more, so that now a child created in this way must grow up amidst the legal, social, and psychological chaos of multiple mothers and fathers. This denies him a fundamental human right. The child becomes a product, whose components are bought on the fertility market. The human right to family lineage must be guaranteed by law.

10.
Digital dehumanization

> *The smartphone is in the saddle, and it rides mankind. Which is why we need a social and political movement — digital temperance, if you will — to take back some control.*
> Ross Douthat, New York Times, March 11, 2017

What a blessing the Internet is! Imagine if the coronavirus pandemic had broken out before the digital transformation and the 2020 lockdown had occurred without the capabilities of digital communication. No working from home, no virtual schooling under the teacher's digital tutelage, no virtual conferences, no Skype calls with family and friends, no online shopping, no remote religious services, no public debate on curtailment of our basic democratic rights through government emergency orders. We would probably have had to set up emergency psychotherapy stations. Thanks to the Internet, despite physical social distancing, we could stay in virtual contact.

But the longer it goes on, the more obvious it becomes that elimination of physical contact fundamentally mangles and reduces people. We are flesh-and-blood people and can only live our humanity if we perceive others with all our senses — see, hear, smell, and touch them.

The corona pandemic has increased to the extreme what the digital revolution had been doing for a long time: uprooting people from time and place, disembodying and vaporizing the real person who is present in the here and now, takes on responsibility and shares joy and sorrow with others. The result is a new kind of digital dehumanization.

Because I'm not a digital native and do not belong to the generation that has curiously tapped buttons and screens from babyhood, I am still astounded at how the Internet has overcome the limits of space and time, which I really didn't expect until the afterlife. I'm happy about the instant exchange of texts, photos, and videos around the world, and I groan under the amount of information that floods my screen solicited and unsolicited.

Technological inventions in themselves are neutral. The big question is whether people have the moral maturity to benefit humanity with them.

Apple brought the smartphone to market in 2007. Since then, more than 4 billion people use them, half of them for more than five hours a day.[182] The smartphone was preceded by the invention of personal computers in the 1980s. (I still remember the huge box under the desk, the tweeting and twittering of the modem, and the constant challenge of learning new devices.) Then came the World Wide Web in the 1990s, and ever more user-friendly manuals.

In 2019, about 6% of 6- to 7-year-olds in Germany had their own smartphone. Among 8- to 9-year-olds, it was 33%, for 10- to 11-year-olds 75%, and among 12- to 13-year-olds 95%.[183]

What is the digital revolution doing to children and teenagers?

Thousands of scientific research studies have examined the effects of the new main activity of most people on Earth. They spend most of their waking hours looking at screens: TV, laptops, tablets, smartphones, and game consoles.

The studies document the damaging effects on children's brain development, on adults' brain functions, on health, the mind, and social behavior with effects throughout society. It looks as if the seemingly limitless technical possibilities for information, communication, entertainment, and manipulation have put humanity into an intoxicated state, where they are blind to the flashers and warning lights.

Sick from digital media

We constantly hear that we must digitize faster, especially the schools. But does shifting learning from the teacher-student relationship to the computer, and shifting social life to social networks, promote development of responsible, capable, amicable, joyful young people?

Here are the risks of excessive smartphone and computer use as summarized by Dr. Manfred Spitzer and documented by many scientific studies:[184]

- Lack of exercise, leading to postural issues
- Nearsightedness
- Obesity
- High blood pressure
- Pre-diabetes
- Lack of sleep (causing daytime fatigue)
- Risky behavior in street traffic
- Attention deficits
- Anxiety
- Depression (including self-harm)
- Suicidal ideation
- Stress
- Addiction (computer, smartphones, internet, games)
- Heavier alcohol and tobacco consumption
- School failure, including dropping out
- Increased aggression
- Less empathy for parents and friends
- Decreased independent decision-making power

The list screams for education and protection measures. Are parents and teens educated about it? No! Are the World Health Organization and the government taking measures to stem the damage to an entire generation? No! Are there campaigns regarding the risks of smartphone use? No! The responsibility falls to the parents who, if they even know the dangers, are desperate to protect their children from the toxic influences of digital media.

The most important factors in the extent of this severe, long-term damage to physical and mental health and social behavior are:

- The age of the media user: The younger, the worse.
- The duration of media use: The more, the worse.
- The socioeconomic background: The lower the economic and social status, the earlier, the greater and the more indiscriminate the media use by parents and children.
- The content: The more brutal, the worse.

Changes in the brain

A newborn's brain weighs 250 grams, more than triples in size in the first year of life, and continues its fast growth until the sixth year. No one learns so much in so little time as a small child. Everything the child experiences, learns, feels, sees, and comprehends forms pathways in the brain. Traumatic experiences in the first year leave indelible marks. Even though the brain pretty much stops growing around age 20, it remains a pliant organ, capable of learning, and changes throughout life. *Use it or lose it* is the brain's motto into old age. If and when an elderly person's brain limits itself to perceiving the immediate present, the onset of dementia also depends on impressions from childhood and the diversity and intensity of the demands on the brain.[185] The brain is never full, but can be "emptied" through media use and be filled with trash.

New imaging processes allow us to look into the brain and determine which areas are more and less active. This allows conclusions to be made on the effects of media use. The New York Times has reported on a study of 3- to 5-year-old children: The more the small children are exposed to the screen — 41% have several devices in their rooms — the worse the development in the parts of the brain devoted to speech and language.[186]

The harm to children's natural, healthy development starts a downward slide beginning when they are small and the child stares mesmerized at the screen, and the "umbilical cord," or communication with the mother, is cut. Instead of constant attention, immediate reaction to his utterances and needs, loving looks and gestures, physical security and comfort, the child is exposed to the solitude of the screen as early as infancy. The less the mother speaks with the child while TV is on, the graver the effects.[187]

In 2017, the German federal government's drug czar, Marlene Mortler, presented the results of the BLIKK study:[188] 5,573 parents and their children, aged 0–13 years, were polled about their interaction with digital media. 70% of preschool-aged children use their parents' smartphone more than 30 minutes a day. The study shows the relationship between media use by parents and children and the child's physical and psychosocial condition. Here are the results:

- Feeding and sleep disturbances in infants if the mother uses digital media when caring for the infant (e.g. she's got Facebook up while she's nursing)

- Language development disorders due to daily digital screen use
- Hyperactivity and concentration problems in children 2–5 years old
- Mental health problems due to restlessness and distractedness (an early sign of later development disorders)
- Mental health problems in children 8–13 who use media more than 60 minutes a day
- Excess weight or obesity due to increased consumption of candy and soda pop combined with lack of exercise. (According to the Robert Koch Institute, 15% of children are overweight, and 6.3% obese — twice as many as 20 years ago.)

The federal drug czar sees a need for action:

> The study shows the health consequences children may suffer if they are left alone to develop their media habits without the help of parents, teachers and pediatricians. It is urgently necessary to raise parents' awareness on the issue of media use. Small children don't need a smartphone. First they need to learn to stand securely on their own two feet in real life. The upshot is that it's high time for more attention to digital media use — by parents, schools and other educational institutions, but also by politicians. In the future, media use must be included in the early detection investigations of children and students.

The results of the BLIKK study confirm the long-term studies of Prof. Christakis and his team in the United States.[189] Early TV consumption between 1 and 3 years leads to attention disorders and hyperactivity (ADHD) at the age of 7. The more media use, the worse the effect. When children watch two hours of TV a day before their second year of life, a third of them have ADHD at 7. In 2007, Christakis conducted another study, of 1,800 American children, that showed that children under 3 sit in front of TV for an average of two hours a day.[190] This impairs their math, speech, and reading ability at age 7, regardless of their intelligence and their parents' social background.[191]

If elementary school children spend many hours a day in front of screens, there is increasing danger of them sliding into the loser life. A research team in New Zealand headed by R. J. Hancox showed in a 2004 and a 2005 study that children between 5 and 15 who spend more than three hours a day in front of TV were less likely at age 26 to have finished school, while those with the lowest childhood TV consumption mostly had a university degree.[192]

The studies by Christakis and Hancox were done before the smartphone took over the world. People didn't have a TV in their jeans pocket yet. Since smartphones have become available, media use for several hours a day by both children and their parents has skyrocketed.

Stressed parents of children stressed by daycare, preschool, and elementary school give their kids over to digital media. This quiets the child down for a while — but at what price! Parents and children pay for the short-term relief with an increasing chance of mental disorders and health problems: continuous restlessness in the child, inability to play independently, sleep disorders, ADHD, poor concentration, overweight, nearsightedness, all the way to addiction.

Media use by parents

The danger to children is not only the duration of their own media use, but also the way their parents use media.[193] The BLIKK study showed that babies have trouble nursing and sleeping if the mother's attention is on her cellphone and not on her child. This precious time is not really spent together if the mother or father is using a smartphone or tablet to cruise the web and only looks over when the child expresses her abandonment through whining, screaming, crying, or other signs of discomfort. Parents then often reply with anger and scolding.

The more that parents use digital media in their children's presence, the more difficult they find their child to be. They don't recognize that their own emotional absence is what is making the child difficult. This starts a vicious circle: Parents' smartphone use, disruptive behavior by the child, more smartphone use by the parents, more media use by the children.... What's up with the child? Why is he so fidgety? Why can't she play by herself? Why does she always look so sad? Why is the school complaining about his belligerence? Shouldn't we take him to a therapist?

Even family meals — which have become rare in many households — don't bring togetherness, because the cellphone on the table constantly interrupts communication. Somebody's always got his nose in the phone — which can be observed wherever people gather: at train stations, airports, playgrounds, in the park, at coffee shops, and on family trips to McDonald's. Parents set the example, and the children follow.

Just a second to look at the text message, just a quick answer, just a fast check of Facebook, I've got to take this quick call ... everything fast and as simultaneous as possible in the mistaken assumption that it won't affect the company one is in at the moment. Actually, the short interruptions kill togetherness. *Multitasking* is what's called for now to keep up with the hectic pace of the digital world. Feed the baby and read messages, eat and check the e-mail, answer phone calls and messages, and always and everywhere with music in the background.

The result is an inability to concentrate. Attention is frayed, and the ability to distinguish what is and isn't important is gone. Many people can no longer bear silence or being alone. However, the ability to concentrate and distinguish what is important are vital conditions for a person's strength of character and ability to make free decisions. They enable critical thinking, self-determination, and goal orientation. How is someone going to learn to set his sights on a goal and focus his energy long-term if he constantly allows himself to be diverted, and as early as preschool can't get absorbed in play?

Lonely and addicted

Children grow up. They want to do what everybody else does, and their parents want to give them what other parents do — namely game consoles and computer games. Almost 40% of 10-year-old boys (16% of girls) have a game console in their room.[194]

What does a child do with a game console? He presses buttons and taps the screen. His fine motor skills don't develop. His breathing is flat, his eyes stressed, muscle activity almost zero, just like perception of the outside world — and there's nothing but isolation and loneliness.

If the game includes virtual networking with other players, there is an illusion of community. But when the console is finally shut off hours later, there's solitude again: no talking, laughing, walking, running, wrestling, no trees, no meadow, no physical effort, no reading, no craft or musical activity — no homework.

The young player absently eats junk food, barely moves, has too little sleep, and doesn't feel like doing anything but that game. The body gets ever fatter and flabbier, the eyes get nearsighted (in South Korea, the country with the highest smartphone density, 95% of people under 20 are nearsighted), the grades drop at school, entry into real groups decreases — is it any wonder that depression is so widespread among the young?

A survey by Bitcom, an interest group on the digital economy, showed that gaming is an everyday part of the vast majority of young people's lives — in fact, an average of two hours a day.[195] Among 16- to 18-year-olds, a third play more than three hours a day, boys considerably more than girls.

One pied piper is the online game *World of Warcraft*. It has been on the market in Germany since 2005 and is permitted for children 12 and over. One of the trailers shows flames of cosmic proportions, scenarios of superhuman threats, satanic grimaces, buxom women, and in between, flashes that say: "A HUNDRED MILLION PLAYERS ... HAVE ALREADY BEGUN THEIR ADVENTURE ... NOW IT'S YOUR TURN." At the beginning, the 12-year-old can play one month for free. After that, it's highly probable he's been bitten by the bug and convinces his parents to pay €11 to €13 a month for continued participation.

World of Warcraft is designed to create addiction. The longer the kid plays, the greater the reward. If he doesn't play regularly, he falls behind. To reach the head of the pack, he has to play for months in a virtual player community that he'll damage if he leaves. The burning pain of loneliness, emptiness, and helplessness of an abandoned child, whether in a tenement or a luxury villa, is deadened by the threatening fantasies of power and violence for the duration of the game, only to emerge again as soon as it's over.

The parents get a few quiet hours a day away from the child. Are they aware of the danger of losing their child to the games? Hancox's studies (see above) show: For every additional hour of screen use, the bond to the parents can decrease by 13%, and the risk of losing connection to peers and friends can increase by 24%.

Gaming has effects on school performance. A study by the Criminological Research Institute of Lower Saxony, headed by Christian Pfeiffer, went into depth on German students' poor performance in the 2006 PISA ratings. About a fifth of the students in Germany — once a nation that set an example — landed in the "risk group" in natural sciences, reading, and mathematics.

What caused that? Social scientists are unanimous: "The more time students spend consuming media, and the more brutal the content, the more their grades in school drop."[196]

Not only the length of play, but the intensity of the violence influences the deterioration of academic performance. The researchers conjecture that: Emotionally stressful content impairs fundamental information processing in the brain and weakens concentration ability.

Violent video games overcome the youthful mind and deaden the senses to finer perceptions and feelings. This impairs the ability to form relationships, which requires the ability to perceive others sensitively.

A person who consumes violence and cruelty on the screen is more indifferent to real violence later.[197] Is that what we want? Do we want no one to help on the playground if someone on the ground is kicked in the face? For everyone in the subway to be silent when an old man gets beaten up? Do we want an ever coarser, more brutal society? No one wants that. Why aren't violent games banned altogether? After the next murder rampage, politicians will again attend the funeral services, seated in the pews with dour faces, and let their spokespeople announce that something must be done about violent games.

Excessive media use can turn to addiction. Whatever the addiction — Internet, cellphone, gaming, sex or drugs, the person has no more control of his behavior. Addiction means a loss of free will. To feel right, the addict has to do something that harms him. The brain's hormonal self-reward system starts to break down, so that the person needs a bigger and bigger fix.

The 2016 study *Game over* by DAK, a German health insurance company, rates 8.4% of young men between 12 and 25 as game addicted, while only 2.9% of girls and women are.[198] Game-addicted young people have less and less contact with friends and family members but instead fight constantly with their parents, barely show up at family meals, and perform worse in school.

Most at risk are young people from less educated classes. The lower the family's social and economic status, the more excessive and uncontrolled the media usage. According to Pfeiffer's study, a 10-year-old boy from a poorly educated family with a migration background in a north German city will consume about four hours of media per school day. A native-born girl from southern Germany who has at least one parent who finished high school, on the other hand, consumes only about 45 minutes of media.

Girls have more interest in social communication and therefore are somewhat ahead in use of social media. Overall, 85% use social networks. Statistical data on daily use of Facebook, Instagram, WhatsApp, Messenger, etc., fluctuate between two and three hours. The more time young people spend romping around in social networks, the fewer real friendships they have. This especially makes girls sad and depressed. It even reduces the size of the brain's area for social interaction, thereby decreasing social skills.[199]

Having lots of online "friends" is a popularity status symbol, but as far as fulfilling social relationships are concerned, they're like trying to satisfy hunger with chewing gum. The constant digital stimulation can hide the emptiness of a person's actual social life and therefore becomes addictive. People may not use real names, and they want to look good in front of their "friends." People show their sunny side or invent a sunny side that doesn't exist in reality — one more reason not to meet up in real life. People can hardly speak openly about serious problems. As soon as someone becomes annoying, people click out or block them from their accounts.

People who have friends in real life, with whom they meet in a real place — often enough and long enough for a relationship to grow and deepen — can also discuss news over social networks without any social ostracism.

Cyber-bullying

In public, there used to be social restraint, because a speaker or writer was visible as a person. But this has fallen away with the anonymity of the Internet. This opens the way for a new kind of social cruelty, cyber-bullying. The Internet has become what the pillory was in the Middle Ages, with the difference that the Internet is visible worldwide. Cyber-bullying affects grownups in the workplace just as it can young people at school. A Forsa survey conducted for a German health insurance company determined that 32% of 14- to 20-year-olds have at one time fallen victim to cyber-bullying, and every fifth elementary school child has been threated or insulted by cellphone. And 10% admit that they have been guilty of the bullying themselves.[200]

Bullying is a type of long-term intentional harassment that one or more group members is subjected to without being able to defend himself. Teasing, ridicule, ignoring, shunning, shoving, nasty looks and comments have always gone on in classrooms, but with the Internet, the possibilities for exposure and humiliation are no longer limited to the immediate social group. There are no boundaries, and they can spread like wildfire. Facebook has a German video, *Aufstehen gegen Mobbing*[201] *(Stand Up Against Bullying)* that deals with the cruelty of bullying.

Under a fake identity, rumors are spread, confidential information is posted, photos are displayed with malicious comments, often with sexist insults, perhaps even nude photos that anyone can see, "like," comment on and share. Before this, there was at least refuge at home, but not in the era of the smartphone.

Everyone wants to belong to a social environment. For this, people are willing to hide their own opinions and howl with the wolves. People can stand being an outsider, but being constantly humiliated by the whole group can have very severe consequences. Absence from school, diminished performance, insomnia, anxiety, helplessness, headaches, stomachaches, long-term depression and even suicide. Once someone becomes a victim of bullying, whatever he does, he can't get back out of that victim role. The bullying victim must turn to authorities outside the group — teachers, assistance organizations, even the police.[202] It is crucial that the victim work together with parents and teachers and that the whole group be included.

It's not just the fat, dumb and unlikable who become victims of bullying — someone can also be targeted for being especially good-looking or very accomplished.

In bullying there is a distribution of roles: In addition to the bully and the victim, there are those who drift along behind, hanging onto a bully's tow rope and feel powerful because of it. Then there are the people who silently stand back, and usually someone courageous who defends the victim.[203]

Cyber-bullying is so widespread that there are many aid and prevention organizations for it. The school should react to the very first sign that a class is disintegrating into bullying. The worst method is to remove the victim from the class, because the bully feels victorious, and the group learns that bullying works, and the victim will be ejected. Bullying is a signal to make a long-term, thoroughgoing issue of social behavior in school, to raise awareness of it, and to impart positive social behavior.[204]

Global manufacturers of awareness

The findings are alarming: Overuse of digital media for entertainment and communication alienates young people from themselves, from their parents and from friends. The formerly central means of engaging the culture, such as reading and writing, deteriorate. Almost 20% of schoolchildren in Germany are functionally illiterate. Only digital tidbits are now exchanged. Fun emojis save people the trouble of forming sentences. Grammar and spelling are truncated or not followed at all, and the students don't have a command of them when things get serious, such as on a written application or oral interview.

Relationships become superficial or break down completely. Loneliness lurks in the unfilled minutes and drives the person — who has now become a *user* — into a vicious circle of ever longer use of digital media with contents that penetrate ever deeper into his personality. The user lives in a delusional world that can never satisfy his true longings, the longing for friendship, for recognition, for love, for liveliness, for an interesting world with exciting challenges that develop their strengths so that they can withstand setbacks and misfortunes and learn from them.

If those things don't happen, the person is putty in the hands of the great manipulators. Everything that drowns out unsatiated longings or satisfies with illusions gains entry into the spirit and psyche of the user, who doesn't know his weaknesses and therefore can't perceive he is being used.

Manipulation is the art of directing others according to your own interests, without them knowing. Edward Bernays, a nephew of Sigmund Freud, explains the methods of mass manipulation in his famous book *Propaganda,* which was published in 1928 (!). The technique for manipulating the consciousness of the masses is called *engineering of consent.* He wrote:

> The conscious and intelligent manipulation of the organized habits and opinions of the masses is an important element in

> democratic society. Those who manipulate this unseen mechanism of society constitute an invisible government which is the true ruling power of our country.... In almost every act of our daily lives, whether in the sphere of politics or business, in our social conduct or our ethical thinking, we are dominated by the relatively small number of persons ... who understand the mental processes and social patterns of the masses. It is they who pull the wires which control the public mind.[205]

Mark Zuckerberg is one of this "small number of people who understand the mental processes and social patterns of the masses" ... and control them. In his wildest dreams, Bernays could not have imagined the manipulation methods available and used after the invention of the Internet 80 years later — by a privately owned company that can direct the consciousness and behavior of (so far) more than half of humanity, without the people noticing.

He founded Facebook in 2004. According to some accounts, he just wanted to network the students at his college, while at the same time always dreaming that one day the whole world would be networked. But he never imagined that "it would be us."[206] In the space of 15 years, Mark the student became one of the world's most powerful men: As of 2019, 2.7 billion people used Facebook (including its other services, 9% growth in one year), 381 million in Europe (half of all residents). The company had revenue of $162 billion with double-digit growth over the previous year, $34 billion in profits, and paid no taxes.

Everything that the 2.7 billion people on Facebook post, like, look at, and search for is saved. The great data alchemists combine that with other services, such as WhatsApp, and transform it into an ongoing profile of each individual user. Many users don't know that their personal data is the currency used to pay for these fantastic "free" services. As the saying goes in the tech industry, "If you're not paying for the product, you *are* the product." You are the goods the Internet giants are selling. Based on personal data gathered from us, news, advertising, and prices for consumer goods can be personally served up, which means they are perfectly tailored to individual taste and — fully undetected — to the Internet giants' socio-political intentions. The independent decision regarding what we want to know is replaced by what we "should" know (see below). Apps make life so simple that we forget how to live simply.

Devices with speech recognition that do anything possible on demand, at the same time record everything we say in private if they are connected to the Internet. The days are over when people thought secret police were responsible for things like that. This all yields *big data*, which can be used for a great many things.

It can inform manufacturers or service providers about our purchasing behavior, so that the prices for an air ticket or a hotel reservation come out differently for a coupon-clipper than for a quality-conscious shopper.

Our data can be sold to banks and companies that want to know something about our creditworthiness.

The data can be sold to politicians who want to win elections, such as through the big data merchant Cambridge Analytica, which got a little careless and had to close down.

Elections can be won through *nudging*: Continuous, inconspicuous little nudges bring the user to a specific voting decision.

Pressure to conform can be created through *likes*: So many of my Facebook friends have liked Greta Thunberg that I think she's cool too, and I'm going to blow off school this Friday to save the world.

The *rankings* of search engines can be manipulated. What appears on the first page of results influences purchase decisions and opinion formation more than what shows up on the third page.

Troll armies can be used to spread targeted false information.

Bots can be used to duplicate news and messages automatically, so that hype builds around a person or an event.

Politically incorrect statements can be classified as *hate speech* and censored.

There's plenty else that can be done without the exploited user having the slightest idea. Manipulation works in the dark and flees the light. Julia Krüger, a scientific expert on Internet politics, writes:

> What should be of the greatest concern is the fact that methods of news selection and coordination are developed and introduced without any transparency or consent. Despite great manipulation risks and problems, Facebook refuses access to

> relevant data by the public, researchers and experts … Experiments on the use of media for political purposes are sold as promotion of freedom and democracy. In truth, this completely lacks the basics of democracy: separation of powers, checks on state authority, and participation.[207]

In other words: Democracy becomes a marionette stage. The people pulling the strings are as hidden in the digital world as the puppeteer is in the theater. Behind the manipulation of opinions, trends, campaigns, needs, purchase decisions and election behavior, there are value judgments. Which ones? Who makes them?

Naturally, Mark Zuckerberg wants only what is best for us. He lets us know:

> We feel a responsibility to make sure our services aren't just fun to use, but also good for people's well-being. The research shows that when we use social media to connect with people we care about, it can be good for our well-being. We can feel more connected and less lonely, and that correlates with long-term measures of happiness and health.[208]

Research and healthy common sense also show that it is detrimental to our health and happiness to spend many hours a day in the virtual world, with virtual "friends," instead of in relationships in the real world with real people.

Mark Zuckerberg thinks an explicit definition of values for the world's population can't be arrived at. It is also not necessary, because the Internet giants, the UN and the EU, most of the media, global corporations, multi-billion-dollar foundations, and the universities all agree: The population must be reduced, abortion is a human right, the LGBTIQ agenda must be supported, dissolution of national identity through migration is a humanitarian imperative, saving the climate is a question of human survival, men are perpetrators and women are victims, the right is evil and the left is good.

Zuckerberg and comrades are creators of the so-called mainstream. He will now generously introduce *user ranking*: Users should judge for themselves whether they trust a given news source. The masses should decide together which news is important, acceptable, and "true." This completes the circle. People are uprooted from those things that form their identity: beliefs, family, nation, gender. They stagger through their young lives with no connection or instruction and seek refuge among people of the same age, who are just as deprived and abandoned. No firm inner core can form to enable them to judge for themselves, but rather the people are internally needy, depressive, and seducible. Thus the population becomes a pliable mass for manipulation by uncontrollable Internet corporations. With such highly developed methods of directing consciousness and behavior, people are imprinted the way the new lords of the world want them to be; then they are granted the "freedom" to decide which information is true or false.

11.
Pornography — defilement of children's souls

It is not the young generation that is deteriorating — they go rotten only if the adults already have.
Montesquieu

"Human dignity is inviolable," says the first article of Germany's constitution. Why does someone have dignity? Because he is a person with free will and reason. He is not an object to be used for just any purpose. To use him is to damage his dignity.

Knowing this requires no constitution or philosophy, but just the question, "Would I like to be used for just any purpose?" Everyone can find the answer in his heart: "No, I do not want to be used — I want my dignity respected."

Using a person means that person is made an instrument for purposes defined by another. He is made into an object.

There is a power gap between the user and the used. Even a child does not want to be used. Good childrearing rests upon the powerful adult respecting the dignity of the powerless child.

The extreme form of disrespect for the dignity of a human being is slavery: You belong to me. The extreme form of respect for the dignity of a human being is love: I belong to you.

Where does pornography fall between these two coordinates? Pornography is visual representation of sexual behavior to produce sexual arousal in the viewer. Sex gets under the skin and affects the person at all levels. If a person tries to separate body from soul, love flees in horror.

In December 2019, anyone googling XXX, the abbreviation for pornography, got 1,420,000,000 hits. In April of 2020, it was 1,900,000,000. Every third Internet search is for pornography. This means that the bright side of our society, in which people have dignity and the right to exist, hovers over a gloomy underworld, in which a person's dignity is crushed — not only the dignity of women who are humiliated, degraded, struck, bound, gagged and tortured to arouse sexual lust in millions of spectators, but also the dignity of those satisfying themselves in front of the screen. They find no peace but may get on a slippery slope to addiction and crime.

Behind it all is a billion-dollar worldwide industry in which men treat women *and children* as refuse. Growth in the child pornography market is booming. In Germany alone, police received 35,000 complaints in 2017. Of them, 14,900 cases were verifiably committed, while only 40% of them were even investigated.[209] Within the EU, hundreds of thousands of children are trafficked. Thousands are abducted and have disappeared forever.[210]

Child pornography is raging through the Internet. On October 7, 2019, the New York Times reported, "Last year, tech companies reported over 45 million online photos and videos of children being sexually abused — more than double what they found the previous year."

When police investigated appalling cases of child abuse in the German town of Bergisch Gladbach in 2020, they came across 30,000 suspects — that's not a misprint, *thirty thousand!* What came to light was "most deeply distressing," said the justice minister of the state of North Rhine-Westphalia. "We have to realize that child abuse on the Internet is much more prevalent than we had previously assumed."

A society swimming in a sewer of smut cannot protect children from pornography. Even if responsible parents don't give their child a smartphone and their Internet access is equipped with filters for porn and violence, some cool kid at school is liable to stick a porn video in front of his nose.

As early as 11 years ago (2009), half of all 11- to 13-year olds had seen pornographic images or movies,[211] many when they were even younger.[212] For young people between 13 and 19, Internet pornography is part of everyday media consumption — and the trend is rising.[213]

The first encounter with sexuality in a context of violence, humiliation, and perversity can be traumatizing — more so, the younger the child is. Girls are generally disgusted by it and are therefore less threatened than boys, but for boys the disgust is soon overpowered by sexual arousal.

In an online article in the German newspaper *Die Zeit*, writer Anselm

Neft describes his own initial sex education at 9 through pornographic images in "an atmosphere of curiosity, shame and degradation."[214] Boys who bragged about already having slept with girls became the heroes, while the girls who had slept with them were "sluts." "I found it disgusting how women were treated in porn, but it also aroused me ... Sex became omnipresent, random, impersonal, obsessive and empty." The author explains that in the complex process of becoming a man, "porn consumption was a fast shortcut to a feeling of manhood ... with no emotional obligation, devotion or vulnerability on my part." A man needs pornography because he feels small, and he feels small because he needs pornography. A first-class business model designed to keep the customers coming back.

Pornography actually does cause addiction and alters the brain. The brain's hormonal reward system is hyperactivated and demands ever-increasing doses. In pornography, the addicting substance is the crossing of sexual boundaries: first women as victims, then children, then babies — and half the world is watching. The most insidious thing about pornography is that even if the person has been able to tear himself away from it, he is pursued by the images over years and decades, because they have been recorded in the brain. In contrast to the body, which can expel certain amounts of poisonous substances, these images that have triggered strong emotions of shock, fear, threat, or sexual arousal burn into the brain. They reemerge in agonizing ways even after the person's sexuality has long since become an expression of loving devotion to a person of the opposite sex.

How horrible it is when a child gets his first impressions of the wondrous phenomenon of sexuality through images of brutal abuse and shameless exhibitions of intimate acts! Nowhere is a person so fragile as in this innermost "garden" where only love should be the key to open if the person's dignity is to be protected. The child is overcome, shocked, ashamed, and feels he is the guilty one and will therefore not entrust this to his parents. But because everything forbidden is attractive, especially for boys, and because becoming a man has something to do with "doing as many things as possible that one really doesn't want to do at first: drinking, smoking, acting cool, hurting oneself and others" (Anselm Neft), a force arises that addicts the beginner to masturbation: Self-satisfaction as short-term satiation of insecurity and emptiness. Sex is uncoupled from its real purpose, devotion to a real person and creation of children. Sex becomes a flight from loneliness into loneliness.

In young people, pornography consumption leads to

- Fixating sexuality on satisfying drives
- Gender stereotypes: the man as brutal and macho, the woman as a humiliated sex object
- Insecurity as a man or woman, because they think they're not virile or pretty enough to meet the standard
- Early, uncommitted, zero-relationship, risky sex with changing partners
- Perverse expectations of the real partner
- Acting out what's seen in the porn
- Sexual abuse of children by children
- Loss of the vision of marriage and family as a model for one's own life[215]

If politicians take up this subject at all, then most of the time it's about stopping child pornography and porn consumption by teenagers. But kids do what adults do. Children are curious, and they want to explore the world. They want to bring adults' secrets to light. Degrading sex also degrades the grownups.

Pornography is a first-order killer of marriage and family. The porn consumer emotionally distances himself from his partner. He becomes incapable of loving, and of expressing his love with tenderness and deep respect. He confronts his wife with perverse sexual requests and eventually loses interest in her and their children. He lives in a continuous state of virtual adultery, which sooner or later becomes real adultery … and finally divorce.[216] [217]

What irony! What hypocrisy! The world speaks of dignity during the day, and then violates dignity at night. The daytime world fights for liberation of women from patriarchal oppression, and the nighttime world degrades women and turns them into objects for brutal sexual exploitation. By day feminism degrades men into wimps and by night calls them rapists.

Could pornography be the revenge of men who are no longer respected as fighters, protectors and fathers?

What can parents do?

There is no simple solution. We are in the midst of the digital revolution and it keeps moving forward. Children must learn media competence, as it's called. Naturally, children must learn to deal with the media, because it's a part of our life. People who want to solve the problem through avoidance would have to live apart, like the Amish, who to this day use no electricity.

Without doubt, children's media use must be monitored: Wait as long as possible to give them a smartphone. Allow them Internet access only in a high-traffic area of the home. Filter for sex and violence. No smartphone at school, no smartphone in the bedroom.

The fact that our society sets no limits on infection by pornography is not a sign of freedom, but one of massive loss of freedom through pornography addiction. Production and use of pornography must be banned and penalized, because it destroys individuals, families, children, and the whole society.

The crucial question for parents is: Has the child succeeded in developing his own internal conscience to distinguish right from wrong, to choose the good, to give priority to real friendships over virtual ones, to true play instead of buttons on a console, to real movement over virtual mobility? For this, the child needs the capacity for self-control, conscience formation, interests as motivation for achievements and the good self-esteem that comes from all of those things. For this, young people need an unbroken bond to their parents who they know love them for themselves.

12.
Divorce — the unbloody sacrifice of children

> *I felt uprooted like a tree whose roots were hanging in the air. My universe was smashed to smithereens.*
> *I became fearful — nothing was sure or predictable anymore. I lost trust in myself and others. I always felt like something bad could happen at any time. There was no more coming home.*
> Testimony of a divorce victim, *Primal Loss*

A man and a woman meet. A spark jumps from heart to heart. People say that Cupid has shot his arrow and created this irresistible attraction. The Latin word *cupidus* means *lustful, passionate.*

It takes the two people time to emerge from the blindness Cupid's arrow has caused, to wake up and to check whether they should really stand before God and the community and promise "I do" until the end of their days. Each passes the test in the eyes of the other. They marry and set off with great anticipation toward the adventure of parenting.

A child is born. With deep amazement, they look at the helpless bundle in their arms, which is fully dependent on their love and care. The parents are prepared to make great sacrifices for the child and reap the deepest joy through the existential and indissoluble bond with the child as he heads into the future.

In the triangle with mother and father, a boy or girl learns what it means to be a man or a woman. They learn how to enter relationships with the opposite sex. They find their place among their siblings. In this fragile form called the family, the child learns and learns, especially from what they see and experience — far more than from what people say.

Every family has conflicts. We're all born selfish and enter marriage with imprints and injuries that can turn everything upside down. There can be disorder and damage in the family home: The power goes out, the furnace goes kaput, doors stick, the cellar is damp — it's the parents' job to bring everything back to order, especially to drain the flooded basement of their psyche. Do the parents show the children by example how to resolve conflicts, how to restore the peace before the sun goes down? Children actually withstand a lot and forgive the parents for almost anything as long as everything can be patched back up and things go back to normal: *We belong together!*

Divorce tears the foundation asunder. Part of the house, maybe even the whole house, becomes unlivable. One or more family members move out forever. *We don't belong together anymore!* Father and mother were the foundation of the child's existence, gave him safety, security, a home, an identity, and a sense of belonging. If the parents break up, the child loses that safety, security, home, identity and sense of belonging. He loses the ground under his feet. For a child, divorce is an earthquake whose aftershocks will continue for decades of his life.

Why does our society consider only the parents' "happiness" and not the children's suffering? Why must children, who still have their life ahead of them, sacrifice their happiness and chances in life so that one of their parents might be happier in a new relationship, or the next one or the next one. The parental relationship rests on a free decision to bind for a lifetime. The child's relationship to the parents does not rest on his own decision and cannot be revoked. He has to live amidst the rubble.

Here are the possible consequences: Depression, anxiety, loneliness, lower self-esteem, failure in school, inability to resolve conflicts, self-injury, suicide, chronic illnesses, drug and alcohol abuse, criminal convictions, early and promiscuous sex, abortion, poverty, inability to bond to others, divorce in his own marriage and thereby another generation of children of divorce.

This is about increased *risk* of disruption in the lives of divorce victims, but it is not inevitable. These risks are documented by a wealth of scientific studies. The initial situation, the scenarios, the divorcing parents' behavior and the children's reaction are different in every individual case. Many children are resilient and can come out more or less unscathed. But all will have the rug pulled out from under them, and they will have to navigate throughout their lives between the divorced parents and their further partners, siblings and all those new "relatives."

Why doesn't society see anything wrong when parents expect their children to endure all this and demand that they accept it without complaint? Living from now on with just one parent; switching homes every two weeks; being the fifth wheel in a patchwork family; having to accept the mother or father's new partner even when it tears at their heart?

The answer is as simple as it is hidden — so that the issue of guilt is never brought up. Many US states eliminated the principle of fault in divorce around 1970. In Germany, it is enough for a couple to live apart for a year, after which one partner can get a divorce even against the will of the other.

A collective no-fault amnesia has taken over. Divorce? No problem! A merry-go-round of lovers, out-of-wedlock children, unmarried cohabitation — no problem for anyone, not even people high in government.

If a father of three daughters discovers his true identity after the age of 50 and enters a new "marriage" to a man, he is lavished with sympathetic understanding in his social circle and the media, maybe even from his own wife, as happened in the United Kingdom's royal family in 2018: Lord Ivar Mountbatten, cousin of the queen, father of three daughters, got divorced from his wife Penny and "married" a man in a church ceremony. His wife Penny accompanied him up the aisle and gave him away to his boyfriend. Did anyone ask the three daughters how it all went for them? But children's feelings don't count. They have to make lemonade.

Law has come down on the side of the adults and guarantees them satisfaction of all sorts of emotional and sexual needs, with the fewest possible complications.

There is no question: There can be emotional, physical and sexual abuse in families that makes separation imperative — even for the sake of the children. But that is just a small portion of the cases — far below 10%. Most of the time the split is justified by "love." Either it's "not there anymore" or it has wandered on. But love doesn't excuse one from guilt. It only veils it. Emotional love is not a magnetic pole to which the conscience can determine its direction — only a fleeting feeling that has no memory and blinds people in the early stages.

Divorce is like an infectious virus for which there is no lockdown. Everybody knows divorced couples and everyone knows children of divorced parents.

The option hovers over marriage like a ghost.

In figures:[218]

- In 2018, there were 20 million registered couples in Germany, of which 83% are married. Of them, 56% have no children. 3.3 million live together unmarried. Of them, 68% have no children.
- In 2017, 74% of minor children grew up with both parents (as biological children, stepchildren, adoptive or foster children).
- In 1961, Germany saw 700,000 marriages and 135,000 divorces. In 2016 it was 410,000 marriages and 162,000 divorces. This means that between 1961 and 2016, the percentage of marriages ending in divorce grew from 19% to 40%.
- Half of the divorced couples had children. In 2016, 132,000 children were divorce orphans. Since 1991, in all of Germany, there have been more than 4 million victims of divorce.
- Between 2007 and 2017, the number of couples cohabitating increased 31%, and the number of those with minor children by 38%, to 934,000.
- Every fifth child — that's 2.4 million — lives with only one parent, in 9 out of 10 cases the mother. The most common cause is divorce. Most single parents receive government assistance.
- The portion of same-sex couples is 1.8%. Among couples with children, 0.15% are same-sex.
- The duration of cohabitation relationships is considerably shorter than that of marriages, and the risk to the children that the parents will part is 90% greater than for children born in marriage.[219] They don't show up in the divorce statistics.

Testimonies from the suffering of children of divorce

How greatly the children suffer can be found in the book *Primal Loss — The Now-Adult Children of Divorce Speak*. (Below, adult children of divorce will be referred to as "ACD.")[220] The editor, Leila Miller, asked these questions, among others, to 70 people whose parents divorced at various points in their childhoods:

- What effect has your parents' divorce had on you?

- What is the difference between how you felt about the divorce as a child and how you feel about it as an adult?
- Has your parents' divorce affected your own marriage or your view of marriage?
- What do you want to say to people who say that "children are resilient" and "kids are happy when their parents are happy" and "kids of divorce will be just fine and will go on to live successful lives"?
- What do you most want adults in our society to know about how divorce affects the children?

This is what adults say years and decades after their parents' divorce:

- It hurts, it hurts, it hurts.
- Children are not resilient. Children are fragile.
- I want adults in society to know that divorce tears children apart. It destroys the fabric of who they are. It permeates every aspect of their lives.
- Get over your selfishness and learn to suffer with each other.

Families cut in half

There's a reason why the word "parents" is mainly used in the plural. Each parent is and remains just a part of the whole. A child needs the space between father and mother to unfold and find himself as a man or herself as a woman.

Divorce is like nuclear fission. There is no longer just one pole, but two poles that mutually repel. All relationships in a divorced family change, and many are fractured even if the parents try to prevent a war, which often doesn't succeed even with the best of intentions.

Even the relationship to the siblings changes. They're no longer one solid community under the parents' roof. They may be torn away from each other and divided among the parents. Are they on opposite sides emotionally? Does an older child suddenly have to take over duties and responsibilities for younger children? Sometimes the siblings can stick together and form a close bond, but they are usually alone in their traumatized feelings.

> *When I was little, I turned off my emotions because it was all too much.* (ACD)

Everyone is forced to take sides: grandparents, siblings, friends and acquaintances. And the kids are torn between it all. They ping-pong between father and mother to maintain their attachment to both parents, and so as not to lose the basis of their own existence.

> *I want to please both of them. I don't want to upset either of them. I want both of them to be happy, so that neither of them will be sad because of me.*[221]

The child's main thought is: My father or my mother has left me. What did I do? Is it my fault? Children torture themselves with subconscious guilt feelings over a situation where they're the real victims.

From one moment to the next, they're alone with one parent, usually the mother. The father moves out. Often, divorce is accompanied by a financial breach between the parents now living apart, which has effects on the children. In Germany, 40% of single mothers receive unemployment compensation. The talk of "child poverty" makes it sound as if the children were independent and obscures the main cause: family breakup. Divorced parents must maintain two households, make support payments and may have to provide financial support for children from the new relationship. Single parents have to work all day, and often nobody's home to take care of the children but the screen.

Everyone involved is overloaded. The mother's pain fills the home like a smoking furnace, and there's no place for the child's pain. No one is there to help him come to terms with his wounded feelings. Even if he's already a teenager when the divorce happens, he still needs both parents help navigate the confusing time through adolescence into adulthood.

> *I was often sad, but I never, ever talked about my feelings or even understood my emotions. I'm not sure if it had anything to do with me becoming promiscuous starting in high school, constantly looking for love and affection.* (ACD)

The child does not want to take sides, but she is forced to, whether directly or indirectly. She has to accept her mother's or father's new partner, and deeply strives to, and she has to share the suffering and loneliness of the abandoned spouse.

Joint custody is also difficult: The parents share custody and support costs, and the child switches back and forth between homes every week or two. One way or another, the child can maintain the relationship with both parents, but at what cost? Pack up your things every two weeks, not be able to meet with your friends where you've been living, have to insert yourself into another family without complaining. Or in some broken American families, the child stays in a permanent home and the father or mother moves out every two weeks to make room for the other custodial parent.

> *We seem resilient because we don't voice our emotions or hurt feelings. Why? Because our parents will negate our feelings with their overpowering, apathetic, anti-my-marriage-to-your-dad/mom propaganda, brainwashing us into a parallel universe that screams, "I HAVE NO RIGHT TO FEEL DEVASTATED THAT MY PARENTS ARE DIVORCED," because my parents are happy about it, and only their feelings count!* (ACD)

The stepfamily

Often the spouse who leaves already has a new partner or immediately falls into a new relationship. He or she makes a break and starts a new life in a new place. A stepfamily arises. Maybe the new partner brings children from a divorce into the relationship, maybe both do, and maybe they end up having children together — like the punchline to the old joke, "Your kids and my kids are beating up our kids." Maybe they get married and the children have to participate in the wedding.

The term invented for this conglomeration of wounded people is "patchwork family." This evokes an image of a beautiful quilt made of many diverse squares of fabric. The word "step" brings up completely different associations, mainly the nasty stepmother in fairytales who is the embodiment of evil. Step relationships are family relationships without the bond of blood. They usually don't go so well.

Stepmothers and stepfathers generally have good intentions as they begin their new role as part of the rag rug that is now their family. Their love for their new spouse makes them willing to accept the spouse's children and to be the extra mother or extra father. The kids may be pampered with gifts. People do their best.

Just *one* mother and *one* father would be enough for the child. And just *one* home. Two houses *don't* make a home. The child's heart bleeds. He feels with every fiber of his existence that this stranger doesn't belong at his mother's or father's side. It hurts him to have to experience this "new happiness," where he's so unhappy and so is his abandoned parent.

> *Also, I'm a 39-year-old man, and I will never, ever be comfortable seeing my mom with another man or my dad with another woman.* (ACD)

Often both parents play tug-of-war with the child. The child wants to do right by both of them, because otherwise he will lose Mom or Dad. He's not allowed to show his suffering, but he does suffer and may act out. He feels he's actually just a drag on the new relationship.

> *The happiness of the current romantic couple always trumps the happiness of the child. Always.* (ACD)

Relationships in a step-family are always complex and tense. Nobody wanted it that way — not the new couple, not the abandoned partner, not the thrown-together children. The new family doesn't rest on a foundation of loyalty, effort, sacrifice, growth and a constant struggle for love, but on a pile of shards left from broken promises, disloyalty, selfishness, and self-actualization at any price. As parents, the man and woman in the new relationship did not have the ability to steer the family ship past the unavoidable rocks, so where will they get the strength, wisdom and selflessness to put the wounded members of the step-family on course?

> *To make matters worse, with all the re-marriage after divorce, there are step-siblings and half-siblings and children from the second and third spouses' first and second marriages, too — all of whom we are*

> *supposed to embrace as "family," even as our parents rejected the very notion and building block of family, namely, lifelong marriage. And then, just to make things extra fun: We have some parents who didn't remarry. So they are alone, lonely, and rely on us to fill that void — which we can't ever fill, because we can't be the ever-present spouse. And then we are made to feel guilty for not being more concerned/present/supportive of their dating/remarrying.* (ACD)

Everybody is wounded. Below the attempt to make everything right, there boils a sea of suffering, reproach, guilt feelings, wrath, jealousy, and contradictory, unresolved loyalties.

> *He idolizes the son from his first marriage and prefers him to me. He says nothing when early Sunday morning the boy turns his CD player up so high that our baby is torn from slumber, and then I have to hear that I don't want the boy here to begin with, that he's just a kid after all, and there's no please or thank you. The second family always plays second fiddle — the child's mother still adores my partner. This pain and anguish in her eyes make me feel guilty for having torn a family apart, the dream of being his number-one woman disappears more and more, now she's brought us the two ADHD boys, because she can't cope with them anymore, they need boundaries, but we have different ideas about that. I'm always the villain, they are shameless and disrespectful toward me, but their father always excuses them — his guilty conscience seems so strong that he doesn't even notice how his new family is drawing ever further away. No, I don't love his son. I count the hours until he's gone again. I'd have left a long time ago if I didn't love this man so much. No matter how you do it, it's always wrong somehow.*[222]

Exposing children's suffering is not to deny that there are also patchwork families that after many years have been able to relax with each other to some degree, celebrate family holidays together, and maybe even build heartfelt relationships. That succeeds only when the participants can forgive, ask for forgiveness, to get back on track in their own lives and acknowledge the suffering of those who had to make room for the new family. The first wife and her children are in the front seat. The second wife will always take the backseat. If she can't accept that she's number two, she may become greedy and want everything for herself when the will is settled. Destructively living out the unfulfillable wish to be the one and only is a distorted image of the yearning of the human heart for true, steadfast love.

For grownups, divorce is a crisis they'll get over sooner or later. Sometimes they're actually happier in their new life and can master the challenges of the second partnership. For the children, the divorce is not a one-time event they can gradually cope with and leave behind, but the landscape of their relationships and living conditions continuously changes. The parents' initial attempt at a soft separation can transform into a full-blown war. The parents get into new relationships, and maybe step siblings and half siblings have to find their place in the new family system, maybe several times. The grandparents take sides, and possibly let the grandchild go. Often the father withdraws from the relationship and from responsibility for the child. The child must continuously adapt to new social and emotional constellations at an age where he needs his energy and the support of his parents to mature into the independence of adulthood.

Science on the suffering of children of divorce

The first social researcher to break the taboo on discussing the suffering of divorce victims was the American psychologist Judith Wallerstein. Starting in the early 1970s, as the divorce rates began to accelerate, she did a long-term study of 130 victims of divorce, in which she questioned them at regular intervals over 25 years.[223]

The normally developed children were between 2½ and 6 years old when their parents separated permanently. The world became dangerous for them. The children felt lonely and abandoned and were left to outsiders or older siblings to be cared for. Twenty-five years later, they told of their sadness, helpless rage and the feeling of exposure. The trauma returned in nightmares for years.

In adolescence, the children had less resistance to drugs, alcohol, and premature sexual activity. A third of those surveyed received no education after high school, and 40% slid below their parents' socioeconomic status. A quarter of all the fathers cut off support after the child was 18, and contact dwindled over the years. Relationships with the step-parents and step-siblings were almost always difficult, and ping-ponging between the two households was exhausting. Children left behind took on emotional responsibility for the abandoned parent. Heavy shadows were cast over their own image of marrying and starting a family. Will I be betrayed or left in the lurch if I let someone get close to me or I ever get married? Will my children also have to go through that? These were their agonizing fears.

Judith Wallerstein stuck a finger in a wound — the notion that only the parents' needs count and that the children have to resign themselves as fast as possible. Courts, lawyers, and youth welfare officers assumed that the child will quickly find his footing again once the actual divorce crisis is over. This is often not the case with spouses who divorce, and almost never the case with children.

> In contrast to the grownups' experience, the child's pinnacle of suffering is not reached when the crisis is most acute and then progressively decline. On the contrary, the divorce is a cumulative experience for the child. Its effects increase as time goes on. At each stage of development, the consequences are experienced differently.... In the first 30 years of the child's life, the effects of the parents' divorce play over and over again.[224]

This does not mean that all children of divorce become sad, failing adults. But the parents' divorce throws a shadow over their existence.

Many studies confirm Wallerstein's results. In the 1990s, Paul Amato and Bruce Keith conducted a meta-analysis (a summary of existing research results) of 92 studies that compared the differences between children from intact families and those of divorced parents. All studies showed:

> The idea that parental divorce has only slight long-term consequences for the child's development contradicts the relevant research.[225]

How do we react when the basis of our existence collapses? Usually with anxiety and depression. And children do, too! The scientific studies show that children of divorce are more likely to feel sad, anxious, depressed or lonely. Their feelings of self-worth and self-confidence go down the sewer. They fear rejection and withdraw from friends and family. Or they may become belligerent and violent, and often self-destructive or suicidal.[226]

Children who steal, punch, stir up the class, make fun of others, spew sexist and racist curses, seldom come from families in which they feel secure and loved, where fathers convey trust and self-confidence, and where boundaries are set.

The trauma of divorce shows up in school performance. A depressed, anxious child who has had his existential foundations shaken can't learn as well. His energy is taken up by the internal and external chaos of his life. Children of divorce usually fall behind in school. They tend to skip school or even completely drop out, and they seldom get training or go to college after high school, because they just can't pull it off.

Mental disturbances show up in physical symptoms. The risk of ADHD (in boys), anorexia and bulimia (in girls), self-injury, asthma, and cancer is considerably higher than among children of intact families. One study has shown that their life expectancy decreases by four and a half years.[227]

What do people do when they can't survive their pain? They smoke, grab a bottle, drink until they black out, take drugs, develop eating disorders, and even harm themselves. Drug abuse is four times higher in children of divorced parents than among children from intact families.

Thus they get on a slippery slope and often fall into criminal activity, especially when the father is absent.[228]

A child of divorce yearns for love and care. He has experienced fractured love between parents, and often one of the spouses was unfaithful. No vision of marriage was conveyed to him. Many hours a day, private life, which should actually be a refuge, is flooded by TV with sexualized dramas of broken relationships. These are *role models* that make all kinds of destructive, unrestrained, selfish behaviors seem "normal."

Once the child has been sexualized at school, puberty opens up the opportunity to flee depression and forlornness through sexual relationships. Usually two poor, wounded teenagers, hungering for love, find themselves in bed — and are soon bitterly disappointed. Sex can become addictive, which will dull the pain in the short term, but will throw the person into even worse inner and outer chaos and do damage to their self-respect.

Early sexual relations are most common among children of single mothers. The earlier the father leaves the house, the greater the probability that the daughter will have sexual affairs and end up pregnant. Girls who grow up without a father have seven times the risk of getting pregnant when they are teenagers.[229]

Children of divorce greatly fear that their own marriage can also collapse. They might poorly trust their own partner and fear that their future marriage will be full of conflict, infidelity, or abuse, and that they will leave their spouse.

Those are justified fears. Children who have lived through their parents' divorce have double the chance of divorcing when they are married.

It should be stressed once again: We're talking about risks and statistical probabilities, not causal inevitabilities. All configurations are unique, as are the reactions of those affected. Sometimes there are helpful people outside the family, sometimes siblings help each other, sometimes the victim of divorce develops a firm resolve toward faithful, indissoluble marriage and parenthood. Some people find their way to God and receive help and healing.

Fathers, where are you?

Millions of children grow up without fathers. In most divorces, the father leaves and the mother remains alone with the children. Children of single mothers often have no consistent relationship with any man into adulthood, not only because almost all their caregivers are women, but also three-quarters of the teachers. The fact that in our educational system the boys are left behind by the girls, get worse grades, and leave school more often without graduating, has been shouted from the rooftops. The reason: Boys are disadvantaged in preschool and elementary school because they're no longer allowed to be boys.

Victims of the dismantling and elimination of fatherhood, children's chances in life are massively impeded. They suffer from:

- more poverty
- more behavioral problems
- more teenage pregnancies

- more sexual victimization
- more drug and alcohol abuse
- more obesity
- more dropping out of school
- more youth delinquency[230]

If one looks at the family background of risk groups, the image is even more drastic. The vast majority of these suffering children and teens come from fatherless families:

- 63% of youth suicide perpetrators
- 76% of school dropouts
- 74% of pregnant teenagers
- 90% of runaways and homeless children
- 70% of youths in government facilities
- 85% of youth inmates
- 75% of youths in drug rehabilitation centers
- 88% of maladjusted children and teenagers[231]

Behind these numbers is great misery that throws the affected children and teens off track in life, with unforeseeable consequences for future generations and for society as a whole. Before long, they'll reach the age of majority and be full citizens of this democracy. How responsibly will they behave? How capable and willing to achieve will they be? What kind of fathers and mothers will they become, if they even want to have children?

For girls, the father is no less important than for boys, but the relationship with the opposite sex is more complicated, because there is an erotic subcurrent that must not overflow the banks. The father is a little girl's first love and her first relationships with men will later be influenced by the dynamic of her relationship with her father. She recognizes her beauty through the eyes of her father. Her self-confidence also significantly depends on whether she admires her father and whether her strong, admired father acknowledges her, encourages her, and has confidence that she can do something remarkable. This confidence of the father is like a blank check for the future that the child will cash as time goes on. Does the father trust only the son or also the daughter to solve arithmetic problems, handle tools, win sports matches and take over responsibility? When the father says, "I'm proud of you," it's a free ticket to success.

No strong father uses verbal or physical power to browbeat or humiliate a child. A strong father sets limits, because he is able to set limits on himself. He demands performance and discipline because he himself is capable of performance and discipline. A strong father has a compassionate heart and respects his child's personality. He does not overpower the child, but explains firmly and patiently what he does and expects from the child. A strong father stands behind his wife and his wife behind him. He protects his family.

Two mothers or two fathers — no difference?

People have gotten so drunk on the spirit of technical progress that they think they can also subject human nature to their power: I decide whether I'm a man or a woman. I decide whether my unborn child can live, must die, or will be produced in a laboratory. I decide what is a marriage and what is a family. I am my own god.

At the beginning of the third millennium after Christ, courts and legislatures have decided that marriage is for *everyone*. Throughout Western history up to now, marriage was the bond between one man and one woman who were ready to give life to children and raise them to adulthood. *Marriage* — the foundation of the family — is, by law, now open to two men or two women, and also to those who were once a woman and are now a man or were once a man and are now a woman. This brings up the question of what actually constitutes life and existence — the linguistic and legal power of politicians and judges, or the reality of a flesh-and-blood body?

Since the Universal Declaration of Human Rights of 1948, a deep transformation has occurred, which Grégor Puppinck, director of the European Center for Law and Justice, describes in this way:

> While the human rights declared in 1948 expressed the natural rights of human beings, since then the spread of individualism has brought about unnatural rights, such as the right to euthanasia and abortion, which for their part have brought about

> new transhuman rights that lead to redefinition of the rights authorized by nature: a right to eugenics, a right to a child, or a right to a sex change. This development attests to a deep-seated change in the understanding of human dignity, which is increasingly reduced to the will of the individual or the spirit of human beings in opposition to their body and represents every denial of nature and the restrictedness of human existence as liberation and progress.[232]

Societies have basic values that hold them together if they are shared by the vast majority of the population. These values have their roots in each society's religion. For the uniquely successful European culture, this was Christianity. People knew that there was a just, merciful God over them who set limits to arbitrary capriciousness. But in the Western world, Christian faith is about to bow out due to an improper attachment to the zeitgeist. This decays the basic values that unified the society. Societies without religion have a short shelf life, because all that's left is individuals who battle over power and privilege. If these privileges are not provided, the cry is ear-piercing: *Human rights! Equality! Discrimination!* The Latin word *discrimen* means distinction. Distinctions are no longer allowed between one social form in which children come into being and that is good for children, and another social form that does not produce children and is bad for them.

And therefore, by court decision and legislative decree, even two men or two women can go to the justice of the peace and marry, be blessed by some Protestant pastors and maybe soon even by Catholic priests, if those prevail who want to transform the church from the last bastion of reason to a running dog of the latest social fad.

Whoever gets married claims to have a "right to a child." If a same-sex couple, who cannot naturally have children are refused, it is then "discrimination" and a violation of a supposed "human right" of *the adult*. But there is no such right to a child in any national constitution and in any international declaration of human rights. It exists only in the individualistic mentality of Western society.

To actually implement it, two men or two women have to take the path of artificial reproduction or adoption.

Two men have to buy egg cells and rent a uterus to have a child. Only one will be the biological father. The imbalance between the fathers is baked in the cake. Who will the child look like?

Two women have to buy semen. Either only one is the mother, or there is a main mother and a secondary mother. Or they practice a type of maternity sharing. One donates the eggs, and the other carries the child. Even here the family dynamic will be steeply slanted between the biological mother and her partner. Who will the child look like? The German minister of justice is proposing a bill to enter two mothers and no father in the birth certificate of the child, even though reason and reality would indicate that there has to be a father *somewhere*.

Another possibility is adoption. Based on the principle of the "camel's nose under the tent," adoption of children by same-sex domestic partners was legalized in Germany in three steps:

In 2005, stepchild adoption: One domestic partner can adopt the other's child.

In 2013, successive adoption: The *adopted* child of one partner can also be adopted by the other.

In 2017, the complete right to adoption: Same-sex partners can jointly adopt non-biological children.

Does anyone ask how things go for the child? A child grows up with a mother and father. The marriage goes bad and the parents split, which is traumatic for any child. The child is granted to the father, who enters a new partnership with a man, or to the mother, who takes up a new partnership with a woman. The child could somehow settle between the separated parents, but adoption by the new partner cuts off the relationship with the father or mother left behind. Because the child is dependent, he or she must accept the new partner as "Father 2" or "Mother 2."

Up to now, conditions have been strict for adoption. Generally, adoptive parents have to be married and able to "emotionally accept the child as their own and offer him or her proper conditions for socialization." Now the child can be adopted by two "fathers" or two "mothers." Not only has he lost his parents, but the archetype of father and mother has been intentionally taken away, and the child must grow up in a homosexual environment, which among men is generally promiscuous.[233]

How will the boy or girl feel when the new parental units come to school or when bringing friends home? How will the child deal with his feelings of sorrow, depression, forlornness, and loss of direction if everyone says, "It's completely normal! Everything's fine! It's all good!" even though nothing is normal and everything is disordered? How will the relationships with relatives be formed, with the many grandmothers and grandfathers the child now has, or with those relatives who reject this lifestyle and who have nothing to do with the child? What view of life does the child form — consciously or unconsciously? What can he trust, and what does he have to build on?

"No difference"?

There are many scientific investigations of how a child fares with same-sex "parents." The problem is that science's primary principle of striving for objective truth is increasingly eroded by political correctness. Money, academic position, and publicity await those who support the LGBTIQ movement's agenda. Those who openly oppose it with sound arguments get neither money nor rank nor publicity, but have to deal with defamation, and possibly lose their jobs in the process. This is why the media present so-called scientific studies that seem to prove that it is all the same to a child whether he grows up with his biological parents or whether a same-sex couple take on the role. Universities and the media trumpet, "No difference!" "No difference!"

In an expert opinion on the US Supreme Court's 2015 same-sex "marriage" decision, renowned professors Loren Marks, Mark Regnerus, and Paul Sullins stated:

> The alleged consensus that children suffer no disadvantage with same-sex parents is a product, not of objective scientific inquiry, but of intense politicization of research agendas in social science associations. ... Given the mounting evidence of harmful outcomes in children raised in households with same-sex parents, state laws restricting marriage to opposite-sex partners have a rational basis....[234]

Social scientist Mark Regnerus became known worldwide, because he had dared to refute the politically correct "no difference" notion based on solid scientific research (*New Family Structure Study*[235]). Attempts were made to put an end to his scientific work, but his results proved watertight against the flood of ideological criticism.

All disadvantages that children from broken heterosexual families have in comparison to those from intact families also occur with children who grow up in same-sex households — plus some additional ones:

Worse performance in school, mental disorders, depression and, as they get older,[236] greater tendency toward suicide, obesity, sexual victimization,[237] identification as gay or lesbian, same-sex sexual partners. As adults, they are more likely to be unmarried, unfaithful, and have sexually transmitted diseases. They more often receive welfare, are more likely to use alcohol, cigarettes and marijuana, spend more time in front of screens, and commit criminal offenses.

No difference? Really no difference?

What is the opinion of the affected, now grown children whom no one asked whether they wanted to be separated from their biological parents and raised by two same-sex partners?

Here is what Katy Faust, who grew up in a lesbian household after her parents' divorce, told the justices of the Supreme Court:

> We are made to know, and be known by both of our parents. When one is absent, that absence leaves a lifelong gaping wound. … Making policy that intentionally deprives children of their fundamental rights is something that we should not endorse, incentivize, or promote. … It moves us well beyond our "live and let live" philosophy into the land where our society promotes a family structure where children will *always* suffer loss.[238]

The victims of reckless assertion of adults' power at the expense of children risk their social and professional existence if they speak about their sufferings. Dawn Stefanowicz, who grew up with a promiscuous homosexual father, nonetheless did:

> As children, we are not allowed to express our disagreement, pain and confusion. Most adult children from gay households do not feel safe or free to publicly express their stories and

> life-long challenges; they fear losing professional licenses, not obtaining employment in their chosen field, being cut off from some family members or losing whatever relationship they have with their gay parent(s).[239]

Again Katy Faust, who tried in vain to soften the hearts of judges who presume to turn society's basic structure on its head:

> We are now normalizing a family structure in which the child from day to day and always is robbed of the influence of one of the two sexes and of a relationship with at least one natural parent. Our culture now tells children that they have no right to a natural family structure and their biological parents, but rather that children must give way to the sexual needs of adults.

What a charming expression: "rainbow family." It's supposed to be colorful and fun in families where children are deliberately withdrawn from at least one parent, in which he is prevented from growing up in "triangulation" between father and mother. In reality, however, these families are not colorful, but monochromatic, because the parents have just one sex. What a stroke of genius to use the symbol of the bond between God and humanity (Genesis 9:8–17) to legitimize a lifestyle that the biblical concept of marriage deeply opposes.

The yearning to procreate through children is anchored in every person's will to life, as is the need to love a child. When this is not possible, whether in a heterosexual or homosexual relationship, the rights of the dependent child are not to be sacrificed to the needs of the adults — out of respect for the child's dignity.

13.
The family — the human biotope

Youth must be treated with respect, because how can one know if the future will not be better than today?
Confucius

Society is at a crossroads: Continue to defame the nuclear family of father, mother, and children as passé, drive families with more than two children into poverty, produce more and more unhappy children with behavioral pathologies, and thus bring forth endless misery and unresolvable problems throughout society — or to take the other route and actually promote the conditions families need to survive and thrive. For this, politicians must finally break the stranglehold of ideologies that destroy the family and the lobbies that promote them. Seventy percent of children in Germany live with their married parents even in this day and age, and more than half of all marriages do *not* end in divorce. They must be strengthened since, according to the Universal Declaration of Human Rights, the family is "the natural and fundamental group unit of society and is entitled to protection by society and the State."

The family is prior to the state. The state depends on the family, not the other way around. Everybody has a father and a mother and owes his existence to the merging of the father's sperm with the mother's egg. The new human being is "bone of the bone" of his biological parents. Therefore, in every human heart there is a burning longing to be loved and cared for by one's parents and see in their unity the mirror image of one's own ontological existence. If the bond between the parents is broken, for whatever reason, it causes great suffering, first of all for the child, but also for the parents whose longing for lasting love is thwarted. This leads to a creeping disintegration of the whole of society. Therefore, the battle for the family is the most important battle of our time.

Concrete action for strengthening the family should include:

- In-depth marriage preparation courses
- Protection of a child's right to life starting at conception
- Family startup loans and support of home ownership with progressive payback reduction per child
- Progressive tax reduction per child down to a full tax exemption
- True freedom of choice between childcare at home and outside care of small children through equal financial support
- Adequate pension credit for years spent in childcare at home
- Effective support for reentry into the workforce after time off for child-care
- Family education rather than sex education in school

There is a country in Europe that has implemented many of these measures in recent years and can be considered a laboratory for their effectiveness — Hungary. The results show that pro-family measures can lead to spectacular changes in just a few years: The divorce rate in Hungary has fallen by almost a quarter, and the number of marriages has risen by nearly half. Abortions have decreased by a third, and the birth rate has gone from 1.23 children per woman to 1.5. This is not yet replacement level, but the ship is turning around.

Even if the politicians in most other European countries are yanking the material and social fundamentals away from families, no one can stop a man and a woman from forming their own family biotope. This requires a vision of life, determination, courage, and trust in the forces for good in life.

A stable, low-conflict marriage is the most important precondition for children to thrive. For this reason, it is crucial to choose a partner conscientiously. When someone says: "I love you," it can be smoke and mirrors. When someone says: "I want to marry you," then it starts to get interesting. Do we share the same vision of life? Do we share the most important values? How will we reconcile family and professional work? How many children do we want? How will we raise them? This book should provide plenty of material for clarifying the positions of potential spouses. It is worthwhile to talk it all through before tying the knot.

If the test is passed on both sides, and both fully and completely agree that "until death do us part," then the foundation is laid for building a solid family. A house of stone is desirable, but a house of love is what determines it all. It should be filled with children's laughter — with play and work, with caring and conversation, reconciliation after conflict, with friends of the children and parents, with music and parties, with unbreakable togetherness — in a word, with life. The parents' love for each other creates the conditions for children to grow and thrive. They see this love as obvious and indissoluble. Family bonds are strong and durable. If they tear, the children are disappointed to the core. Children deserve for them to be reliable.

Parents who want to raise healthy, capable, loving children will succeed in this only if they don't do what "everybody else" is doing and don't allow themselves to be led astray by government and media propaganda.

They will place the child at the center and focus their life's plan on ensuring that the child's basic needs are met.

They will not deliver the small child to collective care by strangers — how could they miss out on their infant's laughter, first step and first words? How could they rob themselves of the experience of their child's unconditional love and not give the child their own unconditional love as father and mother? How could they damage the trust of the child, possibly forever?

They will protect the innocence and purity of their children and not allow sexualization in preschool and elementary school to break their sense of shame and stunt their soul, so that the vision of marriage and family is darkened and the necessary character formation prevented.

They will not accept their child's gender identity as a girl or boy to be intentionally undermined.

In preschool and elementary school, they will defend their rights as parents to raise their child according to their own values.

They will make the richness of real life accessible to their children: discovery of nature, enthusiasm for sports and music, flourishing of their talents, support of their thirst for knowledge, manual skills, and real instead of virtual friendships.

They will teach them media competence, so that the media serve the tasks and life goals of the children, rather than becoming a flat, addictive substitute for an unsatisfied hunger for life.[240]

They will do everything in their power to protect their children's souls from being defiled by pornography or sexual abuse.

They will prepare their children for the cultural battles of our time, so that they are not helplessly exposed to ideological manipulation. This must never be indoctrination on the part of the parents, but education in clear thinking and involvement in open discussion appropriate to their age.

They are determined to grow from the conflicts in their marriage and not to divorce.

All this can only succeed if the children feel loved and secure and respected within in their parents' marriage bond.[241]

What a challenge! What used to be normal is considered a Herculean task today. A majority of the population would want to achieve these goals if the maelstrom of our era's cultural revolution didn't make it so difficult. It is crucial to create and expand networks for families who join forces to support each other in the proper conditions for existence and in practical everyday life.

We need mothers who build a warm nest for their children, and fathers who see protecting the family as their primary task. As the advertisements say, "You don't have to be perfect to be a perfect parent." And there is self-sacrificing love that grows with the children and eventually proves itself by letting them go. Hardly anything challenges the need to transform one's own character and behavior the way raising children does. The reward for the sacrifices parents make will be deep satisfaction of having brought up good and capable children, the love of the grandchildren, and the children's care for their parents when they need it in old age. Every healthy family is salt and light for the world. Every healthy young person is a building block for the future.

14.

Childrearing — making them strong for the future

Interview with Julia Calinescu[242]

Julia is an attractive woman of 37 and the mother of four children between 4 and 13 years old. She wants to give her children love and security, along with the values that will make them strong for the future. That is why she home-schools them.

She has been married to Dan for 14 years. They are Romanian by birth. Julia grew up in Toronto and studied at York University, majoring in French Studies and European Studies. She was hoping for a diplomatic career.

Dan's family emigrated from Romania in 1992, went to a refugee camp in Belgium, was sent back to Romania, and finally immigrated to Canada in 1994. He studied software engineering at the University of Toronto and is currently vice president of an international IT company.

Dan and Julia met in Toronto in 2006. They both came from difficult families and had very stressful childhoods. Julia's parents are divorced. Dan was an atheist, Julia was a non-practicing Catholic who nonetheless always held on to moral values. They dealt with their differing views very intensely, because both were earnestly searching for the truth. After three years, Dan converted and they were married in an Orthodox parish. During their marriage, their path of faith got more and more important. It was the writings of John Paul II that brought them back to the Catholic church.

Despite the difficult time they had growing up, they have a deeply fulfilling marriage and family and counsel others on domestic problems.

People react differently to crises and bad childhood experiences. Many are resilient and take life into their own hands, but others sink into depression and self-destructive behavior. What made the two of you resilient?

Julia: We went through a lot — problems in our original families, bankruptcy, assimilation to foreign cultures — and all that with four small children. We got through it all for just one reason: We always want to grow from what happens. If there's trauma, grow from the trauma! If there's a crisis, grow from the crisis! We have both been through so much that we simply had to work on ourselves. What pulled me through was my faith: Even when it looks bad at the moment, everything can take a turn for the good.

Why did you decide to homeschool your children?
Julia: I'm not the homeschooling mom type. I'm more of an activist, a go-getter. I studied to go into the diplomatic service. At the same time, I wanted to marry and have children. Since childhood, my number-one value in life was to provide my children with a happy, harmonious home. I wanted to make up for the bad I suffered.

When we moved back to Romania, we came to realize that there just weren't any good schools. There's still this vestige of communism. All that counts is that you're better than others and can look down on them. People said, "But you're taking your kids out of the system." And I would say, "Can you name any great Romanians who have come out of this system? Why should I expose my children to it?"

Homeschooling means that you and your husband take full responsibility for raising your children. What makes you so sure you're a good mother and teacher?
Julia: At the beginning, I wasn't sure at all. I remember the first year with Raissa, our oldest daughter. I was full of guilt feelings and doubts. At 23, I didn't feel prepared at all, and feared that everything I did would come out wrong. None of my friends or siblings had kids. I was clueless and wondered what I was even capable of. Then I told myself: Okay, maybe they'll be the dumbest kids in the world, but they'll know what love and security mean and which values count. Math, natural sciences, and history can be googled, but love and security and a happy family life can't be. I chose the worst-case scenario, which naturally didn't happen. Today Raissa explains the electromagnetic spectrum to me and the succession of Chinese dynasties.

As a young mother, there was nothing left but for me to rely on my instinct. I remember how important it was for me to keep things quiet in the house. Babies need soft, harmonious sounds. The first time I took Raissa to a shopping center, she was eight weeks old. I left in a hurry, because it was much too loud and chaotic for her.

When Dan and I argued, I always tried to keep my voice down. Naturally, she didn't understand anything, but I didn't want her to feel the disharmony.

The whole world told me I was crazy and over-protecting. I didn't know if they were right or not. I followed my own intuition.

I remember how I went to the forest with Raissa, carrying her on my body. I would show her the birds, drawing her attention to their chirping. I sang to her and danced with her and always asked myself: What is going on in her mind right now? How is she sensing the world? What can she see and understand?

I always had the conviction that the good things you sow will yield good fruit.

I wanted a home full of peace and joy, because I knew how much I had lacked that. My innocence, my freedom, my curiosity about the world were all so stifled and trampled on that I couldn't wait to see my child thrive and breathe.

Raissa is now 13. She has a very tender, sensitive heart. She doesn't like anything ugly, doesn't want to see aggression in movies, doesn't want to look at any violence or sex. We have never had a TV, but we watch movies with the kids. If something like that comes up, she looks away and protects Caterina, the little one, from it. She also doesn't want to read any books that confront her with evil. Her soul is attracted to the beautiful, the good and the peaceful. Naturally, I'm trying to prepare her for the real world as well.

And how?

Julia: I want them to have sensitive souls, but they need to be strong as well. It's all a matter of the right time. I watch very carefully what the children are ready for and what is suitable for their ages.

They know that there was communist persecution and that people were tortured, but I don't talk about the torture methods. They know about abortion. They have a vague sense, that somehow the woman is getting rid of the child, but they don't know the procedure of it. I would never have the heart to tell my daughter that women do that shortly before birth. I was already grown when I first heard about that, and I remember how much it shocked me. They will find out about all that someday, but I'll tell them these things by and by and won't overwhelm them. I see parents being so reckless with their kids, they just throw everything on them, they expose them to disturbing evils as if they are made of steel. Why instill fear and arouse the curiosity for horror in a child?

For example: I didn't want to tell my 3- and 4-year-old children that there are parents who divorce. I didn't even want them to have the notion that that might happen to Mom and Dad. That is a terrorizing thought for a child: I might wake up one morning and find that Mom or Dad are gone. When they were 7 or 8, I did tell them, some children's parents choose to not live together. Of course, that it is a selfish choice, because the child now has to be bounced around. The child no longer has a home. They were very shocked that parents would do that. At four they would have been horrified; they would have thought there is a danger of that happening to them. At 8 they were able to understand that adults are capable of making that decision, despite their kids.

Later we talked about the reasons people divorce. I didn't say anything about affairs, but I said this: The people think they have a right to happiness. You see that Mom and Dad sometimes have arguments and have to work things out. Look at the four of you. It makes you angry and sad when you're not allowed to play along or when somebody hurts you. If you could, you would probably say: I'm leaving now. I don't like you anymore because you're so mean. And you all have the same parents and the same values. But imagine two people who come from completely different families with completely different life experiences. Is it a challenge for us? Yes! Are we sometimes unhappy? Yes! Angry, sad, upset? Yes! But your brother or sister won't suddenly be gone. You need to work it out together. It's the same thing when grownups are married. If they fail, it's the children who suffer in the end.

So they became very aware of our friends who have gone through divorce, but they were always asking: Mommy, why would they do that? Why can't they just put up with their unhappiness for a time? With a 4-year-old,

I couldn't have had a conversation like that. They know two girls whose parents are divorced, and they are really hard to bear. My kids say: "Maybe, if dad had left us, we would just be the same."

You really have to be careful what you say to a child. We don't realize how fragile a child's heart is. Sometimes I don't know what's going on inside a child. The main thing is that I'm there and talk to them and hold them when they have to cope with something. When I was a child and was crying about something, it was: Quit crying! What's wrong with you?! That was so brutal. Children are very sensitive provided that they are not treated badly and if they are not thrown into all these horrible, grotesque cartoons and children's books full of darkness and occultism.

When is the right time to explain sexuality?

Julia: When I look back on my own childhood, I have a great need to protect their innocence. I keep stories about romantic love away from them. Romantic love is always about drama. They don't need that in childhood. It's been a big blessing that after Raissa we had two boys. They have a strong feeling for the relationship between brother and sister. They learn and play together, but we, the women in the family, have our own interests, as Dad and the boys do. Raissa is now 13.

To this day she looks at boys as brothers, these people, who are always on the go, loud and rambunctious. She has no attraction to "boys." She is still so innocent. The same with our boys. They are very sensitive to immodesty and don't like it when they see women dressed inappropriately.

I didn't know when the right time was to talk to them about sexuality. They actually never asked where babies come from, only how they come out. When I told them, they were surprised, but it didn't injure their sense of shame.

When we were in Rome one time, we met Christine Vollmer, a member of the Pontifical Council for the Family. She studied under Victor Frankl and is founder of an international project called *Alive to the World.* I asked her: When is the right time to tell children something about sexuality?

She answered:

"Children have a wild imagination. If you tell children, their imagination will go much beyond what you told them. They do not understand the physical, nor the emotional aspect of it, nor the spiritual dimension. If you just go with the physical facts, you are placing them in great danger. By the time puberty sets in, when the desire for the opposite sex arises, then it makes sense to tell them about sexuality."

That made sense to me. If you only explain the biological side to children, you separate the experience of body, soul and spirit. Sex is not one thing while love and family are another. Sex, love and family belong together.

Since I don't sense that any of my children are attracted to the opposite sex yet, I'm still waiting before I guide them into this issue of the relationship between man and wife.

Since I am not sensing that any of them have this kind of attraction toward the opposite sex, I am not yet introducing them to this central area of human experience. But we are talking about love, sacrifice, fidelity, long term happiness. They see Dan and me kiss and hold hands and hug, they see that, but it is always associated with marriage. We are teaching them the appropriate affection in different relationships, mother and child, siblings, Mom and Dad. The only reason Raissa wants to get married is because she wants to have children. One day soon she will ask and then she will be told about the beauty and joy of sexuality within marriage.

You said that the Romanian education system doesn't produce any great figures. Do you want your children to achieve greatness?

Julia: I want my children to recognize their purpose in life and to have the strength to fulfill it. To be capable of that, they must have a sharp awareness of right and wrong, and the strength to do good.

I seldom force my children to do something. I show them the consequences of their decisions. We know that children's prefrontal cortex isn't fully developed. They can't assess risks and consequences or plan long-term. The parents are their eyes into the future. The parents have life experience and can tell them: If you do this, there will be these consequences, and when you do that you'll have those consequences. We can see farther ahead than the children. We show them what fruit the correct action will bear, and what the price will be if they take the easy way out.

Parents always say: But they're just kids. Teenagers always do dumb stuff. Boys will be boys. I think to myself: Are you nuts? Do you really think that this person will ever be able to separate his teen years from the rest of his life? I had classmates who were "just teenagers" and are in prison now. How can you as a mother or father not make it clear to the child where a decision is leading? Children have a conscience very early. As early as 2, they know very precisely when they're doing something that's not right.

For example, it was very important to me that my children learn to love a baby. After each sibling was born, I showed the older children what a miracle was unfolding. Look what the baby can do now. Look how helpless the baby is and how dependent on our care. He doesn't know what you know, doesn't have what you have, but you can give it to him. Look how innocent he is — in his smile, you can see a piece of heaven. All my children love babies, even the boys. When they see a baby, they want to hold it. They all love Catarina, our youngest.

My children should know that they aren't the center of the universe. Sometimes the older kids feel I love the baby more than them, because she's always with me, because I'm so patient with her, and do everything she needs. Then I tell the older kids: You're also that way with her. You fight with each other, hurt each other, but you never do that with her. We all love her more because she's so tender and helpless. We give more to the one who needs more.

If you teach children to love babies, then they know what love is — they know the beauty of love and sacrifice.

If love is the most important thing you teach your kids, what is the second most important?

Julia: The second is freedom. God's greatest gift to us is freedom.

That makes us different from animals. We have free will. If all we had was life, we would be like animals. But we have free will, so we are more than animals. In order for us to be truly human, as God wants us to be, we have to be free. When we first we learn about freedom, we learn to say no to things. Our strength is more important than the candy. They learn that saying no is not depriving us, rather we are gaining strength.

I hear people tell me: Just wait until they're teenagers! Hormones are hormones! And I say to them: Since my children were 3 or 4 years old, they have learned that they have a free will and can do without things they would like to have. Once they have practiced saying "no" for ten years, their hormones will not have the same power over them than without this preparation.

Do your children say "no" to you?
Julia (laughing): Of course, they do. Discipline is important. But number one is: There must be joy in the family. We're here to take joy in one another. We do sports together, climb trees, play soccer, go swimming, go on outings and trips. When it's time to clean, I put on happy Latino music. We all clean together, and have fun doing it — at least most of the time. I'd say that at our house it's 80% joy. Learning, playing, eating and working together.

But there are things that have to be done, whether they're fun now or not, and they're not negotiable. I'm pretty tough, and so is Dan. I'm the mother and Dan's the father. My kids know that look from me, and they know there's no way out then. I tell them: If you start to haggle with me, you'll have to do it anyway, and you'll haggle yourself right into trouble. When it's time to clean, it's time to clean. If they're not done with their schoolwork, then they have to do their chores. I decide what's on the table. If they say: I don't like that, then I tell them: I didn't ask. There's one boss here, and it's not you. I do what I can to give them healthy nutrition that they like to eat, but I can't satisfy every one of my children's cravings all the time.

Normally, my children seldom hear "no." I try to prevent confrontation. If they want candy, I say, "Okay, tomorrow after lunch." If they want to play outside, I say, "Okay, after you finish this or that." This way they learn what takes priority. I don't say: No candy! No playtime! Everything has its time. If we hear "no," we shut ourselves off inside and fixate on it. I want to avoid that.

For example: Dominic wants to wear his boots in the summer. I say, "Sure, you can put your boots on when the snow comes. Then we'll build a snowman and go sledding." He imagines all that and completely forgets he wanted to put his boots on. Or Castian, who is the most headstrong of all. I say, "We're leaving in five minutes." He says in a hundred thousand minutes. I say, "Okay, I'll count: 60 thousand, 70 thousand, 80 thousand, 100 thousand." He was happy to get his hundred thousand.

What role does Dad play in your family?

Julia: While Mom is tending to babies, there is someone who tends to Mom. That is a beautiful thing for the couple. Often marriages go down in the first year because the husband identifies with the child: The kids get something I don't get. He should be saying, My wife gives so much to the children. I need to give so much to her. I think the role of the father in the first year is to be a giver, just like the mom becomes a giver.

The older the kids get, the more important the father becomes. When Dan comes home, there's always a big hello. Then I can punch out.

Besides the daily playtime with the kids, Dan takes one of the kids out at least once a month, and the two talk about everything that's on the child's mind. The child has Dad all to himself. There are things they'll talk to him about that they won't tell me.

The father's world of feelings is different. A woman usually holds her baby facing toward her, while the man holds the baby's face to the world. The mother's job is to protect the child, and the father's is to show him the world. A sick child will always need the mother, while the father has a playfulness that most women don't have. Children need time to talk and play with both parents.

What about friends outside the family?

Julia: That's not so simple. My children were at summer camp, and when they came back, they said, "You wouldn't believe how crude the kids are. They always want to be better than the others — that's the only thing that counts. They're always thinking up something their parents are never supposed to find out. The priest explained the Our Father to us and asked, 'Who goes to their father when they have a problem?' Out of the 80 kids, no one but us raised their hand. Then he asked, 'Who goes to their mother?' About 10 answered." Raissa says, "I don't know how we'd live if we didn't have you and Dad to talk to."

Our children trust us. One night at 11 o'clock Raissa came to us crying and said, "Mom, I'm so sad." I asked her why. She said, "Because so many people are suffering, there is just so much pain." I said, "That is true and I am happy that you are aware of it, but you know, you have so many gifts and talents, that you can make life more joyful around you. And if you make life more joyful around you, these people will make life more joyful with those around them, and if you do your part, and I do my part, and Daddy does his part, there will be less suffering."

The next morning, she said: "Thank you, Mommy, for saying that to me last night. I want to do my part." Children need to know that they are heard and listened to. We can't make the suffering go away. But we can be there and listen.

Do you worry about the time when your first child leaves the house?
Julia: No, I can't wait! Honestly, I can't wait for them to be out in the world. There are so many things I want to do. I already work on my plans. I want to build up a cultural center and teach people to make their dreams come true. And I can't wait to see each of them go out and fulfill their missions. I am so excited to see Raissa running her English club at the local library branch. She teaches young children conversational English through inspiring and uplifting stories.

Do you think your children will be equipped to encounter all the evil and temptations?
Julia: Right now, they are not equipped, we still have five or six more years until they will be equipped. I am very trusting. We have invested so much in them, more than enough to deal with the world. Every day we have one hour of theology lesson where I take our faith to illustrate how politics work, how family works and what the Church is all about. I always try to make them understand that there is something greater than pleasure. What has God prepared us for?

They don't know all the horrors of the world, but they understand very well how evil operates and how God operates. When they see evil, they won't be overwhelmed but will know how to stand up to it and do good.

Thank you for the conversation, Julia.

Conclusion
Last but not least

Dear readers,

My warmest thanks for having read this book. It is not easy to expose oneself to the contradiction between reality and the yearnings of the heart, and at the same time perhaps recognize the things where you failed and the things where someone failed you.

It is not going well for a large portion of our children and youth, as the research results on the initial pages of this book show. If a desire has arisen in you to improve the lives of children, then it was worth my having written the book and your having read it. Children need the message: *How wonderful it is that you exist. I want your wellbeing. I am ready to sacrifice for that.* The "yes" that we give to a child is at the same time a healing affirmation to ourselves.

The world we live in — the one children are born into — has smashed to smithereens and exposed the arbitrariness of human decisions. What belongs together has been pulled apart: body from soul, man from woman, sexuality from fertility, procreation from sexuality, the child from its biological parents. Isn't it time to put what belongs together back together? Body and soul, man and woman, sexuality and fertility, parents and child?

The break that caused all the other collapses is the great falling away from God. He could actually exist — the creator of heaven and earth, of each individual person, a merciful God with the best intentions toward people, you and me. The constant hum of God is in the air wherever people are.

Haven't we tried long enough to take everything into our own hands? Hasn't it shown in large ways and in our own small lives, that our understanding is not expansive enough, our horizon not broad enough, our will not selfless enough, our heart not compassionate enough to find solutions to the problems that we have subjected ourselves to?

If we didn't know it before, a tiny virus in 2020 brought us to the limits of our arrogance. It is as if we have rediscovered that we are mortal humans, who have thrown everything precious to us onto the scale — democracy, human rights, freedom of religion, the economic existence of millions of citizens — with unforeseeable consequences.

Suddenly, completely unexpected, from one day to the next, fathers, mothers and children were at home. The whole world was forced to work at home and school at home. Depending on the external and internal relationships, for many parents and children it was a nearly unbearable stress load, and for others a joyful new discovery of family life and a chance for fathers, mothers, and children to reorder the way they use their time. For many who live alone or were shut-ins in a nursing home, the ghost of loneliness became their only companion.

Will we learn from this? Will we recognize the sign of the times? Will we be ready to integrate our lives back into God's proper order? Do we hear Jesus knocking on the door, He who wishes to dine with us, he with us and we with Him (Revelation 3:20)?

I'm aware that it's inopportune to talk about faith. But I have nothing else to say to you if you ask me about the hope that fills me.

> "The rain fell, and the floods came, and the winds blew and beat upon that house, but it did not fall, because it had been founded on the rock." (Matthew 7:25).

Everyone has the choice to keep trying, to build on earthly stability, or to take a great leap of faith and build his life on God's commandments and promises. There is a God, He is love, and he created us out of love. He became flesh, shared the life of the people, was crucified and rose from the dead.

For anyone who believes that, there is no first-class ticket through life and they are subject to unpredictable suffering as anyone else is. But they live with the unshakable hope in Jesus Christ and the repeated flash of a bolt of knowledge: God knows me, God leads me, God surprises me with his mercy.

Gabriele Kuby, July 2020

Endnotes

Afflicted in body and soul

1 DAK Kinder- und Jugendreport 2018. https://www.dak.de/dak/download/kinder—und-jugendreport-2104098.pdf
2 Wolfgang Greiner, Kinder-und Jugendreport der DAK 2018, Schwerpunkt: Familiengesundheit, Folienvortrag, https://www.dak.de/dak/download/folienvortrag-greiner-2104096.pdf
3 https://www.kindergesundheit-info.de/fuer-fachkraefte/grundlagen/daten-und-fakten/kiggs-studie/
4 https://www.bundesaerztekammer.de/fileadmin/user_upload/downloads/04PraeventionstagungLeidl.pdf
5 DAK Kinder- und Jugendreport 2019. https://www.dak.de/dak/download/dak-kinder—und-jugendreport-2019-2168336.pdf
6 Heilmittelbericht des Wissenschaftlichen Instituts der AOK. https://www.aerzteblatt.de/nachrichten/99917/Mehr-Entwicklungsstoerungen-bei-Schulanfaengern
7 Heilmittelbericht des Wissenschaftlichen Instituts der AOK. https://www.aerzteblatt.de/nachrichten/99917/Mehr-Entwicklungsstoerungen-bei-Schulanfaengern
8 https://www.dak.de/dak/download/ergebnisbericht-2090980.pdf
9 Andreas Strom, *Beiträge zur Gesundheitsökonomie und Versorgungsforschung* (Band 23), Bielefeld & Hamburg 2018, Kinder- und Jugendreport der DAK 2018.

Introduction

10 https://www.bundesaerztekammer.de/fileadmin/user_upload/downloads/04PraeventionstagungLeidl.pdf
11 *March of the Penguins,* a film by Luc Jacquet, Oscar 2005.

Chapter 1

12 Joseph Ratzinger, Benedict XVI, *Values in a Time of Upheaval,* Ignatius Press, San Francisco, California, USA, 2006.

13 http://www.medizinfo.de/annasusanna/anatomie/zyklus.shtml.
14 Kathrin Löther, *Journalismus als Familienkiller* ("Journalism as a Family Killer"), in: *Message, Internationale Zeitschrift für Journalismus,* February 2010.

Chapter 2

15 Robert Spaemann, foreword to Gabriele Kuby, *The Global Sexual Revolution — Destruction of Freedom in the Name of Freedom*, LifeSite, Kettering, OH, 2015.
16 https://www.hli.org/resources/contraceptive-brief-condoms/.
17 https://www.welt.de/gesundheit/article196762017/Geschlechtskrankheit-Sprunghafter-Anstieg-der-Syphilis-Faelle-in-Deutschland-und-Europa.htm.
18 https://www.gesundheitsamt-bw.de/lga/DE/Themen/ Infektionskrankheiten/sexuell_uebertragbare/Seiten/HPV.aspx.
19 https://www.spiegel.de/gesundheit/sex/chlamydien-die-unterschaetzte-geschlechtskrankheit-a-1165250.html.
20 Summary here: https://www.hli.org/resources/contraceptive-brief-condoms/#_edn15.
21 Helen Singer-Kaplan, *The Real Truth about Women and AIDS*, Simon & Schuster, New York 1987.
22 https://www.hli.org/resources/the-difference-one-racist-made-margaret-sangers-world/.
23 *Overview*: https://www.hli.org/resources/negative-effects-of-the-pill/
Cancer: Fact sheet of the National Cancer Institute of 01.31.2017: https://www.cancer.gov/about-cancer/causes-prevention/risk/hormones/oral-contraceptives-fact-sheet.
https://www.lifesitenews.com/news/using-contraception-increases-breast-cancer-by-50-new-study-finds
Glaucoma: American Association for Cancer Research (AACR):
https://abcnews.go.com/blogs/health/2013/11/18/birth-control-pills-may-double-glaucoma-risk/
Heart disease:
https://www.goredforwomen.org/en/know-your-risk/risk-factors/birth-control-and-heart-disease
https://www.lifesitenews.com/news/new-contraceptives-raise-risk-of-blood-clots-by-50-to-80-percent-british-st
Embolism, stroke, high blood pressure: https://www.lifesitenews.com/news/new-contraceptives-raise-risk-of-blood-clots-by-50-to-80-percent-british-st
Reduction in fertility:
https://www.timeslive.co.za/sunday-times/lifestyle/2014-07-02-oral-contraceptive-use-could-diminish-fertility-study/

https://www.lifesitenews.com/news/contraceptive-pill-may-damage-womens-fertility-study.

24 https://www.cancer.gov/about-cancer/causes-prevention/risk/hormones/oral-contraceptives-fact-sheet.

25 Lionel Tiger, *The Decline of Males,* Golden Books, New York 1999.

26 Janet Smith, *Contraception: Cracking the Myth,* CD, Lighthouse Catholic Media.

27 https://royalsocietypublishing.org/doi/abs/10.1098/rspb.1995.0087.

28 Frontiers in Neuroscience, 02.11.2019: https://www.frontiersin.org/articles/10.3389/fnins.2018.01041/full.

29 J. D. Unwin, *Sex and Culture,* Oxford University Press, Oxford 1934.

30 Pope John Paul II made it his life's mission to clarify the truth of *Humanae Vitae* with many instructions, such as his encyclicals *Veritatis Splendor* and *Familiaris Consortio.* With his *Theology of the Body,* he left the Church a treasure that his biographer George Weigel called his "time bomb that will change all of theology."

31 Josef Rötzer, *Natürliche Empfängnisregelung. Die sympto-thermale Methode, der partnerschaftliche Weg,* Herder Verlag, München 2013. Extensive literature and advice are available here: Institut für Natürliche Empfängnisregelung, INER: https://iner.org.

Chapter 3

32 Help with unwanted pregnancy: Sundays for Life: https://sundaysforlife.org/de/hilfe/beratungsstelle/de
Tausend plus: https://www.1000plus.net

33 https://www.focus.de/familie/100-000-fehlen-experte-sicher-in-deutschland-treiben-viel-mehr-frauen-ab-als-die-statistik-zeigt_id_6582349.html

34 Manfred Spieker, *Der Verleugnete Rechtsstaat — Anmerkungen zur Kultur des Todes in Europa*, Ferdinand Schönigh Verlag, Paderborn 2011, 2nd edition, p. 17 et seq.

35 https://www.zeit.de/news/2019-02/27/zahl-der-abtreibungen-minimal-gesunken-190227-99-158013
In absolute numbers, most abortions are done in the most populous federal state, North Rhine-Westphalia, at about 22,000. Where births are concerned, it's a different picture. The latest available statistics are from 2017. The highest numbers come from Berlin and Bremen, where 230 and 208 abortions were performed for each 1,000 births. In Bavaria and Baden-Württemberg, on the other hand, there were only 88 and 96 abortions per 1,000 births, respectively.

36 https://www.destatis.de/DE/Themen/Gesellschaft-Umwelt/Gesundheit/

Schwangerschaftsabbrueche/Publikationen/Downloads-Schwangerschaftsabbrueche/schwangerschaftsabbrueche-2120300187004.pdf?__blob=publicationFile.

37 http://curia.europa.eu/juris/document/document.jsf?docid=111402&doclang=DE.

38 European Court of Human Rights on October 18, 2011, in the case of Brüstle versus Greenpeace e.V.

39 This representation of the development of the embryo is based on: Michael Kiworr, *Neun Monate bis zur Geburt,* Bernardus Verlag, Mainz 2016.

40 All Parliamentary Pro-Life Group,House of Commons, UK, *Foetal Sentience & Pain,* March 2020. https://lordalton.files.wordpress.com/2020/03/2020-pro-life-appg-report-on-foetal-pain.pdf.

41 Manfred Spieker, *Der verleugnete Rechtsstaat — Anmerkungen zur Kultur des Todes in Europa,* a. a. O.

42 Judgment of the Federal Constitutional Court of May 28, 1993, 2 BvF 2/90 and 4, 5/92, http://www.servat.unibe.ch/dfr/bv088203.html.

43 Rainer Beckmann, "'Selbstbestimmung' über das Leben Ungeborener", a. a. O., p. 67.

44 Stefan Rehder, "Entschuldigt Euch!," in: *Die Tagespost,* January 15, 2020. https://www.die-tagespost.de/leben/glauben-wissen/Entschuldigt-Euch;art4886,204637

45 Continuing coverage at www.lifesitenews.com.

46 Current reporting at LifeSiteNews.com.

47 Ärzte für das Leben, Post Abortion Syndrom: https://aerzte-fuer-das-leben.de/fachinformationen/schwangerschaftsabbruch-abtreibung/post-abortion-syndrom-pas/.

48 Manfred M. Müller, *Fünf Schritte-Die Heilung der Abtreibungswunden,* Immaculata Verlag, Salzburg 2015, 3rd edition.

Chapter 4

49 https://www.spiegel.de/gesundheit/schwangerschaft/kuenstliche-befruchtung-2015-wurden-mehr-als-20-000-babys-geboren-a-1183272.html.

50 Dietrich von Hildebrand, *Sittliche Grundhaltungen,* Verlag Josef Habbel, Regensburg 1969, p. 20.

51 Since 2018, however, sperm donor anonymity has not been guaranteed in Germany. A nationwide sperm donor registry has been set up, which saves 110 years of personal data on sperm donors and recipients. Children created after 2018 have access to it once they reach age 16. Children born before that have been able demand that the reproduction clinic release the data since 2019. In January 2019, the German Federal High Court decided that the re-

production clinic has an obligation to inform offspring conceived using anonymous sperm donation. The judgment says that the child's right to know his parentage outweighs the father's right to anonymity and medical confidentiality (XII ZR 71/18).

52 The film *The Swedish Theory of Love* shows the misery and loneliness from the loss of love: https://www.youtube.com/watch?v=CfyKYeaZcIM.

53 https://www.welt.de/wissenschaft/article150528268/Ein-Designerbaby-nach-Bauplan-fuer-140-000-Dollar.html.

54 https://www.familienplanung.de/kinderwunsch/behandlung/chancen-und-risiken/schattenseiten-behandlung/.

55 https://www.familienplanung.de/kinderwunsch/seelische-belastungen/partnerschaft/.

56 https://www.ncbi.nlm.nih.gov/pmc/articles/PMC3650450/#FN01.

57 https://www.aerzteblatt.de/archiv/134267/Praenatest-Kleiner-Test-grosse-Wirkung.

58 Karlton Terry, *Implantation Journey — The Original Human Myth:* http://www.ippe.info/publications/articles/implantation_journey.html.

59 Barbara Luke et al., "Risk of severe maternal morbidity by maternal fertility status: a US study in 8 states," in: *American Journal of Obstetrics & Gynecology*, February 2019: https://www.ajog.org/article/S0002-9378(18)30894-9/fulltext

60 Yue-hong Lu, Ning Wang, Fan Jin, "Long-term follow-up of children conceived through assisted reproductive technology," in: *Journal of Zhejiang University Science B,* May 2013: https://www.ncbi.nlm.nih.gov/pmc/articles/PMC3650450/#FN01

61 Theo A. Meister et al., "Association of Assisted Reproductive Technologies With Arterial Hypertension During Adolescence," in: *Journal of the American College of Cardiology,* September 2018: http://www.onlin jacc.org/content/72/11/1267?download=true

62 Ehrentraud Hömberg, "Fertilitastherapie: Produziert sie psychisch gestörte Kinder?," in: *Medscape*, 22.01.2020: https://deutsch.medscape.com/artikel/4902394

63 https://www.dimdi.de/dynamic/de/weitere-fachdienste/samenspender-register/.

64 Children born after July 2028 will be able to view the sperm donor register when they are 16, which means not before 2034.

65 G. Hüther und I. Krens, *Das Geheimnis der ersten neun Monate — Unsere frühesten Prägungen*, Beltz-Verlag, Weinheim 2011, 4th edition.

66 P. Fedor-Freybergh: "Die Schwangerschaft als erste ökologische Situation des Menschen," in: L. Janus et al., *Seelisches Erleben vor und während der Geburt*, LinguaMed, Neu-Isenburg 1997, p. 15.

67 https://www.haufe.de/recht/familien-erbrecht/leihmutterschaft-vom-menschenrechtsgerichtshof-ausgehebelt_220_395494.html.

68 https://www.welt.de/vermischtes/article207998275/Leihmutterschaft-und-Corona-Mehr-als-100-Babys-sitzen-in-der-Ukraine-fest.html.

69 The author is in possession of a photocopied contract between a surrogate motherhood agency, the "potential parents," and the surrogate mother in Ukrainian and English.

70 "Secret diary of a surrogate mother," in: *The Guradian*, 4/27/2013. https://www.theguardian.com/lifeandstyle/2013/apr/27/secret-diary-of-a-surrogate-mother

71 https://www.kath.net/news/60177

Chapter 5

72 https://lifecodexx.com/praenatest-jetzt-in-deutschland-oesterreich-liechtenstein-und-in-der-schweiz-verfuegbar/

73 https://standpointmag.co.uk/issues/may-2016/text-may-2016-catherine-macmillan-saying-yes-to-sara/Also see: *Dear Future Mum:* https://www.youtube.com/watch?v=Ju–q4OnBtNU

74 Louann Brizendine, The Female Brain, New York 2007, Morgan Road Books.

75 Hanne K. Götze, Kinder brauchen Mütter. Die Risiken der Krippenbetreuung — Was Kinder wirklich stark macht, Ares Verlag, Graz 2011, p. 49.

76 Cf. Christa Meves, *Geheimnis Gehirn. Warum Kollektiverziehung und andere Unnatürlichkeiten für Kleinkinder schädlich sind,* Resch-Verlag, Gräfelfing 2005.

Chapter 6

77 UNICEF press release: https://www.unicef.org/press-releases/sweden-norway-iceland-and-estonia-rank-highest-family-friendly-policies-oecd-and-eu

78 Press release of the German Federal Ministry for Families, Senior Women and Youth (BMFSFJ), September 2, 2019.

79 Recommended books on daycare: Hanne K. Götze, *Kinder brauchen Mütter, Die Risiken der Krippenbetreuung — Was Kinder wirklich stark macht,* Ares-Verlag, Graz 2011; Christa Meves, *Geheimnis Gehirn, Warum Kollektiverziehung und andere Unnatürlichkeiten für Kleinkinder schädlich sind,* Resch-Verlag, Gräfelfing 2005; Nicole Strüber, *Die erste Bindung, Wie Eltern die Entwicklung des kindlichen Gehirns prägen,* Klett-Cotta, Stuttgart 2016; Serge Sulz, — *Schadet die Kinderkrippe meinem Kind? Worauf Eltern und ErzieherInnen achten und was sie tun können,* CIP Medien, Munich 2018; — *Risiken der Betreuung in Kinderkrippen, Neue empirische Studien,* CIP Medien, Munich 2018; — *Kinderkrippe als toxischer Dauerstress für Kinder.*

Lecture at the Psychosomatic Congress, Eichstätt 2018: http://dgkjf.de/wp content/uploads/Sulz-Kinderkrippe-als-toxischer-Dauerstress-Psychosomatik-Kongress-2018_2.pdf

80 https://www.berlininstitut.org/newsletter/anzeige.html?tx_news_pi1%5Bnews%5D=730&tx_news_pi1%5Bcontroller%5D=News&tx_news_pi1%5Baction%5D=detail&cHash=444aed4e79d207d7424e91aee9ea9d3bö

81 Rainer Böhm, „Die dunkle Seite der Kindheit", in: *Frankfurter Allgemeine Zeitung,* April 4, 2012.

82 https://www.faz.net/aktuell/feuilleton/debatten/demographie-unser-verschwinden-wuerde-gar-nicht-auffallen-1330352-p4.html.

83 At least since 1992, child care time has been considered in statutory pension insurance. Since 2019, the pension share for children born after 1992 has been about €100 per child per month, and €82 for children born earlier.

84 https://www.i-daf.org/aktuelles/aktuelles-einzelansicht/archiv/2018/01/22/artikel/kinder-und-armut-was-macht-familien-arm.html.

85 https://www.bmfsfj.de/bmfsfj/themen/familie/kinderbetreuung/mehr-qualitaet-in-der-fruehen-bildung/das-gute-kita-gesetz/mehr-qualitaet-und-weniger-gebuehren/das-gute-kita-gesetz—fuer-gute-kitas-bundesweit/128214.

86 Serge Sulz, *Risiken der Betreuung in Kinderkrippen,* p. 10.

87 Quoted in Sulz, Eichstätt 2018.

88 Sulz, *Risiken der Betreuung in Kinderkrippen,* p. 14.

89 NICHD long-term study: D. L. Vandell, J. Belsky et al., "Do Effects of Early Child Care Extend to Age 15 Years?" Results from the NICHD Study of Early Child Care and Youth Development," in: *Child Development,* 8 (3), 737–56.

90 Quebec study. Baker M., Gruber J., Milligan K. (2008), "Universal Child Care, Maternal Labor Supply and Family Well-Being," in: *Journal of Political Economy,* 116, 709–45.

91 Karl Brisch und Theodor Hellbrügge, *Bindung, Angst und Aggression: Theorie, Therapie und Prävention,* Klett-Cotta, Stuttgart 2010.

92 Sulz, Eichstätt 2018.

93 DAK Gesundheitsreport 2019.

94 https://www.aerzteblatt.de/nachrichten/99917/Mehr-Entwicklungsstoerungen-bei-Schulanfaengernhttps:/.

95 https://www.tagesspiegel.de/gesellschaft/panorama/heilmittelbericht-der-aok-jeder-vierte-erstklaessler-erhaelt-sprachtherapie/14992804.html.

96 Manfred Spreng, *Es trifft Frauen und Kinder zuerst, Wie der Genderismus krank machen kann!,* Logos Editions, Ansbach 2016.

97 Sulz, Eichstätt 2018.

98 Wiener Krippenstudie, 2007–2012. https://bildungswissenschaft.univie.ac.at/psychoanalytische-paedagogik/forschung/abgeschlossene-projekte/wiener-kinderkrippen-studie-wiki-die-eingewoehnungsphase-von-kleinkindern-in-kinderkrippen/.

99 Alisa Samuel and Kurt Wedlich, "Zuwendung und ihre Konsequenz für Kinder in Kinderkrippen — Ergebnisse einer psychologischen Pilotstudie zur pädagogischen Grundsituation," in: Serge Sulz (Projektleiter), *Risiken der Betreuung in Kinderkrippen, Neue empirische Studien,* CIP-Medien, Munich 2018.

100 Serge Sulz, Eichstätt 2018.

101 Torsten Kunz, "Gesundheit in Kindertageseinrichtungen," in: Martin R. Textor and Antje Bostelmann (Ed.), *Das Kita-Handbuch*: https://kindergartenpaedagogik.de/fachartikel/ausbildung-studium-beruf/berufsbild-arbeitssituation/1556.

102 Mads Kamper-Jørgensen et al: "Population-Based Study of the Impact of Childcare Attendance on Hospitalizations for Acute Respiratory Infections," in: *Pediatrics,* Vol. 118 No. 4, 2006, 1439–46.

103 Daycare signal of the dgkjf: http://dgkjf.de/wp-content/uploads/dgkfj-Kinderkrippen-Ampel-für-Rat-suchende-Eltern.pdf.

104 Sulz, Eichstätt 2018.

105 Sulz, Risiken der Betreuung in Kinderkrippen, 2018, p. 15.

106 Michael Hüter, „Kindheitsforscher warnt: Hört auf, eure Kinder in Kitas zu geben!," in: *Focus online,* 09.04.2020.

107 Christian Bachmann et al, "The cost of love: financial consequences of insecure attachment in antisocial youth," in: *Journal of Child Psychology and Psychiatry,* 1.10.2019.

108 2 BvR 2347/15.

Chapter 7

109 Quoted in Joseph Christoph Arnold, *Their Name is Today, Reclaiming childhood in a Hostile World,* Plough Publishing House, Walden, New York 2014, p. 16.

110 In 1950, Harvard sociologist David Riesman came out with the book *The Lonely Crowd,* and it became a bestseller. Riesman distinguishes between three types — people who are tradition-directed, inner-directed, or other-directed. The inner-directed person focuses on internal values, such as truth, beauty,and justice. His guiding morals are anchored in the conscience. The other-directed person focuses on the opinions and behavior of others — belonging and being accepted is his most important aspiration. He is guided by anxiety. Riesman could not yet have imagined the extent of mainstream dependence on digital media.

111 https://www.zeit.de/gesellschaft/familie/2019-08/kinderbetreuung-kita-kindergarten-einrichtung-erziehung-kleinkinder/seite-2.

112 http://www.kindergaerten-in-aktion.de/praxis-alltag-in-kindertageseinrichtungen/stress-und-entspannung/stressverhalten-bei-kindern-1.

113 https://www.watson.de/leben/meinung/563489785-kinder-unter-stress-erzieherin-warum-die-kindheit-mit-dem-besuch-der-kita-endet.

114 https://www.nestbau-familie.de/fakten/stress-fuer-kleine-kinder/stressfaktoren/.

115 Manfred Spreng, *Es trifft Frauen und Kinder zuerst,* Logos Editions, Ansbach 2015.

116 "No political force in Germany has worked so hard for the interests of pedophile men as the Green Party. In the mid-1980s, it temporarily operated almost as a parliamentary arm of the pedophilia movement." https://magazin.spiegel.de/EpubDelivery/spiegel/pdf/948655.

117 Christa Meves, *Manipulierte Maßlosigkeit,* Herder-Verlag, Munich 1971; *Wer Wind sät … Folgen der Entschämung und Jugendverführung,* Christiana-Verlag, Stein am Rhein, 1998; *Verführt. Manipuliert. Pervertiert,* Resch-Verlag, Gräfelfing, 2003.

118 Helmut Kentler, *Sexualerziehung,* Rowohlt Taschenbuch 1970.

119 https://www.uni-hannover.de/fileadmin/luh/content/webredaktion/universitaet/geschichte/helmut_kentler_und_die_universitaet_hannover.pdf.

120 https://dx.doi.org/10.18442/129.

121 https://de.wikipedia.org/wiki/Uwe_Sielert.

122 Frank Herrath, "Freundliche Begleitung. Wie man ein Pädagogikfeld bestellt. Beitrag zur Festschrift für Uwe Sielert," Renate-Berenike Schmidt, Elisabeth Tuider, Stefan Timmermanns, (Ed.), *Vielfalt wagen*, Berlin 2009.

123 https://www.isp-sexualpaedagogik.org/downloadfiles/Frank%20Herrath%20-%20Beitrag%20Festschrift%20Uwe%20Sielert%202009_1260308349.pdf.

124 Frank Herrath, Uwe Sielert, *Lisa & Jan, ein Aufklärungsbuch für Kinder und ihre Eltern, Bilder von Frank Ruprecht*, Beltz Verlag, Weinheim and Basel 1991.

125 See the collection of essays *Die missbrauchte Republik. Aufklärung über die Aufklärer,* Ed. Andreas Späth. Verlag Inspiration, Un Limited, London, Hamburg 2010. This also includes Gabriele Kuby "Sexualization of children and teenagers by the state."

126 https://www.kindergartenpaedagogik.de/fachartikel/bildungsbereiche-erziehungsfelder/geschlechtsbezogene-erziehung-sexualerziehung/1197.

127 The parents are acquaintances of the author.

128 This happened shortly before the coronavirus lockdown, so that the dispute over the sex education concept could not be continued right away.

129 https://www.spiegel.de/lebenundlernen/schule/koeln-kita-kuendigt-mutmasslichen-missbrauchsopfern-a-1254158.html.

130 https://de.wikipedia.org/wiki/Original_Play.

131 In a broadcast from the German TV network ARD, *Kontraste*, on October 24, 2019, parents report that their children experienced sexual violence during "original play." Also see: "Friedliches Spiel oder Türöffner für Übergriffe," in: *Der Spiegel,* October 25, 2019.

132 Cf. Michael Felten, *Die Inklusionsfalle. Wie eine gutgemeinte Idee unser Bildungssystem ruinier,* Gütersloher Verlagshaus 2007.
133 https://www.queerformat.de/wp-content/uploads/mat_kita_QF-Kita-Handreichung-2018.pdf, p. 19.
134 https://www.partizipation-und-bildung.de/pdf/Hansen_Knauer_Sturzenhecker_Kinderstube%20der%20Demokratie.pdf.
135 https://www.bertelsmann-stiftung.de/fileadmin/files/Projekte/Jungbewegt/Sommerakademie_2017/Anlage_7_Fachforum_III_Hansen_Wagner.pdf.
136 Lectures at the Congress for Children's rights in February 27, 2020: https://demofueralle.blog/2020/02/27/familie-am-abgrund-videos-der-symposiums-vortraege/.
137 http://www.bagljae.de/downloads/114_sicherung-der-rechte-von-kindern-in-kitas.pdf.
138 A great deal of material can be found at the site of the Bavarian State Institute for Early Education: https://www.ifp.bayern.de/index.php.
139 Huxley, Aldous, *"Ends and Means,"* Oxford University Press, 1946, p. 178.
140 Vgl. https://www.kindergartenfrei.org/index.php?id=3.
141 Mischel, Walter. *The Marshmallow Test: Mastering Self-Control.* United States: Little, Brown, 2014. https://lexikon.stangl.eu/3697/marshmallow-test/.

Chapter 8

142 *Shell Jugendstudie* 2019, Beltz-Verlag.
143 1 BvR 2019/16.
144 Ronald Berthold, "Mau und Frann," in: *Die Junge Freiheit,* May 22, 2020, p. 6.
145 Translator's note: In Germany, because most nouns, including job titles, are marked by grammatical gender, for a long time employers have been required to indicate explicitly on job postings that they are open to both male and female applicants. In the English-speaking world this is not necessary, because job titles are generally the same for both men and women, e.g. "programmer" versus German "Programmierer" (male) and "Programmiererin" (female).
146 Obianuju Ekechova, *Target Africa: Ideological Neocolonialism in the Twenty-First Century,* Ignatius Press, San Francisco 2018. Foreword to the Spanish edition of Gabriele Kuby in homolegens publishers, Madrid 2019.
147 Stefan Timmermanns, Elisabeth Tuider, Petra Bruns-Bachmann, Carola Koppermann, Mario Müller, *Sexualpädagogik der Vielfalt, Praxismethoden zu Identitäten, Beziehungen, Körper und Prävention für Schule und Jugendarbeit,* Juventa-Verlag, Weinheim and Munich 2008.
148 https://demofueralle.blog/eine-seite/.
149 https://www.bzga-whocc.de/fileadmin/user_upload/WHO_BZgA_Standards_deutsch.pdf.

150 For an analysis of the legal contradictions, see Silvia Behrendt, "Sexualpädagogik im Kontext der Schule. Über die Notwendigkeit zur Lösung einer Diskrepanz," in: *Schule & Recht*, No 1, year 2019.

151 Sigmund Freud: "We have seen from experience that ... that any such premature sexual activity impairs the educability of the child." (Gesammelte Werke, S. Fischer-Verlag, volume V, p. 136).

152 https://unesdoc.unesco.org/ark:/48223/pf0000260770 Gabriele Kuby, "Zugriff auf die Jugend. UN-Genderprogrammierung durch Sexualerziehung,“ in: *Die Junge Freiheit,* No. 51, December 14, 2018.

153 https://www.ippf.org/sites/default/files/ippf_framework_for_comprehensive_sexuality_education.pdf.

154 https://www.cdc.gov/std/stats17/adolescents.htm.

155 Pro Familia trains students as young as 15 years old as "peer educators" or "sexperts," who then hold sex education classes in school on their own. Germany's Federal Center for Health Education has instructions that say: Peer Education — a manual for practitioners, Best. No. 13300721. International network: Youth peer education Network (Y-Peer): www.youth-peer.org/web/guest/ypeer-toolkit.

156 Robert Rector and Kirk A. Johnson, *Teenage Sexual Abstinence and Academic Achievement*, October 27, 2015: http://www.heritage.org/Research/Reports/2005/10/Teenage-Sexual-Abstinence-and-Academic-Achievement.

157 Alexander Korte, "Wir erleben einen enormen Zulauf an Jugendlichen, die ihr Geschlecht wechseln wollen," interview in: *Der Spiegel*, July 26, 2019.

158 https://www.centralsexualhealth.org/media/8009/guidance-for-schools-transgender-variance.pdf.

159 https://usports.ca/uploads/hq/Media_Releases/Members_Info/2018-19/Press_Release_-_Transgender_Policy.pdf.

160 Lawrence S. Mayer, Paul R. McHugh, "Sexuality and Gender, Findings from the Biological, Psychological, and Social Sciences," in: The New Atlantis, No. 50, Fall 2016. National Transgender Discrimination Survey, Williams Institute, University of California, Los Angeles 2014.

161 https://www.acpeds.org/wordpress/wp-content/uploads/7.16.19-Surgeon-General-letter1963-v4.pdf.

162 https://www.theguardian.com/lifeandstyle/2017/feb/03/experience-i-regret-transitioning.

163 https://sexchangeregret.com.

164 https://www.change.org/p/save-6-year-old-boy-ja-d-y-from-chemical-castration.

165 https://www.youtube.com/watch?time_continue=81&v=3Ily46yZzsA.

166 *Only Adults? Good Practises in Legal Gender Recognition of Youth.* https://www.iglyo.com/wp-content/uploads/2019/11/IGLYO_v3-1.pdf. A report on that here: https://blogs.spectator.co.uk/2019/12/the-document-that-reveals-the-remarkable-tactics-of-trans-lobbyists/.

167 Cf. Tapio Puolimatka, Transideologie, Ruhland-Verlag, Bad Soden 2019, foreword by Gabriele Kuby.

Chapter 9

168 https://www.bundestag.de/dokumente/textarchiv/2013/45426229_kw26_pa_recht_kinderrechte-212880.

169 https://www.bundestag.de/dokumente/textarchiv/2016/kw04-pa-familie-402682.

170 BT-Drs. 17/10118, 17/11650, 17/13223.

171 Abschlussbericht der Bund-Länder-Arbeitsgruppe "Kinderrechte im Grundgesetz", October 14, 2019. https://www.bmjv.de/Shared Docs/Downloads/DE/News/PM/102519_Abschlussbericht_Kinderrechte.pdf?__blob=publicationFile&v=2.

172 Cf. Michael Tsokos und Saskia Guddat, *Deutschland misshandelt seine Kinder, Mehr als 200.000 Kinder werden pro Jahr Opfer von Gewalt durch Erwachsene*, Droemer-Verlag, Munich 2014.

173 https://de.statista.com/statistik/daten/studie/12982/umfrage/inobhutnahmen-minderjaehriger-durch-jugendaemter/.

174 https://www.faz.net/aktuell/gesellschaft/menschen/kindesinobhutnahmen-nach-der-geburt-getrennt-15806437.html.

175 Alliance Defending Freedom International has provided legal aid to the Wunderlich family: https://adfinternational.org/news/deutsche-homeschooler-erwagen-berufung-nach-entscheidung-des-europaischen-gerichtshofes-fur-mens chenrechte/.

176 Josef Kraus, Wie man eine Bildungsnation an die Wand fährt, Herbig-Verlag, Munich 2017.

177 Steven Bennett, Stolen Childhood, The Truth about Norway's children welfare system, Emira Press, 2019.

178 https://www.youtube.com/watch?v=ePDr1JKzJKY&fbclid=IwAR3lSMn5BK2CLZK8akNzL4x30rJigeNs6-aKqF39SBPlDO9DSH_uvrDK0cc.

179 Robert Clarke, "Norway's Bernavernet and The Future of Parental Rights," in: *The Public Discourse*, October 21, 2019. https://www.thepublicdiscourse.com/2019/10/57789/. In many cases, Alliance Defending Freedom International assists those affected in fighting for parental rights and freedom of religion.

180 https://www.supremecourt.uk/cases/docs/uksc-2015-0216-judgment.pdf.

181 In 1983, the Pontifical Council for the Family presented the *Charter of the Rights of the Family* to the public and to governments. http://www.vatican.va/roman_curia/pontifical_councils/family/documents/rc_pc_family_doc_19831022_family-rights_en.html

Chapter 10

182 Many figures given in this chapter come from books by brain researcher Dr. Manfred Spitzer, who has spent years using his profound knowledge and comprehensive source data from hundreds of scientific studies to battle against *Digital Dementia* and the *Smartphone Epidemic*. I expressly wish to thank Dr. Spitzer for his educational work on the dangers of digitization. Manfred Spitzer, *Digitale Demenz. Wie wir uns und unsere Kinder um den Verstand bringen,* Droemer-Verlag, Munich, paperback edition October 2014 (first published 2012); Manfred Spitzer, *Die Smartphone Epidemie. Gefahren für Gesundheit, Bildung und Gesellschaft,* Klett-Cotta-Verlag, Stuttgart, paperback edition, 2018/2019.

183 https://de.statista.com/statistik/daten/studie/1106/umfrage/handybesitz-bei-jugendlichen-nach-altersgruppen/.

184 *Smartphone Epidemie*, p. 113.

185 *Smartphone Epidemie*, p. 149.

186 http://www.nytimes.com/2019/11/04/well/family/screen-use-tied-to-childrens-brain-development.amp.html; Studie: John S. Hutton et al. "Associations Between Screen-Based Media Use and Brain White Matter Integrity in Preschool-Aged Children", in: JAMA Pediatrics 2019.3869.

187 Alan L. Mendelsohn et al, "Infant Television and Video Exposure Associated With Limited Parent-Child Verbal Interactions in Low Socioeconomic Status Households", *Arch Pediatr Adolesc Med*, 2008 May; 162 (5): 411–17.

188 https://www.drogenbeauftragte.de/presse/pressekontakt-und-mitteilungen/archiv/2017/2017-2-quartal/ergebnisse-der-blikk-studie-2017vorgestellt.html?L=0.

189 Christakis, D.A ., Zimmerman, F. J., Di Giuseppe, D. L., & McCarty, C. A. (2004). "Early television exposure and subsequent attentional problems in children," in: Pediatrics, 113(4), 708–13.

190 Zimmerman, F. J. & Christakis, D. A., "Children's television viewing and cognitive outcomes: A longitudinal analysis of national data," in: Archives of Pediatrics & Adolescent Medicine, 159 (7), 619–25, 2005.

191 Manfred Spitzer, *Digitale Demenz*, p. 138.

192 Hancox, R. J., Milne, B. J., & Poulton, R., "Association between child and adolescent television viewing and adult health," in: *Lancet* 364, 257–62, 2004.

193 Manfred Spitzer, *Smartphone Epidemie*, Chapter 4.

194 Christian Pfeiffer, Thomas Mößle, Matthias Kleimann & Florian Rehbein, *Die PISA-Verlierer — Opfer ihres Medienkonsums,* Kriminologisches Forschungsinstitut Niedersachsen e. V. (KFN), Hanover 2007.

195 https://www.bitkom.org/Presse/Presseinformation/Kinder-und-Jugendliche-zocken-taeglich-rund-zwei-Stunden.html.

196 Christian Pfeiffer et al.

197 Manfred Spitzer, *Digitale Demenz*, p. 199.

198 https://www.drogenbeauftragte.de/presse/pressekontakt-und-mitteilungen/archiv/2016/2016/jeder-12-junge-suechtig-nach-computerspielen.html?L=0.
199 Manfred Spitzer, *Digitale Demenz*, p. 123.
200 Manfred Spitzer, *Digitale Demenz*, p. 12.
201 https://www.facebook.com/BestTrendVideos/videos/588522614986049/.
202 www.schule-atmosfairisch.de.
203 Stefan Korn et al, *Mobbing in Schulklassen — systematische Schikane*: https://www.jugendschutz-niedersachsen.de/wordpress/wp content/uploads/2010/10/korn-mobbing.pdf.
204 https://www.buendnis-gegen-cybermobbing.de.
205 Edward Bernays, *Propaganda,* H. Liveright, New York 1928, p. 71.
206 https://www.facebook.com/notes/mark-zuckerberg/bringing-the-world-closer-together/10154944663901634/.
207 Julia Krüger, *Die öffentliche Meinungsbildung wird für Facebook zum Experimentierfeld*: https://netzpolitik.org/2018/kommentar-die-oeffentliche-meinungsbildung-wird-fuer-facebook-zum-experimentierfeld/.
208 https://www.facebook.com/zuck/posts/10104413015393571.

Chapter 11

209 https://www.bka.de/DE/Presse/Listenseite_Pressemitteilungen/2018/Presse2018/180606_KinderpornografieKlarstellung.html;jsessionid=D6CF159F4C61CAFC19F6EC957FAF5287.live2291?nn=29858.
210 https://ecpat.de.
211 https://www.nytimes.com/interactive/2019/09/28/us/child-sex-abuse.html.
212 https://www.safersurfing.org/mallorca-erstkontakt-zu-pornos-bereits-mit-acht/.
213 Petra Grimm, Michael Müller, Stefanie Rhein, *Porno im Web 2.0. Welche Rolle spielen sexualisierte Webinhalte in der Lebenswelt von Jugendlichen?,* A study done for NLM and BLM: www.hdm-stuttgart.de/grimm/grimm_pornografie_praesentation.pdf.
214 https://www.zeit.de/kultur/2018-03/pornografie-aufklaerung-sexualitaet-frauen-erniedrigung.
215 A report from the Australian government has a good summary of the research: http://aifs.gov.au.
216 Porn consumption is no longer just a male domain. https://www.focus.de/panorama/welt/befragung-aus-grossbritannien-jede-dritte-frau-sieht-sich-mindestens-einmal-pro-woche-pornos-an_id_5496121.html.
217 Tabea Freitag, *Fit for Love? Praxishandbuch zur Prävention von Internet-Ponografie-Konsum*, return Fachstelle Mediensucht Hanover. See also: *Love is more, Safer Surfing*, https://www.safersurfing.org/loveismore/.

Chapter 12

218 Micro-census of the German Federal Statistical Office.

219 Report of the IONA Institute on the *Global Family and Gender Survey*: https://ionainstitute.ie/wp-content/uploads/2019/03/IONA-cohabitation-flyer-LR.pdf.

220 Leila Miller (Ed.), *Primal Loss — The Now-Adult Children of Divorce Speak*, LCB Publishing, Phoenix, Arizona 2017.

221 Anabel, child of divorce, in a film on joint custody: *Heute Mama, morgen Papa — Der Streit ums Wechselmodell*: https://www.youtube.com/watch?v=2sl9 Hruqw78.

222 Quotes from the testimonies of stepmothers on this blog: https://stiefmutter-blog.com/2014/12/05/stiefkinder-sind-die-neuen-schwiegermutter/.

223 Judith S. Wallerstein, Julia M. Lewis, Sandra Blakeslee, *The Unexpected Legacy of Divorce: A 25 Year Landmark Study*, Hyperion, New York, 2000. Summary here: http://www.agsp.de/html/a10.html.

224 http://www.agsp.de/html/a10.html.

225 Paul R. Amato and Bruce Keith, "Parental Divorce and Adult Wellbeing: A Meta-Analysis," in: *Journal of Marriage and Family*, Vol 53, No 1, Feb. 1991, p. 43–59. http://slatestarcodex.com/Stuff/divorce_paper.pdf.

226 The results of scientific studies are documented at this website: https://marri.us/wp-content/uploads/The-Effects-of-Divorce-on-Children.pdf. If other sources are cited, they will be indicated in a separate footnote.

227 Leslie R. Martin, Howard S. Friedman, Kathleen M. Clark, and Joan S. Tucker, "Longevity Following the Experience of Parental Divorce", in: *Social Science and Medicine* 61 (2005): 2182

228 Cynthia Price and Jenifer Kunz, "Rethinking the Paradigm of Juvenile Delinquency as Related to Divorce," in: *Journal of Divorce and Remarriage* 39 (2003).

229 https://cdn2.hubspot.net/hubfs/135704/NFIFatherAbsenceInfoGraphic 071118.pdf.

230 https://cdn2.hubspot.net/hub/135704/file-396018955-pdf/RyanNFIFather-AbsenceInfoGraphic051614.pdf.

231 http://www.vaterlos.eu/wenn-kinder-ohne-vater-aufwachsen/.

232 Grégor Puppinck, *Les droits de l'homme dénaturé*, Le Cerf, Paris, 2018. Quoted from the still unpublished translation into German.

233 Cf. Gabriele Kuby, *The Global Sexual Revolution,* Chapter X.

234 *Brief of amici curiae American College of Pediatricians*, Family Watch International, Loren D. Marks, Mark D. Regnerus and Donald Paul Sullins. Also see: Paul Sullins, "It's Time to Promote Good Social Science on Same-Sex Parenting," in: *The Public Discourse*, May 17, 2019.

235 https://www.focusonthefamily.com/faith/key-findings-of-mark-regnerus-new-family-structure-study/.
236 Mark Regnerus, "The Data on Children in Same-Sex Households Get More Depressing," in: *The Public Discourse,* June 26, 2016. https://www.thepublicdiscourse.com/2016/06/17255/.
237 In his book *Die dunkle Seite der Kindheit* ("The Dark Side of Childhood"), Dirk Bange cites a study by Russell: Every 6th girl who had a stepfather was abused by him before the age of 14, but "only" every 15th girl by her biological father. A study from England and Wales shows that 32% of children growing up with at least one stepparent became victims of abuse, versus 3% of children who lived with their biological parents.
238 Katy Faust, *Dear Justice Kennedy: An Open Letter from the Child of a Loving Gay Parent,* in: *The Public Discourse*, 02.02.2015, http://www.thepublicdiscourse.com/2015/02/14370/.
239 https://www.lifesitenews.com/news/quartet-of-truth-adult-children-of-gay-parents-testify-against-same-sex-mar.

Chapter 13

240 A worthwhile book in English on dealing with media in the family is: Andy Crouch, *The Tech-Wise Family,* Baker Publishing Group, Grand Rapids 2017.
241 Great help for putting all this into practice is the book by Katy Faust: *Them Before Us. Why We Need a Global Children's Rights Movement*, Post Hill Press, New York, Nashville 2021.

Chapter 14

242 The interview was held by the author in English in April 2020.